# AMERICAN JOURNAL
# OF NUMISMATICS

# 21

Second Series, continuing

*The American Numismatic Society Museum Notes*

THE AMERICAN NUMISMATIC SOCIETY

NEW YORK

2009

ISSN: 1053-8356
ISBN 10: 0-89722-308-X
ISBN 13: 978-0-89722-308-9

Printed in China

# Contents

# American Journal of Numismatics

Peter G. van Alfen
*Editor*

Müşerref Yetim
*Managing Editor*

## Editorial Committee

John W. Adams
*Boston, Massachusetts*

William L. Bischoff
*New York, New York*

Jere L. Bacharach
*University of Washington*

Kenneth W. Harl
*Tulane University*

Paul T. Keyser
*IBM T. J. Watson Research Center*

John M. Kleeberg
*New York, New York*

Robert Knapp
*University of California, Berkeley*

John H. Kroll
*Oxford, England*

John Ma
*Oxford University*

Andrew R. Meadows
*American Numismatic Society*

Eric P. Newman
*St. Louis, Missouri*

Ira Rezak
*Stony Brook, New York*

Stephen K. Scher
*New York, New York*

Stuart D. Sears
*Westport, Massachusetts*

Bernhard Weisser
*Münzkabinett*
*Staatliche Museen zu Berlin*

## Editors' Note

In *American Journal of Numismatics* volume 20 (2008) the plates for Giovanni Gorini's article, The Die Sequence of Medma Silver Staters (pp. 143–154), were inadvertently left out. The illustrations for the article can be found in this volume on Plates 14–15.

AJN Second Series 21 (2009) pp. 1–27
© 2009 The American Numismatic Society

# The Northern Syria 2007 Hoard of Athenian Owls: Behavioral Aspects

PLATES 1–3

RICHARD FERNANDO BUXTON*

This article discusses a sample of 2,626 coins from an immense hoard of Athenian tetradrachms deposited c. 400 BC in northern Syria. A vast majority of the coins exhibit multiple types of surface markings. These markings include countermarks, cut countermark-like designs, graffiti, punch marks, cut edges and chisel cuts especially. Such markings are typical of smaller, contemporary hoards containing Athenian coinage found throughout the Near East. However, the large sample size offered by the present hoard further demonstrates that all of these different systems of surface markings conform to consistent patterns in placement and execution. There is nevertheless no similar consistency in the relationship between different marking systems appearing on the same coin. This suggests that each type of surface marking functioned independently but not exclusively as a regularized system of signification and circulation control within the Near East.

## I. Composition and Date of the Hoard

Recently,[1] a phenomenally large hoard of c. 10,000 coins was unearthed in the

*rfbuxton@u.washington.edu

1. For suggesting this project to me while I was a student at the 2007 American Numismatic Society summer seminar and his many helpful suggestions at every stage of its development I owe a tremendous debt of gratitude to Peter van Alfen. I also wish to thank Müşerref Yetim, Wolfgang Fischer-Bossert, Fleur Kemmers, Georges Depeyrot, William Metcalf, Nathan T. Elkins, Stefan Krmnicek and my two anonymous readers for their many helpful comments on earlier versions of this paper. All remaining errors are, needless to say, entirely my own.

area north of Aleppo, Syria.[2] Drawing on multiple sources, it has been possible to gather photographs, weights, and die axes of 2,626 coins from this hoard, representing a little over a quarter of the original.[3] Only about 32% of the hoard sample had been cleaned when the photos were taken and most of the other coins were moderately to heavily corroded (e.g., Plates 1–3, nos. 5, 6, 14, 27, and 31). With three exceptions, the photographed and reported contents of the hoard consist entirely of Athenian tetradrachms (henceforth owls), and the hoard's total worth therefore approaches the impressive sum of 6 2/3rds talents of silver.[4] For the sake of convenience, the term "hoard" will, in what follows, be used to refer not to this north Syrian hoard as a whole, but to the photographed sample of it on which this study is based.

The vast majority of the hoard's owls, some 84% (2,207 coins), is of the mass-produced fifth-century BC standardized type. The type is easily recognized by the mechanical appearance of its design and the diagnostic frontal eye of Athena. This feature conveniently distinguishes such issues from their fourth-century successors in which Athena now sports a profile eye. Standardized fifth-century owls, according to the authoritative chronology of John Kroll, began being minted around the time that the Athenians removed their naval league's treasury from Delos to Athens in 454.[5] They then quickly became the most important and widespread silver currency in both the Aegean and the Near East. Able to export owls of good silver in large numbers thanks to the rich deposits of the Laurium mines in Attica, the Athenians quickly sidelined all other competing silver currencies in or near their empire's orbit through the sheer volume of their money supply. In turn, commercial and state agents throughout the eastern Mediterranean conducting transactions in silver came increasingly to depend on a steady supply of owls.

One consequence of the increasing ubiquity of owls was that by the 420s they had attained a premium in exchange over their bullion value throughout the Near East. In an effort to exploit this opportunity, imitation owls patterned on the fifth-century frontal-eyed type but minted in Egypt and Syria began to appear. This proved fortunate after Athenian owl production collapsed during the last years of the Peloponnesian War starting in 413 when the Spartans disrupted mining opera-

---

2. More specific information about the find spot and deposit context is, unfortunately, unavailable.

3. It is hoped to publish fully this important evidence in a future publication.

4. To give some context for the figure: in Isocrates' *Trapeziticus* of 393 BC the speaker, son of a leading figure in the kingdom of Bosporus, is accused by the famous banker Pasion, an Athenian freedman, of corrupting his slave in order to embezzle this amount (Isoc. orat. 17.12 and 50).

5. For this and the following background see Kroll (1993: 5–8) with further references; cf. van Alfen (forthcoming) and Flament (2007).

tions at Laurium after capturing Decelaea in Attica. The resulting monetary gap was quickly filled by eastern imitations, minted now in ever greater numbers.[6] Minting of these imitation frontal-eyed owls continued in the Near East throughout the fourth century. This was certainly true during the sporadic production of early profile-eyed owls at Athens during the first half of the fourth century. Production even persisted after the Athenians began to mass produce the later *pi*-style of profile-eyed tetradrachms under the financial administration of Eubulus in the 340s.

Imitation owls, recognizable by their slightly off designs and especially their often grotesquely large eyes, make up around 8.5% of the hoard's total. They represent the larger of two significant minority groups within it. Their number is almost evenly divided between random imitations on the one hand (117 coins, e.g., Plate 2, no. 16) and, on the other, owls from two of the three Egyptian imitation types identified by Theodore Buttrey (106 coins). For convenience, I refer to the latter group as Buttrey imitations throughout, retaining his sub-divisions of types B and M (e.g., Plate 3, no. 29).[7] Of particular note among the miscellaneous, non-Buttrey imitations are three coins with die-linked obverses that feature a peculiar bump on Athena's chin (Plate 1, no. 1). Five of the non-Buttrey imitation owls appear to be plated bronze pieces.[8]

In addition to authentic and inauthentic frontal-eyed owls of standardized fifth-century design, a little over 7% of the hoard consists of earlier owls. Almost all of these are from the last two of a series of owl groups identified by Chester Starr. The minting of these earlier owls, henceforth called Starr owls, has been located between the 470s and 450s.[9] Starr owls, which form the hoard's other main minority (191 coins), can be recognized by their more organic designs and, compared with their successors, the smaller helmet ornament for Athena (e.g., Plate 1, no. 2).

Outside of these three main groups of tetradrachms, the hoard contains two archaic owls, one from each of the two latest groups identified by Charles Seltman (groups F and E). These types have been dated by other scholars to the 480s, im-

6. Figueira (1998: 528–535) provides an excellent treatment of the phenomenon. Against this more orthodox position Flament (2003, 2005, and 2007: 57–58) advances the view that many of the owls identified as imitations from this period are, in fact, authentic fifth-century issues, on which more below.

7. See Buttrey (1982a) whose three types—X, B, and M—were revisited by Flament (2001), who added a sub-category to M, type A, not attested in the present hoard.

8. Strictly speaking, the plated pieces are counterfeit coins and not imitations (see van Alfen 2005 for precise terminology, especially table 13.1).

9. The five groups laid out by Starr (1970) remain authoritative, although his dates for their introduction have been revised to those followed here (cf. Kroll 1993: 6 and nn. 10 & 11). See Flament (2007: 47–54) for an excellent distillation of Starr's groups and a summary of views regarding their dating.

mediately preceding the introduction of the Starr owls.[10] The hoard was also ru-
moured to contain a single specimen of an Athenian decadrachm, contemporary
in design and, presumably, minting date with the Starr owls.[11] The photographed
sample of the hoard contains no examples of the profile-eyed Athena found on
fourth-century issues and none were reported to be in the original, full hoard.

A single non-Athenian coin was photographed: an apparently unparalleled
variety of the fifth-century Attic weight standard tetradrachm type from Cyrene
featuring a silphium on the obverse and the head of Zeus Ammon within a circular border on the reverse (Plate 1, no. 3). This type is associated with the reign of
Arcesilas IV (before 462–c. 440?). In terms of style, the bust of Zeus Ammon and
the circular border around it is very close to the latest coins from this series, and so
a date of c. 440 is suggested here for the coin.[12] Unlike these other coins, however,
the legend KYPANAIΩN appears around the outside of the reverse's circular border
instead of the letters KYPA within it. Finally, a reliable source reported that a Syracusan tetradrachm of c. 475 was also included in the original hoard.

The preponderance of fifth-century frontal-eyed Athenian owls taken together with the sizable minority of frontal-eyed imitations and the complete lack of
profile-eyed issues would suggest a date for the hoard of c. 400, before the first
revamped Athenian owls with profile eyes begin penetrating foreign hoards in
either the 380s or 370s.[13] During this period imitations would already be in broad
circulation in order to make up for the shortfall in Attic production in the last decade and a half of the fifth century, although a large amount of authentic Athenian
owls could still be expected to be on hand. Moreover, the large number of Starr
owls, comparable in size to that of the hoard's imitations, argues for as early a date
as possible. After all, such coins would have already by the start of the fourth century been circulating for around fifty years as would also be true of the Cyrenaican
tetradrachm. The Syracusan tetradrachm from the 470s and the two archaic owls
from the 480s point even more strongly in this same direction.

10. The owl groups identified by Seltman (1924) are still accepted, but their chronological
arrangement has been revised by Kraay (1956); cf. Flament (2007: 36–43) for a distillation
and summary of further chronological questions.

11. Starr (1970), 22; cf. Flament (2007), 51–52. See now Fischer-Bossert (2008).

12. Cf. Kraay (1976), Pl. 62.1072 (= Robinson 1927: Pl. 5.16; cf. Pl. 5.17) and his discussion of the coinage on 298.

13. The dating is from Kroll (2006), who conveniently dubs these early profile-eyed issues
as Lentini-style owls, but cf. Nicolet-Pierre (2001) and Nicolet-Pierre and Arnold-Biuchhi
(2000), who argued before the discovery of important new evidence from the Athenian
Agora that the coins are Egyptian imitations based on the later *pi*-style. Building on a suggestion in van Alfen (2005) n. 44 about *pi*-style owls, Kroll on p. 61 suggests that the change
to the profile eye may have been in response to the growing level of imitation owls in Athens. In this manner new genuine issues could, at least for a time, be easily distinguished.

The one serious objection to this proposed dating is the attribution by Buttrey (1982a) of his Buttrey type B to the middle of the fourth century. Buttrey based his dating on the stylistic similarity between type B imitations and the obverse of a marked imitation Egyptian owl whose reverse bears the legend "Artaxerxes Pharaoh" in Demotic. The inscription has to be dated after 343 when Artaxerxes III recaptured Egypt.[14] Christophe Flament (2003), however, has shown that type B and type M Buttrey imitations—the two of the three Buttrey types represented in our hoard—appear in the 1985 Naxos hoard from Sicily which dates to the end of the fifth century. This pushes the date at which these Buttrey types were introduced at least down to the period directly following the drop off in the minting of owls at Athens.[15]

Flament (2003, 2005, and 2007) has also gone on to argue that the presence of these two imitative-looking Buttrey types in the 1985 Naxos hoard suggests that they are, in actuality, authentic Athenian issues. In a recent article, however, Lisa Anderson and Peter van Alfen have convincingly shown that this second point, although possible, need not be accepted as conclusive or necessary. Central to their argument is the observation that the penetration of Near Eastern imitative owls west was a common phenomenon.[16] This is best demonstrated by the preserved 375 Law on Silver Coinage that attempts in part to regulate imitative owls in the Athenian Agora and thus attests to their frequent presence outside the Near East.[17] It seems prudent, therefore, to follow van Alfen and accept the earlier introduction date for the Buttrey types without going on, as Flament has, to recognize them as genuine Attic issues.[18]

Despite the limitations on the amount of knowledge we can extract from this hoard due to (a) the possession of photographs and limited additional information

14. Published, with an excellent photograph, by Mørkholm (1974).

15. The stratigraphy for the 1985 Naxos hoard is not entirely secure and the excavators suggest that it might perhaps date from the early fourth century (see Flament 2007: 222). A 390s date for our hoard is therefore not to be entirely ruled out although as stated the large minority of Starr owls urge the adoption of as early a date as possible.

16. Anderson and van Alfen (2008), 165–166; cf. van Alfen (2004/5), 54–55.

17. For the Athenian Law on Silver Coinage (RO 25 = *SEG* 26.72) and its relation to imitation owl coinage see Buttrey (1981 and 1982b) as well as the *editio princeps* of Stroud (1974). An excellent recent discussion is Ober (2008), 220–245.

18. Such a view may require modification once the Karanis/Fayum hoard from which Buttrey developed his typology is finally published and its relation to the Artaxerxes owl can be clarified. Publication of the hoard is currently being prepared by Carmen Arnold-Biucchi. If Flament is correct and Buttrey types B and M are in fact Athenian from the period 420–405, a c. 400 date for the 2007 hoard remains the most tenable since it would still contain a 4.25% minority of frontal-eyed owl imitations that would most likely stem from the end of the fifth century after the post-Decelaea drop off in genuine Athenian owl production.

Table 1. Distribution of Surface Markings

| | no marks | chisel cut | graffiti | notches | countermark | punch mark | edge cuts | tube mark | cut countermark |
|---|---|---|---|---|---|---|---|---|---|
| obverse only | 1197 | 99 | 158 | -- | 92 | 87 | 7 | 85 | 50 |
| | 45.58% | 3.77% | 6.02% | -- | 3.50% | 3.31% | 0.27% | 3.24% | 1.90% |
| reverse only | 228 | 1496 | 188 | -- | 169 | 75 | 118 | 25 | 3 |
| | 8.68% | 56.97% | 7.16% | -- | 6.44% | 2.86% | 4.49% | 0.95% | 0.11% |
| both | 475 | 142 | 42 | 340 | 14 | 10 | 1 | 2 | 1 |
| | 18.09% | 5.41% | 1.60% | 12.95% | 0.53% | 0.38% | 0.04% | 0.08% | 0.04% |
| Total | 475 | 1737 | 388 | 340 | 275 | 172 | 126 | 112 | 54 |
| | 18.09% | 66.15% | 14.78% | 12.95% | 10.47% | 6.55% | 4.80% | 4.27% | 2.06% |

n.b.: Because each notch is visible on both coin faces, this surface marking type is only recorded under "both." Also, figures in the total column record, for surface markings, the total number of coins affected by a particular marking on either face, but for the "no marks" category only the total number of coins without markings on both faces is given instead.

on the coins, (b) its condition at the time of photographing, (c) our lack of comprehensive die studies for the massive fifth-century frontal-eyed Athenian coinage as well as (d) our poor understanding of the extent of foreign frontal-eyed imitations, the sheer size of our photographed sample presents an invaluable resource for studying the distribution and treatment of Athenian coinage in the Near East at the beginning of the fourth century. Moreover, should a die study of fifth-century standardized Athenian coinage ever be undertaken, the photographs of our hoard could provide an invaluable core sample.

## II. Behavioral Aspects in Surface Marking: Catalogue

One topic about which our hoard can supply an unparalleled amount of information regards the treatment of coinage in the Near East during the Classical period. This is because a high degree of coins in the hoard, around 82%, are affected by intentionally inflicted surface markings of various classes, many of which are largely if not exclusively associated with Near Eastern handling of coinage as determined from hoard evidence (Table 1).[19] Of these there are eight major types, all of them appearing on both faces of coins in the hoard either alone or in combination with one or more of the other kinds of surface markings. They are, in order of frequency: chisel cuts, graffiti, triangular notches cut out of the side of the coin (henceforth notches), countermarks, punch marks, small cuts along the flan bordering a coin's face (henceforth edge cuts), punch-like marks made by a circular tube-like tool (henceforth tube marks), and countermark-like designs cut onto a coin's face (henceforth cut countermarks). The aim of the following is to provide a concise typology of these eight major types, focusing on consistent patterns in the form and placement of each. The eight types are discussed in an order that best allows for points of comparison to be made across categories.

### II.A: Chisel Cuts

By far the most frequent type of surface marking found in our hoard, chisel cuts consist of linear gashes made by hammering a chisel tool into the surface of either coin face. Cuts on the reverse are far more common than those on the obverse, but except for cuts on the obverse of two coins, all the chisel cuts in our hoard on both faces fall into regular patterns of placement.[20]

There are nine regular positions for cuts on the reverse, treated here in order of frequency (Table 2): (1) usually one and occasionally two vertical gashes from the

---

19. Kraay (1976), 286.

20. In responding to a presentation on the topic of chisel cut owls, William Metcalf suggested to me that the pronounced preference for reverse over obverse cuts may reflect a religious anxiety about defacing the image of a divinity.

top of the coin through the area between the eyes of the owl (Plates 1–3, nos. 4,5, 22, 25, 26, and 33); (2) a diagonal gash along the right edge of the owl's wing (Plate 1, no. 5; Plate 2, no. 18); (3) a vertical cut from the bottom of the coin parallel to either side of the owl's right leg (Plate 1, no. 5); (4) a diagonal cut from the bottom right edge of the coin towards its center, usually traversing the epsilon (Plate 1, no. 6); (5) a short diagonal gash through the center of the owl's body (Plate 1, no. 5); (6) a diagonal gash from the coin's top-left edge through the middle of the olive sprig (Plate 1, no. 6); (7) a horizontal gash stretching inward from the center of the coin's right edge and usually traversing the theta (Plate 1, no. 7); (8) a diagonal cut from the top right edge of the coin towards its center, usually traversing the alpha (Plate 1, no. 6); (9) a horizontal gash through the owl's neck (Plate 1, no. 4).

Table 2. Distribution of reverse chisel cuts

| cut type | 1 (eyes) | 2 (wing) | 3 (legs) | 4 (body) | 5 (epsilon) | 6 (olive) | 7 (theta) | 8 (alpha) | 9 (neck) |
|---|---|---|---|---|---|---|---|---|---|
| Number | 1177 | 227 | 162 | 148 | 134 | 131 | 115 | 100 | 74 |
| % of r. cuts | 51.90% | 10.01% | 7.14% | 6.53% | 5.91% | 5.78% | 5.07% | 4.41% | 3.26% |
| % of coins | 44.82% | 8.64% | 6.17% | 5.64% | 5.10% | 4.99% | 4.38% | 3.81% | 2.82% |

On the obverse there are eight regular positions, again treated in order of their frequency (Table 3): (1) a vertical gash from the top of the coin through the area of Athena's olive leaves (Plate 1, no. 8); (2) a vertical cut from the center of the coin's bottom through Athena's neck (Plate 1, no. 9); (3) a diagonal gash from the bottom right edge of the coin passing through Athena's chin (Plate 1, no. 10); (4) a diagonal cut from the top left edge of the coin through the palmette (Plate 2, no. 11); (5) a horizontal cut under or through Athena's eye (Plate 2, no. 12); (6) a vertical gash from Athena's cheek towards her eye (Plate 2, no. 13); (7) a small diagonal cut through Athena's nose (Plate 1, no. 8); (8) a small horizontal gash on Athena's cheek (Plate 2, no. 14).

Table 3. Distribution of obverse chisel cuts

| cut type | 1 (olive) | 2 (neck) | 3 (chin) | 4 (palm.) | 5 (eye) | 6 (v. cheek) | 7 (nose) | 8 (h. cheek) | unique |
|---|---|---|---|---|---|---|---|---|---|
| Number | 86 | 54 | 49 | 22 | 19 | 8 | 6 | 4 | 2 |
| % of o. cuts | 34.40% | 21.60% | 19.60% | 8.80% | 7.60% | 3.20% | 2.40% | 1.60% | 0.80% |
| % of coins | 3.27% | 2.06% | 1.87% | 0.84% | 0.72% | 0.30% | 0.23% | 0.15% | 0.08% |

The cuts above have been described in relation to the owl's iconography and legend. Many reverse punches on owls, however, are struck low, leaving a band of unmarked flan along the top of the reverse strike. Often on these coins chisel cuts occurring in positions that typically cut through iconographic or legend features near the top of the reverse design (e.g., reverse cuts 1, 6, and 8 above) are shifted upwards either partially or entirely to the flan above the reverse stamp. They thus occur where we would expect them to appear had the reverse stamp been properly centered.

Table 4. Number of chisel cuts

|                    | any cuts | 1 cut   | 2 cuts  | 3 cuts  | 4 cuts  | 5 cuts  | 6 cuts  | 7 cuts  |
|--------------------|----------|---------|---------|---------|---------|---------|---------|---------|
| Obverse only       | 241      | 229     | 11      | 1       | 0       | 0       | 0       | 0       |
| % of coins w/o. cuts |        | 95.02%  | 4.56%   | 0.41%   | 0.00%   | 0.00%   | 0.00%   | 0.00%   |
| Reverse only       | 1638     | 1145    | 355     | 105     | 23      | 7       | 2       | 1       |
| % of coins w/r. cuts |        | 69.90%  | 21.67%  | 6.41%   | 1.40%   | 0.43%   | 0.12%   | 0.06%   |

Individual coins can sport up to seven cuts on their reverse and three on the obverse, but the number of examples in our hoard decreases precipitously as the number of chisel cuts increases (Table 4). Chisel cuts in all positions appear on coins without any other chisel cuts while coins with multiple chisel cuts can feature these in any combination of positions.

## II.B: Countermarks

The fifth most common type of surface marking found in our hoard, countermarks appear on reverses almost twice as often as on obverses and rarely on both faces of a single coin. On the obverse countermarks tend to appear in the central, open area provided by Athena's chin while on the reverse most are stamped into the blank space between the owl and legend. Most countermarks on both faces consist of images in a round and occasionally square incuse (Plate 1, no. 8; Plate 2, no. 15, cf. Figure 1, no. 10; Plate 2, no. 22, cf. Figure 1, no. 3; Plate 3, no. 33, cf. Figure 1, no. 13). In addition, obverse countermarks frequently feature one of a variety of letters within a square incuse (Plate 2, no. 16, cf. Figure 1, no. 4), and, in the case of one letter, a circular incuse (Plate 2, no. 17, cf. Figure 1, no. 7). Several of these letters have been attributed by scholars to the Aramaic and Phoenician alphabets and accordingly imply a Near Eastern audience for such markings (see n. 22). Corrosion on many coins has rendered their countermarks illegible, but nos. 1 through 16 in Figure 1 catalogue all legible countermarks appearing in the hoard at least twice.

### II.B.1: The Double-X Countermark

One countermark of particular interest is Figure 1, no. 1, an as yet un-paralleled double-X design that is by far our hoard's most common countermark, appearing on 19% of countermarked coins (52 examples). Along with nos. 2 and 3 in Figure 1 it is the only countermark that appears on both faces, showing up on fifty reverses

Figure 1. Significant Countermarks, Cut Countermarks and Graffiti.*

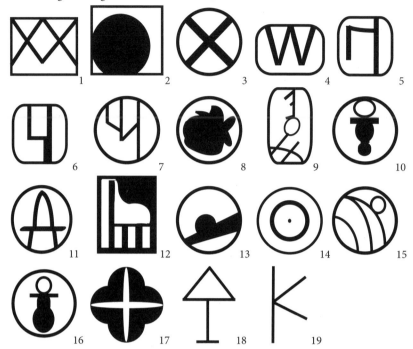

* Cross-references to nos. in other catalogues of countermarks:

3: cf. van Alfen (2000) table 1, no. 1; Hill (1922) 137, no. 53.

4: cf. Elayi and Lemaire (1998) 135, no. 170, identified as Phoenician *zayin*.

6: cf. Elayi and Lemaire (1998) 133, no. 159, identified as Aramaic *tau* or *daleth*.

7: cf. Elayi and Lemaire (1998) 138, nos. 190–196, identified as Phoenician *mem*; Jung-fleisch (1949) 31, nos. 10 and 11, identified as Phoenician *mem*; Newell (1914) fig. 1, no. 3.

10: cf. van Alfen (2000) table 1, no. 17; Hill (1922) 137, no. 105.

12: cf. van Alfen (2000) table 1, no. 14; Elayi and Lemaire (1998) 139, no. 198, identified as Phoenician *mem*.

18: cf. Hill (1922) 137, no. 144.

19: cf. Elayi and Lemaire (1998) Fig. 13, identified as Aramaic *aleph* (fifth-century type).

as against two obverses. On five occasions the stamp appears twice on the same re-verse (Plate 2, no. 18), with the two countermarks also overlapping each other on three of these coins. Only three other coins in the entire hoard display overlapping countermarks, but in these examples the overlapping stamps are never identical types. Moreover, the double-X countermark frequently strays out of the normal open area in which reverse countermarks tend to appear. It is, instead, as in Plate 2, no. 4, often stamped over the owl's body, making the mark far less intelligible.

## Discussion

In an article on two fourth-century owl hoards from Egypt, Peter van Alfen discusses the *quatrefoil* countermark (Figure 1, no. 17).[21] The *quatrefoil* is another stamp of unique frequency subject to the same kind of random placement and multiple, often overlapping stamping as the double-X mark. Van Alfen concludes that the comparatively casual treatment of the *quatrefoil* suggests that it stems from a highly regularized and repetitive control bureaucracy. This bureaucracy would be relatively unconcerned with the intelligibility of a countermark subject to such highly automatic placement.

The unique degree of frequency and apparent carelessness with which the double-X countermark is applied in our hoard suggests that it is the result of a similarly automated process. At the same time the utter lack of evidence for this stamp in other contemporary hoards implies that the regime administering this process was operating on a small scale in relative proximity to the parties responsible for assembling our sample. It may therefore be appropriate to think of the countermark as a local banker's stamp. However, the frequency of owls stamped more than once with this same marking argues against interpreting the stamp merely as a brand indicating private ownership. In such a scenario the multiple double-X countermarks would be redundant.

### II.C: Cut Countermarks

The least frequent type of surface marking in our hoard, cut countermarks are designs or letters incised into the same areas of the obverse and reverse on which countermarks are stamped. The tool employed creates noticeably deeper and thicker lines than graffiti and, consequently, attests to a more technologically sophisticated marking system. There are four cut countermark designs with multiple attestations in our hoard, and although cut countermarks are far more common on the obverse than the reverse, both faces share three of these common types: an X, a V-like figure usually rotated right 90° and a similarly rotated V-like figure bisected between its legs by a horizontal line (Plate 2, no. 19).[22]

### II.C.1: The Arrow-like Cut Countermark

The fourth repeated design, the arrow-like Figure 1, no. 18 (Plate 2, no. 20), is

21. van Alfen (2002b), 67–69. Note that the *quatrefoil* does not appear in our hoard.

22. The second of these three countermarks may perhaps be identified with Phoenician *gimmel* (cf. Elayi and Lemaire 1998: Fig. 14) and the third with *shin* in either Phoenician or Aramaic (cf. Elayi and Lemaire 1998: Fig. 14 for the former and Fig. 13 for the latter).

found on the obverse only of seven apparently authentic owls. Intriguingly, it appears to imitate a countermark attested on contemporary Persian coinage (see n. 22 on Figure 1, no. 18). Further, this arrow-like cut countermark appears on the obverses of two Buttrey-type owls and the reverse of one Cilician stater in a hoard from roughly the same area as ours that was deposited 334–330.[23]

Discussion

Given its recurrence in a later fourth-century hoard, the arrow-like cut countermark is perhaps best understood as a symbol for either private ownership or localized circulation control from the larger area north of Aleppo that endured for much of the fourth century. If so, it provides a fascinating example of a smaller authority employing a comparatively crude technology (the chisel) in order to mark its coinage by mimicking a more sophisticated countermark stamp used by a presumably more developed administrative regime. This phenomenon is also present in the case of several graffiti catalogued below where simple scratches on a coin are used to imitate known countermarks and, in one case, the arrow-like cut countermark itself.

## II.D: Graffiti

Although far less frequent than chisel cuts, graffiti comprise the second most common surface marking type in our hoard. They tend to appear in the same areas on the obverse and reverse as countermarks and cut countermarks while displaying only a slight preference for appearing on the reverse. Coins with graffiti on both faces are not rare. Each graffito consists of a shallow design, often a letter, made by lightly scratching the coin's surface. Seven design types are common to both faces. Among these are three that are identical in form to those cut countermarks described above as also appearing on both obverses and reverses (Plates 2–3, 21 through 23; cf. this last with Plate 2, no. 19). The other four common designs are: (1) two parallel horizontal lines (Plate 1, no. 1, where this figure appears together with an X graffito; Plate 3, no. 33, where this figure is incised over an X graffito); (2) three parallel lines; (3) a Y-like design; and (4) Figure 1, no. 19.[24] A design similar to our letter G appears on several obverses while the legends of a few reverses have been underlined or had their thetas encircled by graffiti lines.[25]

    There are four unique graffiti of particular interest: one is a very complex pentagram on an obverse (Plate 3, no. 24); the second appears on a reverse and imi-

23. Anderson and van Alfen (2008), 172.

24. The Y-like design may perhaps be identified with Aramaic *beth* (cf. Elayi and Lemaire 1998: Fig. 13) or Phoenician *nun* (cf. Elayi and Lemaire 1998: Fig. 14). See n. 22 for the identification of Figure 1, no. 19.

25. This G-like letter is perhaps Phoenician *beth* (cf. Elayi and Lemaire 1998: Fig. 14).

tates the double-X countermark (Plate 3, no. 25; cf. Figure 1, no. 1); the third also appears on the obverse and is the letter found in the countermark of Figure 1, no. 7 (Plate 3, no. 26); and the fourth is an obverse graffito mimicking the arrow-like cut countermark of Figure 1, no. 18 (Plate 3, no. 27).

## II.E: Punch Marks

Like countermarks, punch marks are the result of stamping a coin face's surface except that the stamping tool in this case leaves a blank hole instead of one containing an image. This marking type, the sixth most frequent, also appears in the same areas of obverses and reverses as countermarks, but unlike these shows a slight preference for the obverse. Punch marks do occasionally appear on both faces of the same coin. The vast majority of punch marks in our hoard were created by standardized rounded punches that produce cupola-like indentations of two main sizes (Plate 2, no. 21 and Plate 3, no. 28). Similarly, marks of punch tools with a crescent-shaped head also appear several times on both faces (Plate 3, no. 29). A minority of marks are the result of small, rectangular punches.

## II.F: Tube Marks

More frequent only than cut countermarks, tube marks are produced in a similar manner as punch marks and appear in the same areas of coin obverses and reverses, although overwhelmingly on the obverse and only twice on both faces of one coin. They differ from punch marks insofar as the punch tools used to create tube marks were probably hollow tubes producing incised circular rings of three standardized sizes (Plate 3, no. 30). A minority of tube marks were made by punches creating only a half ring of two regular sizes and on the obverse two of these marks sometimes appear together opposite one another with each opening towards the other (Plate 3, no. 31). Both types of tube markings can potentially be interpreted as letters with the circular marks understood as Phoenician *ayin* and the half-circles as Aramaic *ayin*.[26]

## II.G: Notches

The third most frequent category of surface markings, notches are cut out of a coin's rim and thus affect both of its faces equally. These marks are always cut out from a coin's edge and never chiseled into it, as is apparent from the lack of bunched-up, displaced metal along their edges.[27] As is the case with chisel cuts, more than one notch can appear on a single coin, but the number of recorded specimens decreases with each additional cut. Accordingly, out of 340 affected owls, 239 examples display one notch, 82 contain two, only sixteen carry three and

---

26. See Anderson and van Alfen (2008), 171.
27. An observation well made by Naster (1948), 8.

in a single instance a coin has five notches. However, unlike chisel cuts notches do not appear in predictable positions in relation to an owl's iconography and little can be said about their placement except for two observable tendencies. The first of these is that multiple notches on a single coin tend to be separated from one another by at least 25° along the rim. The second is that on coins with two or more notches, two of these tend to be on opposite sides of the coin's rim from one another (i.e. they are separated by around 180°). The size of notches varies from hardly noticeable indentations (Plate 3, no. 28 at 11:00) to significant cut-out triangles (Plate 3, nos. 27 and 28, both at 4:00). But even in the case of the single coin with five notches, weighing 17 g, the removed metal does not significantly alter the coin's weight from the 17.2 g Attic standard.

### II.H: Edge Cuts

Edge cuts are shallow, short gashes perhaps made by lightly applying a chisel that can appear anywhere along the edge of a coin's face. They are the third least frequent type of surface marking. These marks almost always appear on the reverse where the smaller die stamp of that face tends to leave bands of blank flan along at least one side of the coin's rim on which an edge cut can easily be made (Plate 3, no. 32 at 8:00). As with chisel cuts and notches, more than one cut can appear on a single coin although the number of examples decreases as the number of cuts per coin increases. Accordingly on the reverse, only seven samples show two cuts and two coins contain three whereas 110 possess a single edge cut. On the obverse, five coins contain one cut and only two contain two. Unlike chisel cuts but similar to notches, edge cuts do not appear in predictable positions in relation to the iconography of either face despite gravitating towards bands of blank flan.

## III. Behavioral Aspects in Surface Markings: Discussion

In the area of surface markings, our hoard's importance far outpaces that of its only contemporary Near Eastern peer, the Tell el Maskhouta hoard of 6,000+ owls from Egypt (*IGCH* 1649).[28] This hoard provides an important correlative for our hoard's composition, featuring mainly fifth-century standardized owls mixed with

---

28. A slightly later date for the Tell el Maskhouta hoard is suggested since Naster (1948), Pl. 1.12 is a singular instance of an early profile-eyed piece. Robinson (1947) posits the early fourth century. Flament (2007), 210–212 offers a more recent appraisal and bibliography than *IGCH*. Robinson (1947), Naster (1948), and Jungfleisch (1949) provide the initial and most extensive publications of the material. Buttrey (1982a), 138–139 discusses the presence of Buttrey types X and B in the hoard while van Alfen (2002b), 64–65 discusses imitations and plated owls from the hoard in the American Numismatic Society's collection. Hardwick (2006) is a recent publication of owls belonging to the hoard in the Nicholson Museum at the University of Sydney.

Buttrey and non-Buttrey imitations as well as a few late Starr owls and several plated counterfeits. In stark contrast to our hoard, however, commentators on the Tell el Maskhouta find have repeatedly remarked upon its general absence of otherwise expected and typical Near Eastern surface markings. Indeed, trying to account for the almost total lack of chisel cuts—two or three owls out of 3,800 examined compared with our hoard's majority of 1,737 out of 2,626—Marcel Jungfleisch (1949: 30) could only appeal to the hoard's votive context. He posited that such defaced coins, otherwise common, must have been purposely avoided out of religious scruple. Indeed, only punch marks and notches appear with any frequency in accounts of the Tell el Maskhouta hoard's contents where even countermarks are incredibly rare. It should be noted, however, that the type of punches, notches and even three of the few countermarks recorded from the Tell el Maskhouta hoard can be paralleled in our sample.[29] There are also single examples of a circular tube marking and an X-graffito, both on obverses.[30]

If the Tell el Maskhouta hoard cannot provide a parallel against which to measure the variety, frequency and patterning of surface markings in the current hoard a far smaller but geographically closer hoard of roughly the same date, *IGCH* 1259 from Cilicia, furnishes instructive material for comparison. Although there has been much debate about whether the various coins published by Edward Newell as this Cilician hoard actually form a unity, no one has yet disputed the common provenance or integrity of its 38 expertly published Athenian tetradrachms.[31] As with our hoard we again find a majority of fifth-century Attic frontal-eyed owls with a significant minority of frontal-eyed imitations. A slightly later date for the hoard (c. 380 for Newell) is indicated by the presence of a single early profile-eyed owl and the absence of Starr owls. One coin illustrated in Newell's plates, however, is of the earliest type of standardized owl that directly followed and closely resembles the latest Starr group, a group which is well represented in our sample.

Strikingly, a similar percentage of coins in both our hoard and *IGCH* 1259 suffer from surface markings: 82% as against 83% (Table 5). Moreover, from Newell's catalogue and plates it is clear that all the major types of surface markings familiar from our hoard appear in *IGCH* 1259 aside from graffiti, notches and cut coun-

29. Robinson (1947) mentions seeing an ankh countermark (cf. Figure 1, no. 16); Naster (1948), 8, records an example of Figure 1, no. 10, illustrated in his Pl. 1.5 (cf. our Plate 2, no. 15); Jungfleisch (1949), 34, records Figure 1, no. 7 in his catalogue of countermarks, and two examples of this countermark at Elayi and Lemaire (1998), 138 (countermarks 190 and 193), are identified as "Trésor de Tell el-Maskhuta, don de M. Jungfleisch" (cf. our Plate 2, no. 17).

30. The X-graffito appears on coin no. 3 in the catalogue of van Alfen (2002a): 64–65, while the tube marked owl is no. 4.

31. Newell (1914), 3–7. Flament (2007), 192–193, is the most recent discussion.

termarks (already rare in our sample). Indeed, both hoards share marks from the similar punch, tube and chisel tools as well as two countermarks.[32] Further, the chisel cuts Newell documents both share our hoard's marked preference for appearing on the reverse and appear in the same positions on the owls.[33]

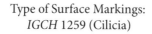

Type of Surface Markings:
*IGCH* 1259 (Cilicia)

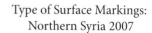

Type of Surface Markings:
Northern Syria 2007

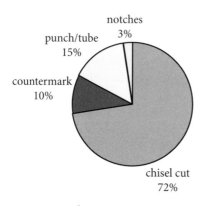

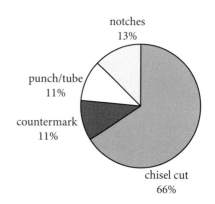

16.67% of coins unmarked             18.09% of coins unmarked

Table 5. Comparison of surface markings with those of *IGCH* 1259[34]

The small size of *IGCH* 1259 should not, of course, lead us to expect direct statistical parallels with our large cousin hoard. Nevertheless, the two hoards are broadly similar in terms of owl types, surface markings and the distribution of these mark-

32. Newell (1914) records chisel cuts as simply cuts and both punch and tube marks as punches, but his Pl. 1.6 and 7 show two different sized punch marks that are both paralleled in our hoard (cf. our Plates 2–3, nos. 28 and 21 respectively) while his Pl. 1.5 displays a half-tube mark also seen in our sample (cf. our Plate 3, no. 31). Coin 30 in Newell's catalogue features an obverse countermark with the same design as our Figure 1, no. 5 and the obverse countermark on coin 31, illustrated in his Pl. 1.4, is the same as our Figure 1, no. 4 (cf. our Plate 2, no. 16).

33. Newell (1914) records the number of chisel cuts on each owl, but not their position. Of the 38 owls in *IGCH* 1259 three contain chisel cuts on both sides, two on the obverse only (including the single profile-eyed owl) and 22 on the reverse. As with our hoard an individual reverse can display up to seven gashes while fewer appear on the obverse (up to two as against three in our hoard). All of the chisel cuts on Newell's plate of owls (Pl. 1.2–9) fit within the regular positions catalogued above. Most striking is Pl. 1.3, which displays reverse cuts in positions 1, 2, 3, 6, and 7.

34. The chart for *IGCH* 1259 is based on the owls in the catalogue of Newell (1914) (coins 2–39), excluding coin 29 (a fragment) and coin 39 (frontal-eyed).

ings (Table 5). This provides a useful indication that our hoard is a representative sample of owls circulating within the connected areas of Cilicia and Northern Syria during the early fourth century.[35]

The owls from our hoard and *IGCH* 1259 also share significant characteristics with those of several similar and well published hoards of the later fourth century from both the same area and the broader Near East. Most relevant are the 1989 Syria hoard (c. 330; van Alfen 2002a), like our hoard from the area of Aleppo, and the ANS Near East hoard from northern Syria (334–330; Anderson and van Alfen 2008). But also of significance are the 1973 Iraq hoard (c. 323/322; van Alfen 2000) and a hoard attributed to the Near East (c. 340; van Alfen 2004/5). All of these hoards contain a mixture of authentic and imitation owls whose majority is affected by the various surface markings listed above (usually around 60–70% of the total). Among these, chisel cuts are always far and away the most prevalent marking type (usually 50–60%) with cuts on the reverse heavily favored. As even a casual glance at the extensive plates from these various hoards reveals, the placement of cuts on their owls fall largely into the patterned positions outlined in our catalogue.[36] Such a regularized and enduring high volume of chisel cut owls may suggest that this treatment of the coinage originated in and was characteristic of the area encompassing northern Syria and Cilicia. Certainly these cuts are found more frequently in hoards from this and surrounding areas than in those of Egypt where, although there is evidence of chisel cut owls, their presence is less strongly felt and several hoards contain no cut owls at all.[37] Such a discrepancy may well reflect Egypt's comparatively easier access to fresh owls, both those directly imported from Athens and those minted imitatively in the region itself.

35. Useful comparative evidence is provided by *IGCH* 1488 buried at Al-Mina during the first quarter of the fourth century and *CH* 8, 73 from Asia Minor deposited c. 400. The 26 owls of *IGCH* 1488 are treated in detail by Robinson (1937), who records that 20 (77%) were affected by surface markings including 15 (58%) with chisel cuts, 5 (19%) with countermarks and 2 (8%) with punches. The one owl with surface markings illustrated as his Pl. 9 no. 11 features a reverse cut in position 1. Little is known about *CH* 8, 73 except that it contained many owls, all of which were reported to be chisel cut.

36. van Alfen (2002a), 6, notes the repeated presence of reverse cuts in positions 1 and 9 from our catalogue above. Anderson and van Alfen (2008), 171–172, point out the repeated presence of these two cuts in combination with a further reverse cut in position 3, a pattern also attested in our hoard.

37. See the remarks on the Tell el Maskhouta hoard above. Also relevant are Milne (1905) on *IGCH* 1651 (54 frontal-eyed owls) and Eddie (1905) on *IGCH* 1652 (68 frontal-eyed and 2 profile-eyed owls). In both cases the hoards are dated to c. 360 and their owls are reported to lack any chisel cuts even though these cuts are found on the non-owl coins of each collection. See also the lack of chisel cuts on the Egyptian owls from two small hoards in the American Numismatic Society's collection published by van Alfen (2002b).

Turning to the distribution of surface markings in our hoard, a few general observations can be made. The first concerns fluctuations in the distribution of these markings over time. As noted in this paper's first section, our hoard contains sizeable minorities of Starr owls and Buttrey-type owls. These coins represent two coherent coin groups that can be dated respectively to the period directly before and after the emission of the standardized frontal-eyed owls that make up the bulk of our hoard. Significant differences between the distributions of surface markings appearing in these two categories of owls, therefore, are likely to be a product of the contrasting stretches of time that these coins were in circulation (Table 6). Accordingly, we can observe that 13% more of the recently circulated Buttrey owls display no markings at all than their older Starr owl counterparts, as would be expected given the latter's longer availability for such modifications.

More tellingly, the bulk of this 13% difference is due not to an across the board increase in the presence of all types of surface markings but instead mainly reflects the sharp difference in the amount of coins in both groups affected by chisel cuts. The longer an owl in our hoard had been circulating, therefore, the more likely it was to gain this one particular type of surface marking. This may suggest that the parties who gathered our hoard were in closer proximity to the agent(s) responsible for administering chisel cuts than to those authorities behind the other categories of marking types. This would further support the argument advanced above that chisel cut owls perhaps represent a distinct practice in the areas of northern Syria and Cilicia. It may equally, however, reflect a larger decline in the popularity of chisel cuts over the time period in which the contents from our hoard were in circulation. Such a decline may in fact be corroborated in the slight drop in chisel cut owls as a share of total owls from our sample's 66% to the consistent 50–60% seen in the later fourth-century hoards from northern Syria discussed above.[38]

Although it is important in discussing the distribution of surface marking in our hoard to foreground the consistent numerical primacy of reverse chisel cuts, this observation must be balanced against another, contrasting one: namely that although surface markings are a common feature on a huge majority of coins in our hoard, coins with no markings at all on either face make up the largest group after those containing chisel cuts. It should accordingly be kept in mind that surface markings were a common but by no means necessary component of owls circulating in a Near Eastern context.

Outside of chisel cuts the distribution of markings between reverse and obverse is far more even, with the second most represented type of markings, graffiti, showing only a minor preference for the reverse. That chisel cuts followed by graffiti and notches are the most represented marking types indicates a correlation

---

38. But note that in *IGCH* 1488, like our hoard from c. 400, only 59% of owls were chisel cut (see n. 36 above).

Table 6. Diachronic distribution of surface marking types

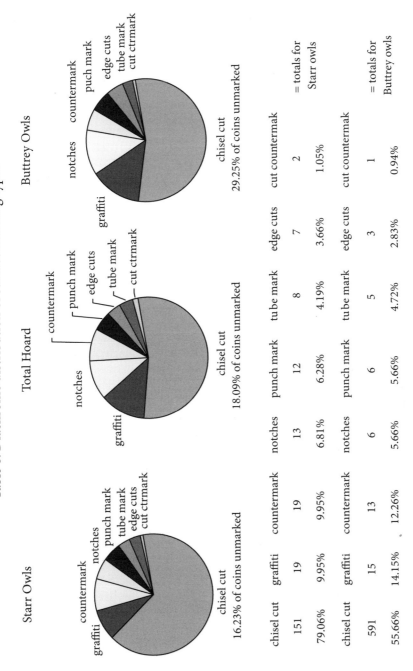

| | chisel cut | graffiti | countermark | notches | punch mark | tube mark | edge cuts | cut countermak | |
|---|---|---|---|---|---|---|---|---|---|
| Starr Owls | 151 | 19 | 19 | 13 | 12 | 8 | 7 | 2 | = totals for Starr owls |
| | 79.06% | 9.95% | 9.95% | 6.81% | 6.28% | 4.19% | 3.66% | 1.05% | |
| Buttrey Owls | chisel cut | graffiti | countermark | notches | punch mark | tube mark | edge cuts | cut countermak | |
| | 591 | 15 | 13 | 6 | 6 | 5 | 3 | 1 | = totals for Buttrey owls |
| | 55.66% | 14.15% | 12.26% | 5.66% | 5.66% | 4.72% | 2.83% | 0.94% | |

between the level of technology required to make a marking and its frequency. The comparably low-tech practice of making gashes, scratching graffiti and cutting notches is simply not on par with the sophistication required to create iconic countermarks, cut complex countermark-like designs (i.e., cut countermarks) or fabricate more specialized tools like punches and tube punches. However, the small gap between the frequency of stamped, iconic countermarks and both notches and graffiti cautions against over-stressing this point (see Table 1).

The differences in technology required for the various categories of surface markings and the disparity in their frequency does, however, invite the question whether they even represent a coherent group of phenomena. Countermarks, cut countermarks and graffiti by their very nature—i.e., as bearing intelligible symbols such as letters and images—reveal themselves as signifiers meant to add information to the coinage on which they appear. By contrast punches, tube punches, notches, edge cuts and especially chisel cuts have often been understood as exclusively serving a metal testing function and not representing systems of signification parallel to other, more sophisticated surface marks.

Certainly the degree of particularized information communicable by countermarks, cut countermarks and graffiti is far greater than that of the other types of surface markings. This is evident from our ability to decode the content if not the meaning of many of the symbols deployed by these three types and even assign a cultural context to some of them. Moreover, as highlighted in the catalogue above, these three surface marking types uniquely share symbols across type boundaries. But although they may be more sophisticated signifiers than the other surface marking types, the sheer quantity of specimens provided by our hoard provides important evidence that other marks share common features as marking systems with countermarks, cut countermarks and graffiti. This is especially true for the extremely well represented category of chisel cuts. Concretely, these shared features are the repeated appearance of identical markings in identical positions allowing for modern classification and, presumably, ancient interpretability.

Chisel cuts, as the largest group of markings in the hoard and the one most frequently dismissed as nothing more than metal testing cuts, are the ideal representative category on which to focus an argument for this interpretation. In Colin Kraay's orthodox formulation from his authoritative *Archaic and Classical Greek Coins*:

> [Test cuts] are savage incisions inflicted with a chisel with no regard for type or legend. Their purpose was evidently the purely practical one of determining whether the coin was made of solid silver throughout; the survival of numerous plated coins (with copper cores) proves that the precaution was necessary. Finds show that such tests were normally performed outside the

Greek world, when the coins ceased to be treated as the currency of individual states and had become so much bullion to be subdivided as required. … Repeated cuts probably represent tests by successive owners; old cuts quickly became tarnished and dirty so that the colour of the metal could no longer be seen, and forgers may have been capable of producing plated forgeries with their flans already convincingly cut.[39]

But, as mentioned, aside from two specimens on the obverse, the chisel cuts on all 1,737 coins from our hoard marked in this manner fell into regular and relatively frequent set positions in relationship to the obverse and reverse designs. These set positions, moreover, can account for all of the chisel cuts on the owl plate from Newell's publication of *IGCH* 1259 and continue to appear with absolute positional regularity in fourth-century owl hoards from northern Syria.[40] Although certain positions appear more frequently than others, all appear independent of all others on multiple occasions. This suggests that each was intended to carry a different meaning that was, on the far rarer number of coins with multiple cuts, combined with that carried by marks in other positions.[41]

Such consistency does not of course disprove that chisel cuts were made to test metal quality nor need it be inimical to such a position.[42] But it does demonstrate that these cuts were regulated by an enduring, widespread and strictly followed standard pattern which in turn suggests the kind of bureaucratic control of coinage also demonstrated by countermarks. The degree to which this control was exercised however was far higher given the much greater frequency of chisel cuts. This is the case even if their crude means of execution suggests at first glance and without reference to either the broad diffusion or enduring regularity of chisel cut patterning a more informal and perhaps even private system of markings. Such cuts accordingly, whether subaerate tests or not, serve like sophisticated countermarks to communicate to Near Eastern handlers of owls that the marked coinage

---

39. Kraay (1976), 16 and n. 4; cf., *inter multos alios*, Robinson (1937), 189–190, van Alfen (2000), 10–13, and Buttrey (1982a), 137: "many of the tetradrachms had been cut upon their surface in antiquity as a test of the metal." Another frequent, if less plausible interpretation of the cuts has been that they served to demonetize currency (Newell 1914: 32). But why this would require applying cuts in often more than one regular position sometimes on one face and sometimes on the other is far from obvious.

40. See notes 34 and 37 above.

41. van Alfen (2002a), 6; Wartenberg and Kagan (1999), 406; and Breglia (1976), 330, make a similar point about chisel cuts in other ancient hoards.

42. The greater likelihood for a coin to suffer a chisel cut the longer it remained in circulation discussed above may in fact be adduced as evidence to support this claim. However, we should also in that case expect older coins to display on average more chisel cuts per affected coin, a finding not corroborated by our sample.

has in some way been made subject to and legitimized by an authority presumably confident its markings would be identifiable to a regional audience.

Against considering such cuts as solely subaerate tests, several pieces of evidence may be presented. Peter van Alfen has productively shown that all ancient testimonia concerning such testing portrays it as not involving the cutting or disfigurement of coins;[43] an argument enhanced by the presence in the Athenian Agora of several plated coins, apparently discarded, without test cuts.[44] Second, four of the five plated coins in our hoard feature chisel cuts, but these were all nevertheless admitted, suggesting a lack of correlation between the cuts and their supposed testing function. Third, sizable minorities of the chisel cuts in our hoard are either too shallow to have functioned effectively as core tests or so deep as to have blown entirely through the coin, reaching a depth unnecessary for testing the interior. Such disparities in cut depth instead suggest the product of a highly automatic marking system where, as with countermarks, the placement and not the depth of the mark is of paramount importance. The result for both chisel cuts and countermarks is, accordingly, a fluctuation of shallow and over-deep markings around a median standard of impression depth. Indeed, some coins even show different depth cuts side by side on the same or opposite faces.[45]

Regardless of the ultimate status of chisel cuts as testing devices for bronze cores, one interesting observation can be made that perhaps helps explain why examples of cut owls rarely appear in western hoards despite being widespread in the Near East. The discrepancy is curious, especially given the comparative ease with which unmarked imitations from Syria and Egypt made their way west. However, the 375 Athenian Silver Coinage Law stipulates that whenever a coin has been deemed to be subaerate (i.e., *after* it has been tested), it should only then receive a chisel cut and be removed from circulation by being dedicated to the Mother of the Gods (see n. 17). Indeed, during the Athenian Agora excavations plated owls with such chisel marks were found in the area of the Metroon.[46] Therefore in Athens, at least after 375, cutting a coin destroyed its value as currency, and the literary evidence assembled by van Alfen (see n. 43) suggests that this was a widespread phenomenon in Classical Greece. Accordingly, owls that had been marked in this manner while in the Near East could not reenter Aegean circulation, accounting for their poor showing in Greek-speaking areas. An implication of this is that such coins were not acquired, as has often been posited for owls in the Near East, in or-

---

43. van Alfen (2002a), 6–7 and n. 11 citing Bogaert 1976.

44. Kroll (1993), 4, where discarded subaerate pieces without chisel cuts (four) outnumber those with (two), not counting the pieces found near the Metroon (for these see below).

45. Plate 1, no. 6 is an excellent example of a single coin with two rather shallow cuts and one excessively deep one.

46. Kroll (1993), 9.

der to conduct business with Greek mercenaries or merchants.[47] This would seem then to provide another piece of evidence for a domestic Near Eastern market for owls as coins, or at least as not just so much bullion (following Kraay's formulation quoted above).

If the above arguments for the semiotic value of chisel cuts are accepted, their applicability to the last two, still unconsidered types of surface markings—namely notches and edge cuts—remains ambiguous. Edge cuts, with their largely consistent appearance as a single mark along bands of unstamped reverse flan, could conceivably be interpreted as representing an easily intelligible sign of either private ownership or, less likely, circulation control. Such shallow cuts after all could in no way serve instead for subaerate testing. Moreover, the rarity of multiple edge cuts on a single coin, the lack of patterning in such instances and the scarcity of any edge cuts on obverses raises the possibility that these particular instances of edge cutting simply represent random, incidental markings. Such cuts would accordingly be unrelated to the semiotic purpose behind the common, straightforward single edge cut placed along un-stamped bands of reverse flan.

A modified version of the position advanced above for edge cuts seems tenable in the case of notches: smaller wedges probably could not perform a metal testing function, and although it could be argued that larger notches did, compared with chisel cuts they seem an inefficient and, on coins where both markings types coincide, redundant mechanism for doing so. Moreover, even if larger notches tested for metal, this would still leave the purpose of smaller wedges unknown. Explaining these markings as ownership or circulation control signifiers is therefore easier. Further, because multiple notches on a single coin are common, we can posit a system in which the number of notches alone is responsible for transmitting the surface marking type's meaning. Unlike with chisel cuts, the position of the notches would here carry no significance. Alternatively, because notches uniquely among surface marking types involve removing a part of the coin, they may represent a form of tax or a circulation control designed to discourage the re-export of owls from a set area through diminishing their value.[48]

The case has been made that all eight categories of surface markings outlined above represent systems of signification, and for many of these categories their semiotic status is beyond doubt. It remains to consider how these various communicative systems and the authorities behind them interacted with one another. Unfortunately, the picture we can draw of this interaction from the data is exceptionally murky and inconclusive since there are no clear correlations between different surface marking types that do or do not appear with each other on individual coins.

---

47. Figueira (1998), 533–534.

48. As noted in the catalogue, however, even large notches did not remove a significant amount of silver from an owl. But their intended effect may have been psychological.

Each of the eight marking types appears alone on at least one coin from our hoard and all but four of the possible combinations of two surface marking types occur exclusively with one another on at least one owl. Three of these unattested combinations, moreover, involve cut countermarks, the rarest type of surface marking in our hoard and therefore the most likely for which evidence would be absent. The fourth involves tube marks, our hoard's second rarest surface marking type.[49] Further, even the four pairs of surface marking types unattested in exclusive combination appear together on coins featuring more than two categories of markings. These observations about attested type combinations are meant to suggest that no hierarchy of markings can be readily extracted from our hoard: rarer types of markings do not exclusively appear on coins also marked with more common surface marks and, accordingly, no *cursus honorum* or progressive sequence of surface modification for a Near Eastern owl is forthcoming. Our north Syrian hoard, instead, is a heterogeneous mix of owls that have reached it untouched by any marking regime, only affected by one, or, rather frequently, by any but no necessary combination of two or more.

This impression of heterogeneity is only strengthened when we look closely at coins with marks from multiple categories that either overlap each other or seem to react to one another in a way that allows us to plot out which came first on the individual coin. In some examples punches and countermarks are superimposed atop graffiti (Plate 2, no. 22) while on other coins with similar combinations it is the graffiti that is scratched on top of these markings (Plate 3, no. 33). On other occasions, by contrast, a graffito has moved from its usual location undoubtedly because a countermark or punch already occupied the usual spot for it (Plate 3, no. 34). The only pattern that does emerge in fact is that lower technology marks more consistently overlap more sophisticated devices. Accordingly, of nineteen coins where a relationship between chisel cuts and other markings is evident, seventeen show the cut overlaying countermarks, punches, tube punches and graffiti (Plate 2, no. 18). In the remaining two cases cuts and notches overlap in situations where priority is impossible to determine.

In conclusion we can say that although the surface marking of owls is a phenomenon that can be characterized as Near Eastern in scope, this Near Eastern context cannot be reduced to any simple system tied to a single authority. Countermarks, cut countermarks and graffiti both in our hoard and in others show that various surface markings were employed to address several cultural groups of the contemporary Near East. Moreover, some marking types used on our owls like chisel cuts, the double-X countermark and the arrow-like cut countermark even seem to have been tied to an area proximate to the hoard itself. At the same time

---

49. A cut countermark never appears exclusively with a countermark, a tube mark or an edge cut. No coin in our sample contains a countermark alone with a tube mark.

the seemingly random combinations of marking types exhibited by our hoard's uniquely large sample demonstrates that the owls subject to these varied semiotic regimes freely circulated between them. But by being collected together in hoards regardless of the various surface markings to which they were subject, these coins also indicate that they nevertheless retained their intelligibility and significance as owls at all stages of this process.

References

Anderson, L. and P. G. van Alfen. 2008. A fourth-century BCE hoard from the Near East. *American Journal of Numismatics* 20: 155–198.

Bogaert, R. 1976. L'essai des monnaies dans l'antiquité. *Revue Belge de Numismatique.* 122: 5–34.

Breglia, L. 1976. Contromarche monetarie e monete "sfigurate." *Annali dell'Istituto Italiano di Numismatica* 23/24: 325–331.

Buttrey, T. V. 1981. The Athenian currency law of 375/4 BC. In *Greek numismatics and archaeology: essays in honor of Margaret Thompson,* O. Mørkholm and Nancy Waggoner, eds., pp. 33–45. Wetteren, Belgium: Cultura.

———. 1982a. Pharaonic imitations of Athenian tetradrachms. In *Proceedings of the 9th International Congress of Numismatics, Berne, September 1979,* vol. 1, T. Hackens and R. Weiller, eds., pp. 137–140. Louvain-la-Neuve and Luxembourg: Association Internationale des Numismates Professionels.

———. 1982b. More on the Athenian coinage law of 375/4 BC. *Numismatica e Antichità Classiche* 10: 71–94.

*CH* 8 = Wartenberg, U., M. Jessop Price and K. A. McGregor. 1994. *Greek hoards. Coin hoards* 8. London: Royal Numismatic Society.

Eddie, S. 1905. Les monnaies dites cisaillées. *Rassegna numismatica, finanziaria e tecnico-monetaria* 2: 51–55.

Elayi, J. and A. Lemaire. 1998. *Graffiti et contremarques ouest-sémitiques sur les monnaies grecques et proche-orientales.* Glaux 13. Milan: Edizioni ennerre S.r.l.

Figueira, T. 1998. *The power of money: coinage and politics in the Athenian Empire.* Philadelphia: University of Pennsylvania Press.

Fischer-Bossert, W. 2008. *The Athenian decadrachm.* Numismatic Notes and Monographs 168. New York: American Numismatic Society.

Flament, C. 2001. À propos des styles d'imitations Athéniennes définis par T. V. Buttrey. *Revue belge de numismatique et de sigillographie* 147: 39–50.

———. 2003. Imitations athéniennes ou monnaies authentiques? Nouvelles considérations sur quelques chouettes athéniennes habituellement identifiées comme imitations. *Revue belge de numismatique et de sigillographie* 149: 1–10.

———. 2005. Un trésor de tétradrachmes athéniens dispersés suivi de considérations relatives au classement, à la frappe et à l'attribution des chouettes à des ateliers étrangers. *Revue belge de numismatique et de sigillographie* 151: 29–38.

———. 2007. *Le monnayage en argent d'Athènes: de l'époque archaïque à l'époque hellénistique (c. 550–c. 40 av J. -C.)*. Louvain-la-Neuve.

Hardwick, N. 2006. *IGCH* 1649: Tell el Mashkouta (anc. Pithom-Heroopolis), 17 km. W of Ismailia, 1947–1948. *Numismatic Chronicle* 166: 382–385.

Hill, G. F. 1922. *Catalogue of Greek coins in the British Museum: Arabia, Mesopotamia and Persia*. London: British Museum.

*IGCH* = Thompson, M., O. Mørkholm and C. M. Kraay, eds. 1973. *An inventory of Greek coin hoards*. New York: American Numismatic Society.

Jungfleisch, M. 1949. Remarques sur une trouvaille de tétradrachmes athéniens faite au voisinage de Pithom. *Revue Numismatique* 11: 27–34.

Kraay, C. M. 1956. The archaic owls of Athens: classification and chronology. *Numismatic Chronicle* 16: 43–68.

———. 1976. *Archaic and classical Greek coins*. Berkeley: University of California Press.

Kroll, J. H. 1993. *The Athenian Agora vol. XXVI: the Greek coins*. Princeton: The American School of Classical Studies at Athens.

———. 2006. Athenian tetradrachms recently discovered in the Athenian Agora. *Revue Numismatique* 162: 57–63.

Milne, J. 1905. A hoard of coins from Egypt of the fourth century BC. *Revue Archéologique* 5: 257–261.

Mørkholm, O. 1974. A coin of Artaxerxes III. *Numismatic Chronicle* 14: 1–8.

Naster, P. 1948. Un trésor de tétradrachmes athéniens trouvé à Tell el Maskhouta (Égypte). *Revue belge de numismatique et de sigillographie* 94: 5–14.

Newell, E. T. 1914. A Cilician find. *Numismatic Chronicle* 14: 1–33.

Nicolet-Pierre, H. 2001 (2004). Retour sur le trésor de Tel el-Athrib 1903 (*IGCH* 1663) conservé à Athènes. *Arkhaiologike ephemeris* 139: 173–187.

———, and C. Arnold-Biucchi. 2000. Le trésor de Lentini (Sicile) 1957 (*IGCH* 2117). In *Pour Denyse, Divertissements numismatiques*, S. Hurter and C. Arnold-Biucchi, eds., pp. 165–171.

Ober, J. 2008. *Democracy and knowledge: innovation and learning in classical Athens*. Princeton: Princeton University Press.

RO = Rhodes, P. J. and R. Osborne. 2003. *Greek historical inscriptions: 404–323 BC*. Oxford: Oxford University Press.

Robinson, E. S. G. 1927. *Catalogue of the Greek coins of Cyrenaica*. London: British Museum.

———. 1937. Coins from the excavations at Al Mina (1936). *Numismatic Chronicle* 17: 182–196.

———. 1947. The Tell el-Mashkuta hoard of Athenian tetradrachms. *Numismatic Chronicle* 7: 115–121.

*SEG* = 1923–. *Supplementum Epigraphicum Graecum*. Amsterdam.

Seltman, C. T. 1924 [1974]. *Athens, its history and coinage before the Persian invasion*. Chicago: Ares.

Starr, C. G. 1970. *Athenian coinage, 480–449 BC*. Oxford: The Clarendon Press.

Stroud, R. S. 1974. An Athenian law on silver coinage. *Hesperia* 43: 157–188.

Van Alfen, P. G. 2000. The "owls" from the 1973 Iraq hoard. *American Journal of Numismatics* 12: 9–58.

———. 2002a. The "owls" from the 1989 Syria hoard with a review of pre-Macedonian coinage in Egypt. *American Journal of Numismatics* 14: 1–57.

———. 2002b. Two unpublished hoards and other "owls" from Egypt. *American Journal of Numismatics* 14: 59–71.

———. 2004/5. A new Athenian "owl" and bullion hoard from the Near East. *American Journal of Numismatics* 16/17: 47–61.

———. 2005. Problems in ancient imitative and counterfeit coinage. In *Making, moving and managing: the new world of ancient economies, 323–331 BC*, Z. Archibald, J. Davies and V. Gabrielsen, eds., pp. 322–354. London: Oxbow.

———. (forthcoming). The Coinage of Athens, 6th–1st c. BC. In *The Oxford handbook of Greek and Roman coinage*, W. Metcalf, ed. Oxford: Oxford University Press.

Wartenberg, U. and J. H. Kagan. 1999. Some comments on a new hoard from the Balkan area. In *Travaux de numismatique grecque offerts à Georges Le Rider*, M. Amandry and S. Hurter, eds., pp. 395–407. London: Spink.

*AJN* Second Series 21 (2009) pp. 29–49
© 2009 The American Numismatic Society

# Athenian Tetradrachms from Tel Mikhal (Israel): A Metallurgical Perspective

PLATE 4                HAIM GITLER, MATTHEW PONTING, AND OREN TAL

This paper uses the analytical results from inductively-coupled plasma atomic emission spectrometry (ICP-AES) and lead isotope analysis (Q-ICP-MS) of a group of Athenian-style tetradrachms found in the excavations of Tel Michal to investigate their origins. The majority of these coins are thought to be Eastern imitations based on style, but the analysis suggests that all these coins may actually be authentic Athenian issues. This is because they were clearly produced from bullion that came from the silver mines of Laurion in Attica. Given the stylistic variability of the Athenian tetradrachms from Tel Michal, we can assume that they are representative of the 'owls' that were circulated in Achaemenid Palestine. Therefore, although it would be premature to argue that the term Eastern imitation is an erroneous scholarly convention, this paper demonstrates that it is a clear possibility.

Tel Mikhal is located in the southern Sharon plain, on the central coastal strip of Palestine.[1] The site has been excavated extensively, revealing in the main Persian (Achaemenid) period remains of the fifth and fourth centuries BC that relate to a series of fortresses on the mound, including cult, service, and possibly domestic buildings on the hills that surrounded the mound and a cemetery on the plain to its northeast.[2]

---

1. This study and its publication were supported by the 'Ancient Israel' project (New Horizons programme) of the Institute of Archaeology, Tel Aviv University.

2. E. Stern (ed.), *The New Encyclopedia of Archaeological Excavations in the Holy Land, 3* (Jerusalem, 1993), s.v. Tel Michal; A. Gorzalczany, The 1996 Excavations along the Northern Hill at Tel Mikhal (Tel Michal), *'Atiqot* 52 (2006), pp. 1–21.

Among the finds retrieved in the course of the latest (salvage) excavation in 1996 are eleven Athenian and Athenian-style tetradrachms found in three adjacent loci (Plate 4, B1–B11).[3] The excavators described these finds as 'a dispersed hoard.' The three loci apparently represent fills.[4] The hoard report mentioned that there are no die-links between the eleven tetradrachms and that no graffiti were noticed on them.[5] According to Ariel, the low level of wear of most of the tetradrachms suggests that they belong to roughly the same date. He also suggested that they were contemporary with three silver Sidonian coins allegedly belonging to the 'hoard' and attributed to 'Abd'astart I/Straton I.[6] In fact, two of the Sidonian coins should be attributed to Ba'alšillem II (c. 401–366 BC), namely the single Sidonian coin illustrated in the publication (Plate 4, B12), and another similarly described coin (no. B13).[7] The third (no. B14), which is plated, may well also be attributable to Ba'alšillem I, though it is hardly legible. The 'hoard' also included a posthumous bronze of Alexander the Great (Plate 4, B15) which dates to 323–317 BC.[8] This coin was retrieved from Locus 464 which formed part of the 'hoard,' though it was overlooked by the excavators when they set a deposition date 'close to the mid-fourth century BC' on the basis of their dating of the Sidonian coins. We do not believe that the Athenian tetradrachms form part of a hoard, at least not in the sense that they were buried together with the Sidonian coins and the posthumous Alexander bronze.[9]

---

3. D. T. Ariel, Coins from Tel Mikhal (Tel Michal), 'Atiqot 52 (2006), pp. 71–88.

4. The relevant loci are 464, 473, and 509, though the latter is missing in the plan and loci list of Gorzalczany (n. 2), pp. 6, 15–16, which gives an overview of the 1996 excavation finds.

5. However, our inspection of these tetradrachms did reveal graffiti on some coins, notably a Phoenician-Aramaic *gimmel* or Greek *lamda* on the reverse of B7 (cf. Ariel [n. 3], Figure 2; and see for comparison J. Elayi and A. Lemaire, *Graffiti et contremarques ouest-sémitiques sur les monnaies grecques et proche-orientales* (Glaux 13; Milan, 1998), p. 64, no. 151, Pl. 18). There are also graffiti on the right reverse field of B2 and on Athena's cheek on coin B11. It should also be noted that test-cuts which are commonly found on Athenian-style coins in the Levant are not found on these tetradrachms.

6. Ariel (n. 3), pp. 73–75, 83–85, nos. B12–B14.

7. J. Elayi and A. G. Elayi, *Le monnayage de la cité phénicienne de Sidon à l'époque perse (Ve–IVe s. av. J.-C.)* (Transeuphratène, Supplement 11; Paris, 2004), Type IV.1.3.c, nos. 851–1191, pp. 136–174 (cf. esp. no. 928).

8. M. J. Price, *The Coinage in the Name of Alexander the Great and Philip Arrhidaeus: A British Museum Catalogue* (Zurich and London, 1991), Tarsus, no. 3063, p. 378.

9. In fact, on the basis of stylistic comparanda we are inclined to date the Tel Mikhal tetradrachms to the second half of the fifth century BC, much earlier than the Sidonian and posthumous Alexander issues. Kroll dates this type of Athenian coin to 454 to c. 415–413 BC, as he associates the beginning of the conventionalized style and the mass striking of this series with the removal of the Athenian League treasury from Delos to Athens in 454 BC,

Authentic Athenian or Athenian-style tetradrachms have been retrieved from several controlled archaeological excavations in Israel, including Bethsaida, Kh. Qastra, 'Atlit, Dor, Megiddo, Kh. 'Eleq, Bet She'an, Tel Zeror, Samaria, Mt Gerizim, Aphek, Wadi ed-Daliyeh, Tell en-Naṣbeh, Ashkelon, Kh. 'Etri, Beth-Zur and La-chish.[10] The present study aims to present an archaeo-metallurgical study of the silver content and trace elements (especially gold and bismuth) of the Athenian owls discovered in Tel Mikhal, and to compare them with those of contemporary indigenous Philistian coinage of the Persian period, in order to assess the origin of the metal ores. Earlier studies have shown that the metallic composition of several Athenian tetradrachms usually taken as ancient imitations (of Buttrey Style B and M)[11] does not differ from that of genuine coins.[12] These analyses however were made on coins purchased in the antiquity market whose place of retrieval is unknown.

Given that the Tel Mikhal tetradrachms are stylistically varied and given that the archaeological context of their find spots (three different loci) suggests that they most probably did not belong to a hoard, it seems likely that, although they were found in one site, they can be taken as representative examples of the issues of the Athenian owls which circulated in Palestine during the second half of the fifth and the first half of the fourth centuries BC.[13]

## Results

The coins were analyzed by the use of inductively-coupled plasma atomic emission

and its most probable termination with the decline in silver bullion income from Athens' allies and the Laurion mines (J. H. Kroll, *The Athenian Agora* 26: The Greek Coins [New Jersey, 1993], pp. 6–7, esp. no. 11, and *id.*, A Small Find of Silver Bullion from Egypt, *American Journal of Numismatics* 13 (2001), p. 3, n. 2).

10. For a detailed list, see Ariel (n. 3), pp. 75–78, Table 1; H. Gitler and O. Tal, *The Coinage of Philistia of the Fifth and Fourth Centuries BC: A Study of the Earliest Coins of Palestine* (Collezioni Numismatiche 6; Milan, 2006), pp. 23–30, Table 2.1.

11. T. V. Buttrey, Pharaonic Imitations of Athenian Tetradrachms, *Proceedings of the 9th International Congress of Numismatics, Berne, September 1979*, I (Louvain-la-Neuve, 1982), pp. 137–140.

12. Cf. C. Flament, A propos des styles d'imitations Atheniennes definis par T.V. Buttrey, *Revue belge de numismatique et de sigillographie* 147 (2001), pp. 37–50; C. Flament, Imitations athéniennes ou monnaies authentiques? Nouvelles considerations sur quelques chouettes athéniennes habituellement identifiées comme imitations, *Revue belge de numismatique et de sigillographie* 149 (2003), pp. 1–10; C. Flament and P. Marchetti, Analysis of Ancient Silver Coins, *Nuclear Instruments and Methods in Physics Research* B 226 (2004), pp. 179–184.

13. However, only a few of the Tel Mikhal tetradrachms show low level of wear and this may support the idea that they circulated in Palestine (and beyond?) at the time, and may be seen as a representative group of southern Levantine Athenian owls.

Table 1. Silver bullion content of the Tel Mikhal tetradrachms

| No. (Cat. No. in Ariel 2006) | Weight / Axis | Bullion | Reg. No. |
|---|---|---|---|
| 1 (B1) | 16.29 g / 9 | 99.0 | IAA 81274 |
| 2 (B2) | 16.09 g / 9 | 98.2 | IAA 81277 |
| 3 (B3) | 16.25 g / 9 | 98.9 | IAA 81278 |
| 4 (B4) | 16.66 g / 9 | 99.8 | IAA 81275 |
| 5 (B5) | 16.28 g / 9 | 99.4 | IAA 81283 |
| 6 (B6) | 16.20 g / 7 | 99.8 | IAA 81284 |
| 7 (B7) | 16.71 g / 9 | 99.7 | IAA 81276 |
| 8 (B8) | 16.85 g / 7 | 99.9 | IAA 81280 |
| 9 (B9) | 16.24 g / 7 | 99.6 | IAA 81281 |
| 10 (B10) | 14.37 g / 7 | 97.8 | IAA 81282 |
| 11 (B11) | 16.41 g / 6 | 99.4 | IAA 81279 |
| Total N | 11 | 11 | 11 |
| Mean | 16.21 g | 99.2 | |
| Minimum | 14.37 g | 97.8 | |
| Maximum | 16.85 g | 99.9 | |
| Std. Deviation | | 0.7 | |
| Total N | | 11 | 11 |
| Mean | | 99.2 | |
| Minimum | | 97.8 | |
| Maximum | | 99.9 | |
| Std. Deviation | | 0.7 | |

spectrometry (ICP-AES) on turnings obtained by drilling into the edge of the coin. Details of the analytical technique are given in the Appendix below.[14]

## Silver Content

Silver produced by traditional methods in antiquity is not chemically pure but

14. Describing coin no. B9, Ariel (n. 3), p. 83, notes that "In the plate, on the reverse, there appears a circle-like symbol close to the owl in the right field. In fact this is an area of corrosion that was removed after the photography. There is nothing in the right field of the reverse besides the inscription." Recently an Athenian tetradrachm with a symbol which seems to be an intaglio Θ in the right field between the owl and the Greek legend was found at the excavations of Tel Dor (Yoav Farhi, personal communication). Coin B9 in the Tel Mikhal hoard may have a similar symbol.

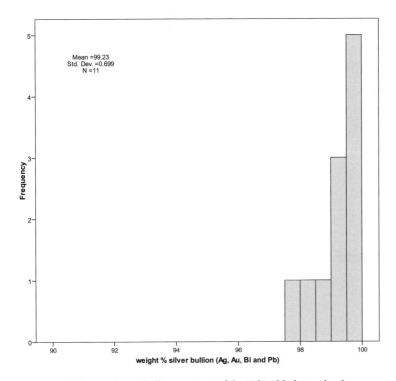

Figure 1. Silver bullion content of the Tel Mikhal tetradrachms.

contains traces of other metals that relate to the ore smelted or the subsequent refining process. It is therefore a more accurate estimate of the silver bullion content
of ancient coins to regard the proportion of silver metal in an alloy as the combined total of elemental silver together with traces of the geochemically related
elements gold, bismuth and lead. The silver bullion content of the coins analyzed
here is presented graphically in Figure 1. The average bullion content for the Tel
Mikhal tetradrachms is 99.2% with a standard deviation of only 0.7, suggesting
well-controlled production, or at least a consistent source of supply. There is no
significant difference in fineness between the single coin (B4) identified as au-
thentically Athenian (although it appears with a question mark i.e., "Autonomous
Athens?") and three coins (B5, B9, and B10) defined as "Autonomous Athens or
imitation" in the original report and the remaining tetradrachms which were defined as imitations (B1, B2, B3, B6, B7, B8, and B11).[15]

15. Ariel (n. 3 above), pp. 74–75, 83–85. It should be noted that B10 is of a slightly lower bullion content and its weight is significantly lighter that the rest of the analyzed tetradrachms.

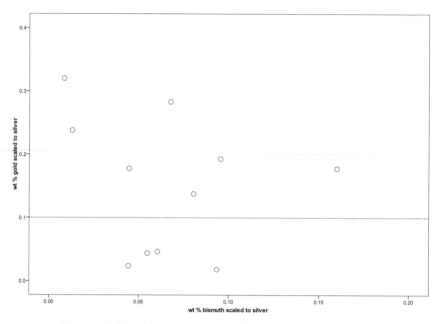

Figure 2. Gold and bismuth contents of the Tel Mikhal tetradrachms.

## Trace Elements

As well as gold, bismuth and lead, other metallic elements may also relate to the original ore, such as copper, tin or nickel; however, these elements may have been added to the metal as, or as contaminants within, the major alloying components. In particular, in cases where copper is present at levels greater than 0.5–1.0 %, it is likely that it was added as an alloying component and that any tin or nickel present would have come as contaminants within it. Only the gold and bismuth can be reliably regarded as associated solely with the silver source/s, while the lead relates to the technology and scale of the refining process. The gold levels are not significantly altered by smelting and refining whilst the bismuth levels are altered only slightly. For these reasons the gold and bismuth traces are regarded as the most useful trace elements in ancient silver.[16] In the coins analyzed here, the gold and bismuth contents suggest two groups: one with a gold content of between 0.1% and

16. H. Mackerrel and R. B. K. Stevenson, Some Analysis of Anglo-Saxon Associated Oriental Silver Coinage, in E. T. Hall and D. M. Metcalf (eds.), *Methods of Chemical and Metallurgical Investigation of Ancient Coinage: a Symposium held by the Royal Numismatic Society in London on 9–11 December 1970* (London, 1972), pp. 195–209. E. Pernicka and H. G. Bachmann, Archäometallurgische Untersuchungen zur antiken Silbergewinnung in Laurion, *Erzmetall* 36 (1983), pp. 592–597, conducted more rigorous experiments that both confirm and dispute Mackerrel and Stevenson's work.

0.45%, and another with a lower gold content of less than 0.08% (Figure 2). The group with lower gold content contains the only coin in Tel Mikhal that has been identified by Ariel as an authentic Athenian coin; the majority of coins (7 or 64%) are in the group with higher gold content.

Useful comparanda are to be found in the analyses of a sample of coins from the Asyut hoard (*IGCH* 1644), deposited in Egypt about half a century before the beginning of our period in around 475 BC. This hoard of about 900 coins appears to be a representative sample of coins circulating in the eastern Mediterranean at the time and comprises primarily coins of Athens and Aegina, together with coins of the Orrescii, Thasos, Acanthus, Corinth, Chios, Samos, Cyprus and Cyrenaica, as well as Persian sigloi.[17] Analyses were conducted on 120 coins from this hoard, representing all the issuing authorities, with the aim of identifying the sources of silver and determining how the coins of the different authorities related to one another.[18] The study presented the results of both bulk chemical analysis (by neutron activation and atomic absorption spectroscopy of drilled samples) and lead isotope measurements (by thermal ionisation mass spectrometry). This combination of chemical and isotopic analysis is a particularly powerful analytical approach which can enable conclusions based on one set of data to be clarified, expanded and often confirmed by the other. The interpretation of these analyses revealed at least three sources of silver used for coin production: Laurion in Attica, Siphnos in the Aegean, and at least one unidentified source. Athenian coins were made exclusively from silver from Laurion, while Aeginetan coins were initially made predominantly from Siphnian silver but gradually started using Laurion silver later in the fifth century BC. Corinth and Samos used bullion from both Laurion and Siphnos and may thus have used Aeginetan coins or a combination of Aeginetan and Athenian coins as its source. The coins of Acanthus and Thasos were more problematic, but appeared to be produced from silver from at least one other unknown source, while the coins of the Orrescii have a unique isotopic signature and a tightly defined chemistry suggesting a relatively small local source, possibly on Mount Pangaeon, which is reported by Herodotus to have had silver deposits.[19] Likewise and unsurprisingly, the Persian sigloi appear to be made of silver from neither Laurion nor Siphnos. Since this publication, further work has established the isotopic signature for the silver mines on Thasos and shown that this silver source was used to make a significant proportion of Thasian silver coins.[20]

17. M. Price and N. Waggoner, *Archaic Greek Coinage: The Asyut Hoard* (London, 1975).

18. N. H. Gale, W. Gentner, and G. A. Wagner, Mineralogical and Geographical Sources of Archaic Greek Coins, in D. M. Metcalf and W. A. Oddy (eds.), *Metallurgy in Numismatics* 1 (RNS SP 13; London, 1980), pp. 3–49.

19. Herodotus, V, 23; VII, 112.

20. G. A. Wagner and G. Weisgerber (eds.), *Antike Edel-und Buntmetallgewinnung auf Thasos*, *Der Anschnitt* Beiheft 6 (Bochum, 1988), esp. pp. 212–223 by N. H. Gale, O. Picard, and J.-N. Barrandon.

The Tel Mikhal coins fit the Asyut chemical data remarkably well. The two groups distinguished by their differing gold and bismuth content correspond with Asyut coins struck from what appears to be, respectively, Laurion silver and Siphnian silver. Figure 3 shows all the data together and clearly shows the two main fields separated by gold content of below and above 0.1%.

The predominantly Athenian group is composed of the majority of Asyut coins which have a Laurion lead isotope signature and can be chemically defined as having low gold and low bismuth. The group also includes some coins with a non-Laurion signature such as the coins of Thasos and Acanthus. This group contains four of the Tel Mikhal tetradrachms, including the coin regarded as an authentic Athenian issue (B4); the other three are classified as imitations by Ariel (B6, B7, and B11). This may imply as well that B6, B7, and B11 are authentic Athenian issues.

The so-called 'Siphnian' group comprises the Asyut coins attributed by lead isotope analysis to silver ore sources in Siphnos but also includes the Aeginetan coins and the coins of Corinth, Zankle, Samos and Caria that also have a 'Siphnian'-type lead isotope signature. This gold/bismuth group also includes the Persian sigloi and a group of Lydian silver staters and half-staters from sixth century Sardis made from silver *parted* from electrum from the river Pactolus,[21] as well as the remaining seven tetradrachms from Tel Mikhal. It is quite clear, therefore, that the simple gold/bismuth plot is not sufficient to separate all the sources of the silver in these coins, but it does clearly separate Laurion and so-called 'Siphnian' silver, although this latter compositional group clearly includes non-Siphnian coins. Further study of the graph shows that, although the silver used by the Orrescii has a gold and bismuth content within the broadest confines of the Laurion cluster, the coins cluster tightly enough together to suggest that the source of the silver is different; a suggestion confirmed by the quite different lead isotope signature that these coins have.[22]

The 'Siphnian' group can also be sub-divided; the Aeginetan coins cluster tightly together with the Corinthian, Zankle, and Carian coins attributed to Siphnian silver by lead isotopes, but are also joined by one Persian siglos and the Lydian staters, while the Tel Mikhal tetradrachms cluster with the other two Persian sigloi and the Corinthian, Samian, and Lycian issues also attributed to a Siphnian silver source by lead isotope analysis. It is worth noting that one of the early Lydian staters appears far to the low bismuth/high gold end of the scatter, suggesting the existence of a third compositional group, situated between the Laurion group and the 'Siphnian' group, consisting of the Tel Mikhal tetradrachms with more than 0.1% gold, one of the early Lydian staters and two of the Persian sigloi. Both of these sub-groups, however, also contain coins that have been attributed by lead

21. A. Ramage and P. T. Craddock, *King Croesus' Gold* (London, 2000). The data for Lydian silver used in these analyses are from this publication.
22. Gale *et al.* (n. 18), p. 44.

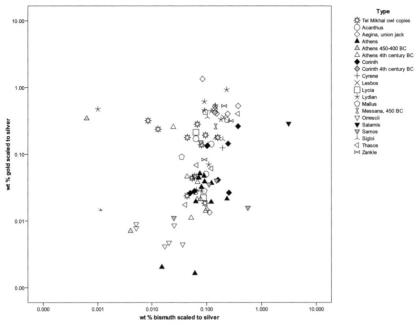

Figure 3. Comparison of the composition of the Asyut hoard coins
and the Tel Mikhal tetradrachms.

isotope analysis to the island of Siphnos, although the number of these are in the minority (less than one-third in group 1 and less than one-quarter in group 2). The bulk of the Asyut hoard coins in both groups (68% and 78% respectively) are either attributed by lead isotope analysis to the 'intermediate' group according to Gale *et al.* or to Lydia by the archaeology.[23] Furthermore, Gale *et al.* speculate that some of these 'intermediate' lead isotope group coins could be produced from silver from either Macedonia (Mount Pangaeon), a view supported by subsequent lead isotope analyses, or from Lydia,[24] while suggesting that those coins struck by Lesbos, Salamis, and Lycia are from a source that 'should probably be sought rather in Anatolia.'[25]

Comparison of the gold and bismuth content of the Tel Mikhal coins with the published work on the Asyut and Sardis material therefore suggests that they can be divided into two groups; those with low gold and low bismuth corresponding to silver with a Laurion lead isotope signature (B4, B6, B7, and B11) and those with high gold and low to moderate bismuth that largely correspond to coins with a non-Laurion signature and that include coins with a Siphnian and 'intermediate'

23. *Loc. cit.*
24. *Ibid.*, p. 42.
25. *Ibid.*, p. 45.

(between Laurion and Siphnos) signature. The majority of the Tel Mikhal coins are found in this second 'non-Laurion' group.

Other chemical elements measured in the Asyut and Tel Mikhal coins can also provide useful information. The lead can be seen as an indictor of technological differences in silver refining, while the copper and nickel can be used to indicate when copper was intentionally added to the silver.

The lead contents plotted against the gold contents allow some separation of the two main groups on the basis of technology. The coins of the Orrescii stand out as containing relatively high lead with an average of 2.1% indicating quite poor cupellation. The Aeginetan coins, on the other hand, are characterised by particularly low levels of lead (average 0.3%, but with the majority containing less than 0.1%), suggesting good cupellation technology. The bulk of the early Lydian staters also stand out as a group with relatively low levels of lead (average 0.2%). All the Athenian tetradrachms from the Asyut hoard appear to fall into lower and higher lead groups that correspond to a fourth century BC group (plus four fifth century coins) and a group made up of solely fifth century BC coins, an interpretation being that cupellation technology improved with time. It is therefore worth noting that, with one exception (B11), the low-gold Tel Mikhal tetradrachms all fall within the earlier higher lead sub-group and include the only Athenian coin identified as authentic (B4), although the type is clearly of late fifth century date.

The copper contents of Greek silver coins of this period are generally quite low; the plot of copper against nickel (Figure 4) shows that the bulk of the Asyut coins have copper contents which are mostly less than 1% and thus might at first glance be assumed to have been present in the original ore rather than intentionally added. However, it should also be noted that in the majority of cases where the copper content of Asyut hoard coins reaches between 0.5 and 1% or more, the copper is correlated with nickel. This suggests that copper at these levels and above was intentionally added because the strong correlation shown is typical of copper metal from certain sources; indeed Gale *et al.* also notice this phenomenon and comment that copper from Siphnos appears to contain in the order of 1.5% nickel.[26] However, the Tel Mikhal tetradrachms show no evidence of a similar correlation, despite the fact that four coins have copper contents equal to or greater than 1%. Such an amount of copper is unlikely to be a naturally occurring contaminant, especially if these coins are produced from silver stocks comprising largely remelted Athenian and other Greek coins—though there are some Asyut coins, even Athenian, with high copper contents—and so may have been intentionally added. The fact that the copper in these coins is not correlated with the nickel indicates that its source is not the same as that of the copper added to the Asyut coins. This is supported by the fact that the level of arsenic and cobalt measured in the Tel Mikhal tetradrachms is generally greater than that in the Asyut coins (Figure 5).

26. *Ibid.*, p. 21.

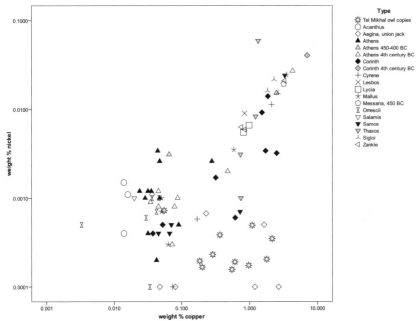

Figure 4. Copper and nickel contents of the Tel Mikhal tetradrachms and the Asyut hoard coins.

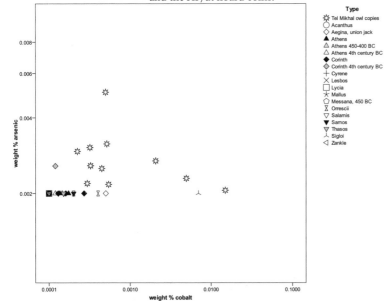

Figure 5. Arsenic and cobalt contents of the Tel Mikhal tetradrachms and the Asyut hoard coins.

Table 2. ICP-AES analyses of the Tel Mikhal tetradrachms. All data are in weight percent. Where an element was not detected, or the measured value was below the 3σ limit of detection, a value of half the limit of detection was used (see Appendix for technical details).

| | sample ref | silver | arsenic | gold | bismuth | cobalt | chromium | copper | iron | manganese | nickel | lead | antimony | tin | zinc | bullion |
|---|---|---|---|---|---|---|---|---|---|---|---|---|---|---|---|---|
| B1 | IAA 81274 | 98.2 | <0.002 | 0.314 | 0.008 | 0.0050 | <0.00005 | 0.974 | 0.002 | <0.00003 | <0.0002 | 0.462 | <0.002 | <0.002 | <0.0001 | 99.0 |
| B2 | IAA 81277 | 96.9 | <0.003 | 0.172 | 0.043 | 0.0021 | 0.00016 | 1.792 | 0.005 | 0.00007 | <0.0002 | 1.057 | <0.002 | <0.002 | <0.0001 | 98.2 |
| B3 | IAA 81278 | 98.2 | <0.003 | 0.234 | 0.013 | 0.0005 | 0.00034 | 1.097 | 0.003 | 0.00032 | 0.0005 | 0.412 | <0.002 | <0.002 | <0.0001 | 98.9 |
| B4 | IAA 81275 | 97.7 | <0.002 | 0.018 | 0.091 | 0.0003 | 0.00020 | 0.201 | 0.002 | 0.00020 | <0.0002 | 1.934 | <0.002 | <0.002 | 0.0003 | 99.8 |
| B5 | IAA 81283 | 98.0 | <0.003 | 0.135 | 0.079 | 0.0004 | <0.00006 | 0.612 | 0.003 | <0.00003 | <0.0002 | 1.134 | <0.002 | <0.002 | <0.0001 | 99.4 |
| B6 | IAA 81284 | 97.1 | <0.003 | 0.045 | 0.059 | 0.0003 | <0.00006 | 0.185 | 0.003 | 0.00005 | <0.0002 | 2.571 | <0.002 | <0.002 | <0.0001 | 99.8 |
| B7 | IAA 81276 | 98.2 | <0.003 | 0.023 | 0.043 | 0.0003 | 0.00019 | 0.288 | 0.002 | 0.00018 | <0.0002 | 1.454 | <0.002 | <0.002 | 0.0006 | 99.7 |
| B8 | IAA 81280 | 97.8 | <0.003 | 0.174 | 0.156 | 0.0002 | <0.00006 | 0.056 | 0.004 | 0.00009 | 0.0007 | 1.833 | <0.002 | <0.002 | 0.0010 | 99.9 |
| B9 | IAA 81281 | 98.7 | <0.005 | 0.190 | 0.094 | 0.0005 | <0.00012 | 0.368 | 0.005 | <0.00006 | <0.0002 | 0.646 | <0.004 | <0.002 | <0.0001 | 99.6 |
| B10 | IAA 81282 | 96.8 | <0.002 | 0.274 | 0.066 | 0.0005 | <0.00005 | 2.151 | 0.004 | 0.00017 | 0.0003 | 0.688 | <0.002 | 0.053 | <0.0001 | 97.8 |
| B11 | IAA 81279 | 98.5 | <0.002 | 0.043 | 0.054 | 0.0150 | 0.00059 | 0.552 | 0.002 | 0.00006 | <0.0002 | 0.830 | <0.002 | <0.002 | 0.0004 | 99.4 |

## Lead Isotope Analyses

It is clear that elemental analyses alone cannot provide answers to all the questions posed by these enigmatic issues and so the samples taken from the Tel Mikhal coins were submitted for lead isotope analysis.[27] This form of lead isotope analysis is less accurate than traditional thermal ionisation mass spectrometry (TIMS) or multi-collector ICP-MS, however direct comparison of data using multi-collector ICP-MS and the system used here from the same samples indicate that accuracies of 0.1% can be obtained for most isotope ratios, whilst those based on Pb204 can be as poor as 1%. However, for the purposes of the discussion here, it is felt that these data are adequate.[28] The results are presented in Figures 6 and 7 and clearly show the majority of the Tel Mikhal coins to have a lead isotope signature consistent with Laurion metal. There is a slight extension of the field created by the Tel Mikhal coins out of the Laurion field and into the areas covered by the Halkidiki and Macedonian isotope fields, suggesting that some of the silver is of a mixed origin. Indeed, there are examples of lead/silver ores from Turkey that also have similar isotope signatures.

The low-gold low-bismuth group of Tel Mikhal coins that so closely matches the Athenian tetradrachms from the Asyut hoard (B4, B6, B7, and B11) is not differentiated from the high-gold group by the lead isotopes to any significant degree. This suggests that there are two groups of metal with a Laurion lead isotope signature that can only be distinguished chemically and this may have a technological rather than provenance-related explanation. Lead metal was usually added to scrap silver metal during melting in order to separate the silver from any added copper; the silver would dissolve in an excess of lead and the resulting silver-rich lead would then be cupelled to extract the silver in the usual way, leaving any copper or other impurities behind with the oxidized lead. The effect of this process would be for the lead isotope signature of the added lead to effectively obscure the underlying lead isotope signature of the original silver source. If Laurion lead was added to refine foreign silver, then the lead isotope signature of the refined silver would be that of the Laurion lead and not of the silver source. However, because of its low chemical reactivity, the concentration levels of the gold in the original silver ore will be carried through the smelting and refining processes largely unchanged and therefore remain as an indicator of the original ore source (Pernicka and Bachmann 1983, n. 16).

27. The authors are extremely grateful to Dr. Scott Young (School of Biosciences, University of Nottingham) for undertaking the lead isotope analyses.

28. Since this paper was submitted the Tel Mikhal samples have been re-analyzed by multi-collector ICP-MS by the NERC Isotope Geochemistry Laboratory of the British Geological Survey. Whilst the increased accuracy is evident, the conclusions and interpretations presented here are confirmed and supported. The new data are to be published elsewhere.

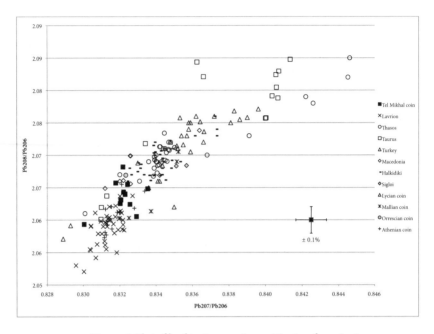

Figure 6. Plot of lead isotopes ratios 208/206 and 207/206.
The point with error bars represents the estimated error of the analyses.

The high-gold Tel Mikhal coins group nicely with Asyut hoard coins from Cyrene, Acanthus, Lycia, and two of the three Persian sigloi and therefore suggest a northern Greek and/or Anatolian origin. It should also be stressed that the lead isotope abundances for certain of the Tel Mikhal coins in this high-gold group (B1, B2, B3, B8, and B9) also fall on the edge of or just outside the Laurion lead isotope field. This may suggest that these coins are made of mixed metal from other Greek sources, the most likely of which appear to be Macedonia and/or Halkidiki or even sources in Anatolia. This would fit with the 'intermediate group' suggested by Gale et. al.[29] If future lead isotope and chemical analysis attributes additional 'Eastern owls' to this group, rather than to the Laurion field, it would provide important evidence for further discussion of the origins of these coins and their relationship to the tetradrachms of Athens proper.

29. Gale *et al.* (n. 18), p. 44.

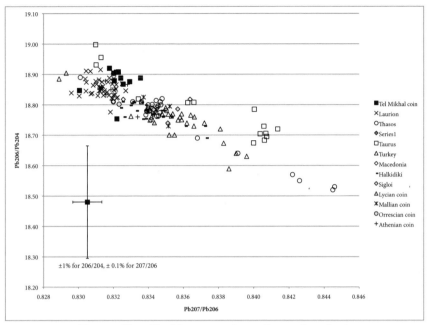

Figure 7. Plot of lead isotopes ratios 206/204 and 207/206.
The point with error bars represents the estimated error of the analyses.

Table 3. Quad-ICP-MS lead isotope data (see Appendix for technical details).

| Sample | 207/206 | 208/206 | 206/204 | 208/204 | 207/204 |
|--------|---------|---------|---------|---------|---------|
| B1 | 0.832 | 2.064 | 18.907 | 39.023 | 15.736 |
| B2 | 0.833 | 2.062 | 18.868 | 38.913 | 15.709 |
| B3 | 0.832 | 2.064 | 18.754 | 38.714 | 15.607 |
| B4 | 0.832 | 2.066 | 18.920 | 39.083 | 15.737 |
| B5 | 0.832 | 2.063 | 18.903 | 38.990 | 15.728 |
| B6 | 0.832 | 2.068 | 18.907 | 39.103 | 15.734 |
| B7 | 0.832 | 2.063 | 18.879 | 38.949 | 15.708 |
| B8 | 0.832 | 2.066 | 18.888 | 39.013 | 15.723 |
| B9 | 0.833 | 2.061 | 18.876 | 38.894 | 15.722 |
| B10 | 0.830 | 2.059 | 18.847 | 38.812 | 15.644 |
| B11 | 0.834 | 2.065 | 18.888 | 39.000 | 15.744 |

## Conclusions

These analyses present a complex picture of silver procurement in Persian-period Palestine. It seems clear that much of the silver for both Tel Mikhal tetradrachms and the Philistian and Edomite coinages[30] probably originated in the Greek world, especially Athens. There are close compositional links between the Tel Mikhal tetradrachms and the Philistian and Edomite coins and it seems possible that the same sources of bullion were being used for both coinages.[31] Both the chemical and lead isotope analyses reported here indicate that a significant proportion of this bullion came from the silver mines at Laurion in Attica, as original bullion or in the form of melted Athenian and other Greek city coins used for making Eastern owls.[32] Other Greek silver sources are also indicated, in particular Halkidiki and Macedonia. However, the use of Greek silver is only part of the picture. The analyses of the Tel Mikhal coins also suggest that some of the silver may also have had its origins in the imperial coins of Persia and the earlier issues of Lydia. This is, of course, not surprising. It is rather the fact that so much Greek silver was finding its way into the Athenian copies from Tel Mikhal which is of interest and which corroborates the economic links with the Greek world already attested by the dominance of the Athenian owl as the prototype of choice.[33]

---

30. See H. Gitler, M. Ponting, and O. Tal, Metallurgical Analysis of Southern Palestinian Coins of the Persian Period, *Israel Numismatic Research* 3 (2008), pp. 13–27.

31. *Ibid.*

32. Here one must refer to the *kršn* (*karsh*), *š* (*šheqels*) and *ḥ* (*ḥallures*) denominations used for the weighing of silver ores(?) carried in Ionian ships sailing to Egypt mentioned in the *Customs Account* of Elephantine, dated to year 11 of Xerxes I—475 BC or Artaxerxes I—454 BC. For the published edition, see B. Porten and A. Yardeni, *Textbook of Aramaic Documents from Ancient Egypt, 3: Literature, Accounts, Lists* (Jerusalem, 1993), §C3.7. The information from this document concerns maritime trade, including the kinds of ships sailing to and from Egypt and the kinds of goods they carried, as well as the system of duty collection and royal accountancy in Egypt at the time; see A. Yardeni, Maritime Trade and Royal Accountancy in an Erased Customs Account from 475 B.C.E. on the Aḥiqar Scroll from Elephantine, *Bulletin of the American Schools of Oriental Research* 293 (1994), pp. 67–78; P. Briant and R. Descat, Un registre douanier de la satrapie d'Égypte a l'époque achéménide, in N. Grimal and B. Menu (eds.), *Le commerce en Égypte ancienne* (IFAO, Bibliothèque d'Étude 121; Cairo, 1998), pp. 59–104.

33. The Athena/owl motif was borrowed by the southern Levantine societies (Philistian, Samarian, Judean, Edomite) because it symbolized the accepted currency of the period; it probably had no mythical connotations for them. The prototype for the local Palestinian Athenian-style issues was the tetradrachm. This is evident from the fact that in local issues of all denominations (sheqels ['tetradrachms'], quarter-sheqels ['drachms'], one-eighth sheqels ['hemidrachms'], *ma'ehs* ['obols'], half-*ma'ehs* ['hemiobols'], and even smaller denominations: see O. Tal, Coin Denominations and Weight Standards in Fourth-century

However, it should be stressed that, on the basis of the analyses presented here, it is also possible that all the Tel Mikhal coins are authentic Athenian coins, although only B4 is considered a possibility from a stylistic point of view and B5, B9 and B10 were classified as 'Autonomous Athens or imitation.'[34] If we accept the attribution of these coins in Ariel's report, then the Eastern owls will have been produced from either Greek ores or melted Athenian and other Greek city coins.[35] The other interpretation of the data could be that the attribution of these coins on stylistic grounds is erroneous and that they are in fact authentic Athenian issues.[36] Two considerations support this notion. First of all, why would anyone melt an authentic Athenian tetradrachm in order to produce a tetradrachm which looked almost identical?[37] In case chopped, cut or worn authentic Athenian coins were used for this purpose one would expect different chemical composition and a lower level of pure silver. This holds true for other types of 'intermediate' phases in which melted authentic Athenian coins were used. Secondly, the number of late sixth and fifth century BC coins retrieved from controlled archaeological excavations in Israel is relatively small, and the same can be said of stray finds in the

BCE Palestine, *Israel Numismatic Research* 2 [2007], pp. 17–28) a crescent appears in the upper left field between the olive and the owl. In the authentic Athenian issues the crescent occurs only on the tetradrachms.

34. Ariel (n. 3), p. 74.

35. Palestine has no silver sources of its own so all silver used in the region must have come from outside.

36. For example, the attribution of Roman *denarii* to mints was traditionally based on stylistic criteria, which have a number of limitations and need to be supplemented by metallurgical analysis. Thus, although chemical analysis has revealed that traditional attributions of Severan *denarii* are generally accurate, it has also shown that about 10% of attributions are false, and has allowed a significant proportion of uncertainly attributed *denarii* to be given definite attributions: see H. Gitler and M. Ponting, *The Silver Coinage of Septimius Severus and his Family (193–211 AD): A Study of the Chemical Composition of the Roman and Eastern Issues* (Glaux 16; Milan, 2003), esp. pp. 52, 63–78).

37. One might note that the 17.2 g theoretical weight of the Athenian tetradrachm (see H. Nicolet-Pierre, Metrologie des monnaies grecques. La Grèce centrale et l'Egée aux époques archaïque et classsique (VIᶜ–IVᶜ s.), *Annali* 47 [2000], p. 41; J. Elsen, La stabilité du système pondéral et monétaire attique (VIᶜ–IIᶜ s. avant notre ère), *Revue belge de numismatique et de sigillographie* 148 [2002], p. 23) is some 4% heavier than the average weight of our coins which is 16.5 g (B4 is 16.66 g; B6 is 16.20 g; B7 is 16.71 g; and B11 is 16.41 g. But, given the relative scarcity of Eastern owls found in controlled archaeological excavations or as strays in Palestine (Gitler and Tal [n. 8], pp. 23–30), such a small difference would not have prompted the melting down of Athenian coins in order to produce lighter local coins with the same types since the profit would be too low and would hardly cover the cost of the procedure.

region.[38] One might thus argue that too few Greek city coins reached the region to support the production of Eastern owls in any great quantity. Nonetheless, hoards containing relatively large numbers of early Greek coins have been found both in the southern Levant and Egypt,[39] and it may be that most such coins were consigned to the melting pot to produce local coins before they had had a chance to circulate.

Our metallurgical analyses thus cast some doubt on Ariel's identification of ten of the Tel Mikhal tetradrachms as Eastern imitations and suggests that many of the owls which circulated in Palestine could in fact be authentic Athenian coins. Given the stylistic variability of the Tel Mikhal tetradrachms, it is reasonable to assume that many of the Athenian-style tetradrachms found in Palestine will reveal similarly complex metallurgical results. It would be premature however to argue that the term Eastern imitations—and its derivatives i.e., Eastern/Palestinian/southern Levantine owls—is an erroneous scholarly convention of mental rationalization based on their 'non-canonical' craftsmanship, given the relative small number of analyzed coins and their provenance in a single site.

The mean silver content of all 11 tetradrachms is 99.2% and the lowest silver content is 97.8% which is still higher than the average silver content of Philistian coinage analyzed by the same method (ICP-AES).[40] This suggests that the silver content of the Eastern owls was as strictly controlled as authentic Athenian tetradrachms and provides further evidence to support the view that these coins are either authentic Athenian products or some form of centrally minted eastern issues produced from Greek silver. Given the stylistic variability of the Tel Mikhal tetradrachms and our metallurgical analyses, it seems that authentic Athenian and

38. Gitler and Tal (n. 10), pp. 13–30.

39. See e.g., H. Gitler, A *Hacksilber* and Cut Athenian Tetradrachm Hoard from the Environs of Samaria: Late Fourth Century BCE, *Israel Numismatic Research* 1 (2006), pp. 6–7, Table 1 *passim*.

40. Cf. Gitler, Ponting, and Tal (n. 26), Table 2. This is also true of southern Palestinian coinages analyzed by a different method (XRF); thus the average silver bullion (= Ag + Au + Pb + Bi) of the 271 Philistian issues analyzed in the course of Gitler and Tal's work on the Philistian coinage (Gitler and Tal (n. 10), pp. 329–334 *passim*) is 95%; the average silver content of the 66 Samarian issues analyzed in Gitler and Tal's work on new Samarian coin types (H. Gitler and O. Tal, Coins with the Aramaic Legend *Šhrw* and Other Unrecorded Samarian Issues, *Schweizerische Numismatische Rundschau* 85 [2006], Table 1) is 92.5; the average silver content of 24 Edomite 'drachms' (plated coins excluded) discussed in H. Gitler, O. Tal, and P. van Alfen, Silver Dome-shaped Coins from Persian-period Southern Palestine, *Israel Numismatic Research* 2 (2007), Table 4, is 97.5%; and the average silver content of the 32 Persian-period *yhd* coins discussed in H. Gitler and C. Lorber, A New Chronology for the Ptolemaic Coins of Judah, *American Journal of Numismatics* 18 (2006), Table 4, is 97.7%.

Eastern owls could hardly be distinguished from one another, so that that Eastern owls would be readily acceptable in Athenian and other Greek markets. Who then would benefit from the production of Eastern owls? Some have argued that the minting of silver bullion in the earliest stages of the monetary economy in the southern Levant was connected with payments to the army—that is, funding for the activities of the Phoenician fleet on behalf of the Achaemenids, or for the major urban centers responsible for supplies to the army.[41] Others have claimed that the minting of Athenian-style Eastern issues was intended to address the lack of Athenian coinage in the markets of the Near East after the Peloponnesian War.[42] Both suggestions may well explain the high standard of production of the Eastern owls. If they were aimed at Greek markets (mercenaries and merchants), we may suggest that the Achaemenid authorities controlled their production and circulation in order to facilitate international interactions and trade. The Eastern owls were produced at the same time as the local Philistian, Samarian, Judean, and Edomite (autonomous) coinages. Their function however differed: the latter formed part of an intra-city or intra-regional monetary system for they are rarely found outside the political boundaries of the issuing authorities,[43] while the former formed an international currency since they are found well beyond the boundaries of the Fifth Satrapy. Elsewhere we have argued that much of the silver for the Philistian and Edomite coinages originated in the Greek world, most probably from Athenian coins.[44] It would thus be reasonable to suggest that the Philistian minting authority was one of the production centres that made the Eastern owls for the Achaemenid and Greek markets, while at the same time producing a local coinage with a lower bullion content. The fact that the first production stage of Philistian coinage shows a high degree of similarity in weight, flan, fabric, and even in some of the motifs shown in the Eastern owls may suggest that some of the latter were locally produced and may be regarded as the forerunners of local Philistian types or contemporary counterparts. Palestine had a long tradition of using bronze, silver, gold, and different metal alloys in trade, as the *Hacksilber* hoards found at biblical sites in Palestine attest.[45]

41. Cf. Babelon, *Traité* II.2, p. 671; J. Elayi, L'ouverture du premier atelier monétaire phénicien, *Bulletin du Cercle d'Études Numismatiques* 32 (1995), pp. 73–78.

42. Cf. J. P. Six, Observations sur les monnaies phéniciennes, *Numismatic Chronicle* 67, Part II (1877), pp. 177–239; J. G. Milne, The Origin of Certain Copies of Athenian Tetradrachms, *Iraq* 4 (1937), pp. 57–58.

43. Gitler and Tal (n. 10), pp. 49–51.

44. Gitler, Ponting, and Tal (n. 30).

45. Gitler and Tal (n. 10), pp. 9–12.

## ANALYTICAL APPENDIX

The coins selected for analysis were first sampled by drilling into the edge of the coin with a 0.6 mm diameter drill and collecting the turnings. The first millimetre or two of metal was always discarded to avoid contamination by corrosion products and unrepresentative surface metal. Approximately 10 mg of the sample was weighed into a glass vial and dissolved according to the procedure devised by Hughes *et al.*[46] The dissolved sample was made up to a final 10ml volume with purified water (18.2 M$\Omega$) and centrifuged to ensure that all the precipitated silver chloride settled out. Silver was calculated by difference and checked by atomic absorption spectrometry. Analysis was conducted on a Perkin Elmer DV3000 series inductively coupled plasma atomic emission spectrometer (ICP-AES) which was calibrated using matrix-matched multi-element standards. Instrumental drift and analytical precision were monitored by specially prepared quality control solutions which were measured after every ten samples. Accuracy was checked by the use of two certified standard reference materials (SRMs): Bundesanstalt für materialprüfung No. 211 and Silver standard Gliwice AG5-chem. The relative accuracy based on two analyses of both SRMs at the beginning and at the end of the analysis is better than 8% for all major and minor elements (copper <1%), with the exception of lead (9.2% error at a concentration of 0.74%). The relative accuracy of the trace elements is better than 10%, again with the poorer values occurring when the concentrations approach the limits of detection (i.e., manganese with a 13.5% error on a certified value of 0.0019%). Instrumental precision (coefficient of variation across three replicate analyses of the same sample) is generally better than 3%, while analytical precision (coefficient of variation of two analyses of the same SRM across all analyses) is generally better than 3% for major, minor and trace elements over all analyses, with the exception of manganese, antimony, and bismuth, which are poor because the certified values are close to the limit of detection (LOD). The LODs for the analysis (expressed as parts per million), calculated at 3 σ, are:

| Ag | As | Au | Bi | Co | Cr | Cu | Fe | Mn | Ni | Pb | Sb | Sn | Zn |
|---|---|---|---|---|---|---|---|---|---|---|---|---|---|
| 0.001 | 0.039 | 0.005 | 0.013 | 0.002 | 0.001 | 0.041 | 0.001 | 0.0004 | 0.003 | 0.013 | 0.029 | 0.029 | 0.002 |

Lead isotope ratios were determined by quadrupole ICPMS (*Thermo-Fisher Scientific* X-Series[II]). The dwell times used were: 10, 10, 2.5, 2.5 and 2.5 ms for $^{202}$Hg, $^{204}$Pb, $^{206}$Pb, $^{207}$Pb and $^{208}$Pb respectively. These represent a compromise between the need for stability for individual isotope count rates and an attempt to minimise 'plasma flicker' during each run. The isotope $^{202}$Hg was included to provide an isobaric correction for $^{204}$Hg on $^{204}$Pb. Ten analytical runs per analyte were employed.

46. M. J. Hughes, M. R. Cowell, and P. T. Craddock, Atomic Absorption Techniques in Archaeology, *Archaeometry* 18 (1976), pp. 19–37.

Isotope ratios were determined from blank-corrected cps data. Mass bias correction (K-factors) of raw cps data was undertaken by running the isotopic reference NIST-981 after every four samples and calculating K-factors for each sample by extrapolation. Quadrupole stability was checked from a plot of K-factor against mass difference ($\Delta$mass) for the isotope ratios (K-factor = 1.0 at $\Delta$mass = 0). Detector 'dead time correction' was optimised by running several concentrations (5 – 40 µg L$^{-1}$) of NIST-981 at the start of each experiment and adjusting to minimise variation in the ratio $^{206}Pb/^{208}Pb$ across the concentration range. (Information on the instrumentation and procedures employed for the lead isotope analyses was kindly provided by Dr. Scott Young).[47]

47. Comparative lead isotope data are from the following: Gale *et al.* (n. 18); I. L. Barnes *et al.*, Isotopic Analysis of Laurion Lead Ores, in C. W. Beck (ed.), *Archaeological Chemistry* (Washington, 1974), pp. 1–10; G. A. Wagner *et al.*, Early Bronze Age Lead-Silver Mining and Metallurgy in the Aegean: The Ancient Workings on Siphnos, in P. T. Craddock (ed.), *Scientific Studies in Early Mining and Extractive Metallurgy* (London, 1980), pp. 63–80; N. H. Gale, Some Aspects of Lead and Silver Mining in the Aegean, *Thera and the Aegean World*, II (London, 1980), pp. 161–195; V. E. Chamerlain and N. H. Gale, The Isotopic Composition of Lead in Greek Coins and Galena from Greece and Turkey, in E. A. Slater and J. O. Tate (eds.), *Proceedings of the 16th International Symposium on Archaeometry and Archaeological Prospection* (Edinburgh, 1980), pp. 139–155; N. H. Gale, W. Gentner, and G. A. Wagner, Mineralogical and Geographical Silver Sources of Archaic Greek Coinage Special, *Publications of the Royal Numismatic Society* 13 (1980), pp. 3–49; N. H. Gale and Z. A. Stos-Gale, Cycladic Lead and Silver Metallurgy, *The Annual of the British School at Athens* 76 (1981), pp. 169–224; *id.* Thorikos, Perati and Bronze Age Silver Production in the Laurion, *Attica Miscellanea Graeca* 5 (1982), pp. 97–103; E. Pernicka *et al.*, Archaometallurgische Untersuchungen in Nordwestanatolien, *Jahrbuch des Romisch-Germanisches Zentralmuseums* 31 (1984), pp. 533–599; Z. A. Stos-Gale, N. H. Gale, and G. R. Gilmore, Early Bronze Age Trojan Metal Sources and Anatolians in the Cyclades, *Oxford Journal of Archaeology* 3 (1984), pp. 23–44; N. H. Gale, O. Picard, and J. N. Barrandon, The Archaic Thasian Silver Coinage, *Der Anschnitt* Beiheft 6 (Bochum, 1988), pp. 212–223; K. A. Yener *et al.*, Stable Lead Isotope Studies of Central Taurus Ore Sources and Related Artifacts from Eastern Mediterranean Chalcolithic and Bronze Age Sites, *Journal of Archaeological Science* 18 (1991), pp. 541–577; Z. A. Stos-Gale, N. H. Gale, and N. Annetts, Lead Isotope Data from the Isotrace Laboratory: Archaeometry Data Base 3. Ores from the Aegean: Part 1, *Archeometry* 38 (1996), pp. 381–390.

AJN Second Series 21 (2009) pp. 51–88
© 2009 The American Numismatic Society

# The Eras of Pamphylia
# and the Seleucid Invasions of Asia Minor

PLATES 5–7

ANDREW MEADOWS*

This article attempts to identify eras by which the Pamphylian cities dated their posthumous Alexander coinage of the late third and early second century. The following start dates are suggested: Perge – c. 223/2 BC; Aspendos – c. 213/2; Phaselis – c. 213/2. It is argued that the beginning of the issues of Perge and Aspendos, as well as of their eras, are connected with Seleucid military activity in Pamphylia. The same reason is suggested for the over-representation in hoards of certain issues of the mints of Perge and Aspendos. A connection between the arrival of Antiochus III in Asia Minor in 203 is further proposed as the possible context for the beginning of the coinage of Side with autonomous types. The posthumous Alexander coinage of Phaselis is suggested, on the basis of its pattern of hoarding, to be a different phenomenon, to be regarded as more truly civic in nature. The Seleucid coinages of Seleucus III and Antiochus III previously given to Seleucia ad Calycadnum (*SC* 916 and 1016) are reattributed to Termessos.

The posthumous Alexander coinage produced in the region of Pamphylia in southern Asia Minor poses a familiar problem.[1] The issues in question form part of the

*meadows@numismatics.org. The following standard abbreviations are used: *IGCH* = M. Thompson et al., *Inventory of Greek Coin Hoards* (New York, 1973); *CH* = *Coin Hoards*; *SC* = A. Houghton, C. Lorber et al. *Seleucid Coins* vols. I and II (Lancaster, PA, 2002 and 2008); *CSE* = *Coins of the Seleucid Empire from the Collection of Arthur Houghton* vols I and II (New York, 1983 and 2007); Price = Price (1991). Where numbers appear in parentheses after the names of coin hoards these refer to entries in *IGCH* or *CH*.

1. I must here express my sincere thanks to Cathy Lorber, Andrew McIntyre and Oliver

broader phenomenon of the posthumous Alexanders of the late third and early second centuries BC, but distinguish themselves by the appearance thereon of a series of sequences of numbers, generally identified as years of civic eras, attributable to a number of issuing cities. The two most readily identifiable are the issues of Phaselis (with mint mark Φ) and those of Aspendos (mintmark ΑΣ) Plate 5, nos. 1–2).[2] A third large mint used no mint mark, but is generally regarded (since its treatment by Seyrig)[3] to be that of Perge (Plate 5, no. 3). Three other mints have also been identified as Sillyon (mint mark ΣΙ), Magydos (M) and Termessos (T) (Plate 5, nos. 4–6), and a fourth, identified by a Φ in combination with o, will be discussed by Andrew McIntyre in a forthcoming study, but these last will not concern us here (Plate 5, no. 7).[4]

The issues of Perge run from year 1 to 33 (with gaps in years 3, 5 and 6); those of Aspendos from year 1 to 29, (gap in year 13); those of Phaselis from year 1 to 33, (gap in year 29).[5] Given the general stylistic similarity of the issues, the geographic proximity of the cities and the similar spans covered by their eras, it is *a priori* tempting to regard all of these eras as identical, and to recognize the Pamphylian era as something of significance beyond the merely civic. Such indeed was the assumption of earlier scholars, including Seyrig. But the hoard evidence, as has been clearly demonstrated by Christof Boehringer, Martin Price and most recently Andrew McIntyre, tells a different story. Between the eras of Perge and Aspendos there is, without a shadow of a doubt, a difference of 10 years, the era of Perge having begun first.[6] The evidence for Phaselis emerges less clearly, but has seemed in the past to suggest that its era began shortly after that of Perge, and a little before that of Aspendos; we shall return to this question below. But if this much is clear,

Hoover who have generously provided me with unpublished material and who have all read this paper in an earlier version, provided me with detailed reactions and saved me from a number of errors. For those that remain, *mea culpa*.

    2. A die study of the Alexanders of Phaselis is included in Heipp-Tamer (1993). To date no such study of the mint of Aspendos has been published.

    3. Seyrig (1963). The key to attribution was the appearance on issues dated to year 20 of a mint mark depicting a sphinx, bearing stylistic similarities to that which appears on the bronze coinage of Perge. For a die-study and commentary see Colin (1996), pp. 17–33.

    4. For Sillyon see Price (1991), pp. 366–367, nos. 2976–2981 (years 3, 4, 5, 6 and 11 are recorded). The evidence for the 'Magydos' issues has now been collected by McIntyre (2007), but the attribution remains uncertain. For Termessos see McIntyre (2006) and below.

    5. For a summary see Price (1991), p. 348; for the gap in year 3 at Perge see also McIntyre (2007), p. 93, n.3 (where, however, there is a mistake in the discussion of years 1 and 2. Both are attested by a single obverse die; it is the second die attributed by Colin to year 1 not year 2, for which Colin records only one die, that is to be regarded as a forgery).

    6. The difference of 10 years, at minimum, emerges from the study of shared dies by McIntyre (2007). The hoard evidence, as we shall see, suggests that it is highly unlikely to be longer.

the absolute chronology of when these eras began and ended remains uncertain. Two reconstructions currently vie for consideration.

The first is that proposed by Christof Boehringer who in 1972 collected the evidence for known specimens of the Alexanders of Perge and noted what appeared to him to be a falling-off of production after year 29. This fact he combined with the limited hoard evidence, which also showed a group of four hoards closing with Perge year 29. To these observations he added the hypothesis that the battle of Magnesia, which he dated to November/December 190 BC, was the historical event behind these two patterns. From this he was able to posit a start date for the era of Perge 29 years before 190. The era thus began in 219/8. Based on the probable gap of 9–10 years between the eras of Perge and Aspendos, he further posited a start date for the latter city's era in 210/209 BC.[7]

Martin Price, on the other hand, while accepting the approximate dates of Boehringer's reconstruction, did not believe such precision was possible on the basis of the hoard evidence, and instead sought an answer, like Seyrig before him, in immediate political events near the beginnings of the supposed eras. Like Seyrig, he alighted upon the aftermath of the death of Ptolemy Euergetes in 222 BC, and a hypothesized Ptolemaic loss of Pamphylia in the following year, as the start date of the era of Perge.[8] For Aspendos he suggested 'a date in the period 214–210 BC, following the defeat of Achaeus' (p. 353).

Both of these reconstructions seem plausible, yet both rely in part on inferences from supposed historical circumstances, rather than numismatic evidence for their absolute dates. It is not, therefore, easy to choose between them. To resolve the matter new evidence is clearly needed, and in fact appeared over ten years ago with the publication of two important new hoards from the Levant.

In Part I of this article, I shall discuss the ramifications of this new evidence and re-examine some of the older hoard evidence with a view to establishing a chronology for the Pamphylian eras that is based first and foremost on the numismatic evidence. In Part II, I shall investigate how this hoard-derived chronology fits with what is otherwise known of the history of Pamphylia in the late third and early second centuries BC, and what additional light the evidence of the coinage may throw on the matter.

## Part I. The Hoard Evidence

The first 'new' hoard referred to above had in fact previously been noted under the title 'Syria 1971' as *CH* 2. 81. Details of the group had been recorded in commerce by P. Girardi and preserved in the interim by A. Houghton. The publication by Le

---

7. Boehringer (1972), pp. 52–56 (Perge) and 59 (Aspendos). Cf. Le Rider (1972), pp. 254–255, Mørkholm (1978), pp. 69–70 and Price (1991), p. 347 for summaries.

8. Price (1991), p. 347; cf. Seyrig (1963), pp. 41–42.

Rider (1998) now allows the following summary of its contents:

**Syria 1971**
 Antigonus Doson 1 tetradr. (Poseidon/Apollo on prow)
 Philip V 1 tetradr. (Shield/club in wreath)
 Posthumous Alexander tetradrs.
  Megalopolis 1 (Price 752)
  Sinope 1 (Price 1257)
  Heraclea Pontica 1 (Price 1281)
  Pergamum 1 (Price 1490)
  Miletus 2 (Price 2171, 2180)
  Chios 3 (Price 2393, -,-. Bauslaugh [1979] 50A, -,-)
  Samos 2 (Price 2446–7)
   Rhodes 4 (Price 2511, 2517–8, 2520; Kleiner [1971], III, XI, XII, XIII)
   Phaselis 5 (to Yr. 19)
   Aspendus 3 (to Yr. 18)
   Perge 6 (to Yr. 26)
   Aradus 5 (to Yr. 195/4 BC)
   Gerrha 3 (Price 3957)
   Uncert. Mints 3
 Ephesus 3 drs.
  Kinns (1999) Class F?
 Alabanda
  1 tetradr. (Series 1, ΤΙΜΟΚΛΗΣ)
 Side 22 tetradrs.
 Syria
  Antiochus I 2 (*SC* 308a; 379.6a)
  Antiochus II (*SC* 587.4b)
  Antiochus Hierax 3 (*SC* 835.6; 855.1; 879.4)
  Antiochus III 11
   Uncert, mint 49 (Phrygia) 1 (*SC* 1004)
   Soli 2 (*SC* 1019.2a; 1021.2)
   Tarsus 1 (*SC* 1031.2)
   Laodicea ad mare 1 (*SC* 1071.2)
   ΔI mint 2 (*SC* 1112)
   Uncert. Mint 67 (N. Mesopotamia) 1 (*SC* 1132.6)
   Uncert. Mint 68? 1 (*SC* 1137)
 Egypt
  Ptolemy II 2
  Ptolemy IV 1
  Ptolemy V 2

The hoard is remarkable in a couple of respects and the full ramifications have yet to be appreciated.

The appearance of Ptolemaic issues in a hoard otherwise composed of Attic weight coinage is not unique, but certainly out of the ordinary and is, as Le Rider noted, strongly suggestive of a provenance on the borders of Seleucid and Ptolemaic territory.[9] This likely provenance is further supported by another component of the hoard, the posthumous Alexanders from the mint of Arados. As, again, Le Rider noted, the hoard contained five such coins, all marked with the city's era, which began in 259 BC. Years 61 (1 specimen), 64 (1 specimen) and 65 (3 specimens) were all represented: 'étant donné le peu d'abondance du monnayage de cette époque, la présence dans le trésor de cinq exemplaires d'années voisines n'est peut-être pas sans intérêt pour la détermination du lieu de trouvaille'.[10] He went on to suggest a find-spot within the Aradian Peraea or close to its borders.

There can be little quarrel with this analysis of the hoard, but having established the likelihood of a provenance from the Aradian Peraea or its environs, we can surely take a step forward in the determination of the date of the deposit of this hoard, and thereby clarify the chronology of some of its contents. If the hoard was indeed found in the Aradian Peraea, then the issues of Aradus should be the most recently produced coins present. The pattern of representation of Aradian issues, with three of the five consecutively dated specimens having been struck in year 65, strongly suggests a date of deposit in 195 or 194 BC.

We may begin by noting that this is a good general fit with the Seleucid contents of the hoard, amongst which were two issues of the mint of Soli, which can only have opened after the capture of this city by Antiochus III in 197 BC, and the ΔI mint, active in Syria from around the same date.[11] The tetradrachm of Philip V, which had traveled furthest of all the coins in the hoard had been struck perhaps a little before 197 BC.[12]

The hoard also contains issues of the dated Alexander coinages of Phaselis (to year 19), Perge (to year 26) and Aspendos (to year 18). The latest years of both Perge and Aspendos are represented by two coins each (compared to one for all other years), and the latest two coins of Perge were struck probably from the same obverse die. It is likely, therefore, that the latest coins of these two mints were produced fairly close to the date of the hoard's deposit. Taking the date of deposit

---

9. Two analogous hoards, Dniye 1952 (*IGCH* 1538) and Ras Baalbek 1957 (*IGCH* 1593), are from 15 miles E and 50 miles SE of Aradus respectively.

10. Le Rider (1998) 95–6.

11. The hoard also contained an issue of uncertain mint 68 (N. Mesopotamia), *SC* I. 1132.6. The opening date of this mint is also given in *SC* as 197 BC, however the style of the coins may suggest an earlier date of issue.

12. Boehringer (1972), pp. 116–8.

for the hoard as 195/4 BC, we can see that the era of Aspendos must have begun by *c*. 212/1 BC at the latest, while that of Perge, which, as McIntyre (2007) has demonstrated, started 10 years earlier had begun by 222/1 BC at the latest. Since the coins were moving from Pamphylia to Phoenicia, we can, of course, only take these dates as *termini ante quos* for the beginning of the two eras. In any case, it seems that Boehringer's low dates of 219/8 and 210/09 must be ruled out.

The second new piece of hoard evidence applies less directly to the Pamphylian coinage but has, as will become clear, considerable significance for the dating of a number of other hoards, on which the dates of the Pamphylian issues rest. To clarify this significance it will be necessary to focus briefly on the Seleucid coinage of Antioch.

E. T. Newell divided the coinage of Antioch under Antiochus III into four groups. The dates of these he assigned on historical grounds, and essentially without the benefit of hoard evidence. In 1972 C. Boehringer assembled the hoard evidence then available and noted that this evidence suggested a somewhat later series of dates for the beginnings of Newell's second, third and fourth groups. In *SC* I, the lowering of dates was resisted partly on stylistic grounds.[13] However, in his die-study of the mint of Antioch, published in 1999, G. Le Rider had noted the important evidence of a new hoard found in excavation at Oylum Höyüğü in northern Syria (Kilis province, in modern Turkey).[14] The latest coins in this hoard are probably a fresh Alexander of Perge of year 19, and an equally fresh autonomous coin of Side, of one of the city's earlier issues. The publishers of the hoard arrived at a *terminus post quem* for burial of c. 200 BC, on the basis of the issue of Perge, and assuming Boehringer's chronology. We may allow, on Price or Seyrig's chronology a date a couple of years earlier, or on the chronology that will be proposed in this paper, a *terminus post quem* of 205 BC. But this last date is the earliest that could be tolerated for the burial of the Oylum Höyüğü hoard.

As Le Rider pointed out, the value of this hoard lies in its circumstances of discovery: it is certainly complete, and this fact allows us to make some inferences concerning the Seleucid content with some confidence:[15]

> It is notable... that the hoard contains no tetradrachms of Antioch of series II nor of series III or IV. While the composition of hoards must be interpreted with care, it would seem that Boehringer was right to lower a little for each series the dates proposed by Newell. Series III and IV ought not to have begun much before 200, and their beginning could be connected with the preparations for the campaign that ended with the victory at Panion

13. Newell (1941), pp. 134–155; Boehringer (1972), pp. 8–9 and 95–97; *SC* I, pp. 358–9 and 394–6.
14. Le Rider (1999), pp. 157–8; Özgen and Davesne (1994), pp. 45–64 (*CH* 9. 501).
15. Le Rider (1999), p. 158, my translation.

over Ptolemy (V) in 200, and the annexation of Phoenicia and Coele Syria. Another explanation would be that this coinage was inaugurated in anticipation of the great expedition of Antiochus III in Asia Minor, of which the first act took place in 198.

Table 1. Proposed dates for Antiochus III's issues at Antioch

| Series | SC Nos. | Obv. dies | Newell | SC | Boehringer | Le Rider |
|---|---|---|---|---|---|---|
| I | 1041–2 | 11 | 223–213 | 223–211/10 | 223–208 | 223–208 |
| II | 1043 | 8 | 213–208 | 211–208 | 208–203 | 203–198 |
| III | 1044 | 17 | 208–200 | 204–197 | 203–195 | |
| IV | 1045–6 | 22 | 200–187 | 197–187 | 195–187 | 198–187 |

The absence of the substantial series II, III and IV from a hoard just to the north of Antioch is surely significant, and Le Rider is correct to push the dates of these series downwards. If we are to fit all three series in the period after c. 205–203 BC, then the second of the alternative reconstructions that he proposed seems most likely to be correct. A synopsis of the various proposed dates for these groups is presented in Table 1.

The net effect of Le Rider's down-dating is to lower the start dates of groups II and III. When combined with the new evidence for the beginning of the Pamphylian eras, this will have a significant impact on the dating of a number of hoards, as we shall see. Not least, it makes sense of the Seleucid contents of a group of hoards conventionally dated to the late 190s, but which contain issues only down to Antioch series III.[16]

With this new evidence summarized, we may now turn back to the identity of the Pamphylian eras. To achieve further precision in the assignment of dates to these eras, it will be necessary to take a closer look at two categories of hoard evidence: first, a group of fairly closely dateable hoards that do not contain the Alexanders of Perge and Aspendos, and second a group of similarly dateable hoards that are the earliest to contain them.

The first of these groups is summarized in Table 2. Before beginning to interpret this table, it is important to bear in mind the point, recently highlighted by McIntyre, 'that Perge produced very little Alexander coinage before year 7.'[17] We must allow for the fact that the absence from the hoard record of the first 6 years or so of Perge's era may be due to the relative absence of these issues from circulation.

16. See for example: Mektepini (*IGCH* 1410: 190 BC, to Ser. II); Sardis Pot (*IGCH* 1318: 190 BC, to Ser. III); Pisidia (*IGCH* 1411: 190 BC, to Ser III); Kosseir (*IGCH* 1537: 190 BC, to Ser. III). Further discussion of these hoards and their (revised) chronology will be found below.

17. McIntyre (2007), p. 1, n.3.

Table 2. Late third–early second century hoards with no Pamphylian Alexanders

| Hoard | Date | Dateable content |
|---|---|---|
| Tartous (1530) | 229–220 | Price 2509 (Rhodes); Aradus Yr. 23 (237) |
| 'Seleucus III'[a] | 225/224 | SC 921; SC 928 (225/4 BC?) |
| Syria? (1531) | 225–220 | Ant. Doson (Poseidon/Apollo+prow) |
| Asia Minor/N. Syria (1.74) | 215–210 | SC 1042 (223–208) |
| Gordion V (1405) | 217–210 | SC 1042 (223–208); SC 1160 (220–211/10); Aradus Yr 43 = 217 |
| Homs (1532) | 220–210 | SC 1042 (223–208); SC 1069 (223/210) |
| Syria (1533) | 216–210 | SC 1042 (223–208); SC 1025 (216–213) |
| Syria (1535) | 220–210 | SC 1042 (223–208) |
| Basra 'A' (1786)[b] | 210 | SC 1041 (223–208); SC 1162 (211/10) |
| 'Antiochus III'[c] | 196 | SC 1044 (198–187); SC 1164 (211/10) |

[a] SC II.2, pp. 142–150.
[b] On the two separate parcels that make up the listing in *IGCH*, and the need to separate them see SC II.2. pp. 126–127.
[c] SC II.2, p. 150. See Lorber and Houghton (2009) for a full publication of the hoard and discussion of burial date (c. 196 BC) and contents.

The general conclusion that we may draw from this table is that Pamphylian Alexanders tend to be absent from hoards in Asia Minor and the Seleucid kingdom that were deposited in the period c. 229–210 BC. In two cases at least, this absence is likely to be significant. The massive Seleucus III hoard deposited in 225/4 would surely have contained Pamphylian Alexanders had they existed at this time.[18] The Gordion V hoard, buried at some point between 217–210, may also be significant, since the slightly later Gordion I hoard, buried c. 210 BC (see Table 3 below), did contain Pamphylian issues. Given the relatively light striking of Pergaean issues in years 1–6, the absence from Seleucus III can suggest to us only that the era of this city is unlikely to have begun before c. 231 BC. On the other hand, the absence from Gordion V, if pressed, suggests a somewhat later *terminus post quem* of c. 224 BC. This latter date sits comfortably enough with the evidence of the Syria hoard discussed above, which provides a *terminus ante quem* of 222/1. The period c. 224–221 BC begins to look promising as the period within which the era of Perge may have begun.

Against this background it is worth considering for a moment the picture that emerges from the other hoards in Table 2 from which the Pamphylian issues are absent. By 215 BC at the latest, Pergaean issues were being produced with regular-

18. As Cathy Lorber points out to me, it contained earlier coins of Perge, in the form of 5 tetradrachms of Artemis Pergaia type. On the date of this hoard, see Lorber and Houghton (2009).

Table 3. The Earliest hoards containing Pamphylian Alexanders

| Hoard | Date | Perge | Phaselis | Aspendos | Sillyon | Aradus | Seleucid content |
|---|---|---|---|---|---|---|---|
| Syria (1535) | 210–205[a] | 13 | | 1 | | | 1042 (223–208) |
| Diyarbakir (1735) | 205–200[b] | 10 | | | | 44 = 216 | 1041 (223–208) |
| Gordion I (1406) | 210–205[c] | 14 | | | 11 | 42 = 218 | 1042 (223–208); 1162 (211/10) |
| Asia Minor (1426) | 215–205[d] | 15 | | 2 | | 44 = 216 | Uncertain |
| Pergamum (1303) | 210–205[e] | 15 | | | | | 1161 (220–211/10) |
| 'Achaeus'[f] | 204–199 | 20 | | 9 | | 53 = 207 | 1206 (223/2) |
| Oylum Höyüğü (9.501) | 205–200[g] | 19 | . | 2 | | | 1042 (223–208); 1160 (220–211/10); 1063 (205–200) |

[a] Boehringer (1972), p. 158 dated this hoard to 'the last decade of the third century' but, as Houghton and Lorber point out (SC I.2, p. 101), the Seleucid content might suggest a date no later than 210 BC. With the revision of the dates of the Antioch mint suggested above, we may bring this date down to 208 or shortly after.

[b] The date is based on the inclusion of a Rhodian Alexander (Price 2522), the production of which is likely to be connected to Rhodian military activity c. 205–200 BC. Seleucid content, as well as that of Side, suggests that a later date is unlikely.

[c] For the date, derived from the Seleucid content, see SC I.2, p. 88.

[d] The date is based on the fresh, dated specimen of Aradus.

[e] The date is based on the Seleucid content and the presence of just the earliest issues of the mint of Side, and none of the later Alexanders of Rhodes.

[f] For a provisional listing of the hoard's contents see SC II.2, pp. 150–151. Full publication will follow in CH 10. The terminus post quem for burial of the hoard is provided by the Aradian issue. The meager representation of coinage of Antiochus III suggests that it cannot date much later. If this hoard was deposited in Western Asia Minor, as the presence of Achaeus' issues suggests, then it is likely to have been buried before, or perhaps in the context of, Antiochus' campaign of 203. See further Meadows and Lorber (forthcoming).

[g] The contents of this hoard bear a similarity to those of the Pergamum hoard (above, [n. e]), however the presence of issues of the mint associated with Antioch (SC 1063) in Oylum Höyüğü may suggest a slightly later date.

ity, yet we find a series of seven hoards that might have been deposited after this year, but which contain none. Most, if not all of these hoards were deposited to the east of Pamphylia, either in Syria, or further east still.[19] It seems, therefore, that at this early period in Pamphylian production, coins were not circulating widely, and not moving eastwards in significant quantities.

19. The exception is perhaps the Antiochus III hoard, which may have been deposited in N.W. Asia Minor. See Lorber and Houghton (2009).

Examination of the earliest hoards to contain Pamphylian Alexanders suggests that this pattern changed only gradually (Table 3).

First we must note the pattern of distribution of the hoards from this phase of Pamphylian production. In all likelihood, four of the seven hoards were concealed to the north or west of Pamphylia. Just three provide evidence for eastward movement. An interesting anomaly also emerges. At this period, there is no evidence for the circulation of the issues of Phaselis, which are entirely absent from these hoards, even though on the conventional chronology, which sees the era start shortly after that of Perge, the mint is likely to have been producing coin throughout this period.[20] This may suggest that the Phaselite issues, at least in this period, constitute a different phenomenon from those of Aspendos and Perge; it may also suggest that we should re-examine the chronology of the Phaselite era.

The hoards in Table 3 seem for the most part to have been buried within the decade 210–200 BC.[21] Ostensibly they span ten years of production too, from years 10–20 at Perge and 1–9 at Aspendos. They also span at least the decade of years 42–53 (218–207 BC) at Aradus. Combined, these three decades provide us with another range of possible dates for the start of the Pergaean era. If 210 equated to year 10 of Perge, then it would suggest a start in 220. If 218 BC equated to year 10, then it produces a start in 228. The range of 228–220 certainly does encompass the period that we have derived above by other means, but caution is required. This new range is based in part upon approximations of hoard burial dates combined with the presence of coins within hoards that have travelled some distance from their points of origin. Of more help perhaps is the observation that emerges from consideration of the four hoards that contain Seleucid issues of the mint of Antioch: none apparently contain any issues that postdate c. 208 BC: specifically, series II, III, and IV of this mint, struck c. 208–198 and c. 198–187 BC on the chronology proposed above (Table 1), are all absent. This impression is bolstered by the representation of issues of the mint of Seleuceia on the Tigris in three of the hoards, which seem to cease around 210 BC.

It may have taken a while for the later Seleucid issues to enter circulation, particularly further west where the Pamphylian Alexanders were circulating and a number of these hoards were deposited. But it seems highly unlikely that any of these hoards belong after the campaign of Antiochus III into Asia Minor in 203 BC.[22] In fact it is tempting to suggest that a number of these hoards represent

20. However, we should note that one of the important results of McIntyre's (2007) detachment of the 'omicron' issues from the main sequence of Phaselis' Alexanders is to reduce the size of the latter issues considerably. For the first 15 years of production Phaselis used on average just one die per annum.

21. The only possible exception is the Asia Minor hoard (*IGCH* 1426), but our record of this so incomplete as to render it almost worthless as a chronological indicator.

22. For discussion of this campaign see further below, Part II.

Table 4. Later hoards containing Pamphylian Alexanders deposited during the probable period of their production

| Hoard | Perge | Phaselis | Aspendos | Aradus | Seleucid SC and date |
|---|---|---|---|---|---|
| Latakia (1536) | | 10 | | 61 = 199 | 1121 (213–203); 1112 (197–187) |
| Syria (2. 81) | 26 | 19 | 18 | 65 = 195 | 1019         1132 (197–187) |
| Mektepini (1410) | 29 | 18 | 19 | 64 = 196 | 1043 (203–198); 1063 (205–200) |
| Sardis pot (1318) | 29 | 5 | 20 | 62 = 198 | 1044 (198–187); 1063 (205–200) |
| Pisidia (1411) | 29 | 25 | 18 | 43 = 217 | 1044 (198–187); 1063 (205–200) |
| Ayaz-In (1413) | 29 | 26 | 20 | 63 = 197 | 1045 (198–187); 1020 (197–187) |
| Unknown 2000[a] | 29 | 24 | 20 | 65 = 195 | 1046 (198–187); 1021 (197–187) |
| Cuenca (8. 375)[b] | 29 | | | 65 = 195 | 1041 (223–208) |
| Kosseir (1537) | 20 | 24 | 19 | 69 = 191 | 1044 (198–187) |

[a] For a summary see *SC* II.2, pp. 77–8, where the hoard's findspot is designated as 'Pamphylia or Cilicia,' an inference based on contents. I am grateful to Oliver Hoover for a full listing of this hoard prior to publication, which will occur in *CH* 10. Hoover includes in his listing an issue of Seleucus IV (*SC* 1298), which seems to me to be intrusive.

[b] Alicante (8.411), with identical contents to the Cuenca hoard (8.375) published by Villaronga (1984), appears to be a doublet included in *CH* 8 in error, and should consequently be deleted. Interestingly, the bulk of the Roman Republican content of this hoard seems to predate 200 BC, on Crawford's chronology (denarii to *RRC* 128 with one example of *RRC* 171). The burial date of the hoard is in fact determined by the Aradian (and Pergaean) content (Villaronga, loc. cit., pp. 136–7).

deposits made in anticipation of, or in reaction to the beginning of this campaign, and thus reflect circulation down to as late as 204 or 203 BC in areas that had fallen out of direct Seleucid control. This is particularly attractive, as has been noted above (page 59, table note f), in the case of the Achaeus hoard, the only hoard known to have contained coins of the usurper, which otherwise seem to have been purged from circulation within the Seleucid realm. Therefore, in place of the ranges 210–205 suggested above for a number of these hoards, we might more reasonably substitute c. 210–203 BC. That being the case, we produce a range of dates for the beginning of the Pergaean era of c. 230–223 BC.

If we set this possible range of c. 230–223 BC, which emerges from consideration of the hoards in Table 3, alongside the range of c. 224–221 BC that we deduced from consideration of Table 2, then we see that the years 224 and 223 BC emerge as the most likely for the commencement of the Pergaean era. With this possibility in mind, we may turn to a second group of hoards containing Pamphylian Alexanders, and perhaps begin to view some old friends with new eyes (Table 4).

This table presents an overview of hoards that seem likely to have been buried within the 190s BC, and thus within the period in which, on any chronology that has been proposed for the Pamphylian eras, the Alexanders of Perge, Aspendos and Phaselis were all still in production. We may start with some general observations. First, setting aside the Latakia hoard (1536), which may be slightly earlier than the rest,[23] an interesting pattern emerges. All hoards but one end either with year 29 of Perge or the contemporary year 19 of Aspendos. The remaining hoard, Syria (2.81), ends with year 18 of Aspendos. Second, all but one (5 of 6) of the hoards that end in years 29 or 19 with identifiable find-spots were buried to the north and/or west of Pamphylia.

The question is, how to interpret this intriguing pattern? *Prima facie*, it might appear that all of these hoards closed at the same time and are to be linked to a single event such as a battle or invasion. But two facts argue against this hypothesis. First, the hoards are not all from the same region: one is from Spain (Cuenca), two are from Phrygia (Mektepini and Ayaz-In), one is from Lydia (Sardis), one from Pisidia and one from Syria (Al-Qusayr). Second, it is only the issues of Aspendos, Perge and (as we shall discuss), Aradus that give this impression of contemporaneity. As can be seen very clearly from Table 4, the Seleucid content of the hoards shows a clear chronological progression that strongly suggests that the hoards from Mektepini through to Unknown findspot 2000 were buried over a period of time, not within a single year. A similar impression emerges from the Sidetan content. Mektepini contains only issues signed by AP, A, and ΔI that had appeared in the earlier Pergamum Asklepieion (1303) and Oylum Höyüğü (9.501) hoards included above in Table 3, and belonging most probably to the last few years of the third century. Unknown findspot 2000 and Ayaz-In both contain later issues struck by ΔEINO, ΔIOΔ, and ΣT (with variants).

If these hoards were not buried at the same time it seems that the Aspendian and Pergaean contents of these hoards are skewed and the explanation for the homogeneity of content of these two mints across such a broad geographical area is to be sought not in the circumstances of burial of these hoards, but rather in the phenomenon of circulation of these particular Alexanders. Whereas these coins had enjoyed only limited circulation during the early years of their production, right down to the last years of the 3rd century BC (Table 3), suddenly, and during a period that apparently ends in year 29 of Perge = 19 of Aspendos, there was a release of coin of these mints into circulation such that they penetrated into Asia Minor and even as far as Spain, but also moved back eastwards to Syria. Put another way, year 29 = 19 did not see an increased instance of hoarding, rather it marks the end of a period of enhanced circulation of Pamphylian coinage.

---

23. Seyrig (1973) inclined on the basis of the three coins of Aradus 'en excellent état et l'absence des années 62, 63 et 64, pourtant commune' to date the hoard c. 198, but was pulled towards a later date by the inclusion of Alexander issues of Rhodes with full magistrate's names. These latter issues were probably not as late as Seyrig thought, however, and a date of c. 198 BC appears more likely.

Significantly, this pattern of overrepresentation which has been deduced here from the end date of Pergaean content across a number of hoards from disparate regions, finds full support in the study of this mint by Colin (1996). From his die study of the Alexanders we may produce the following figure detailing survival rate of coins of each year, expressed as a ratio of known specimens to observed dies (Figure 1). The result is startling, but not unexpected.

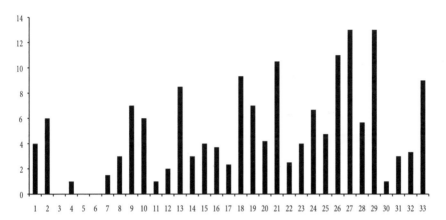

Figure 1. Number of known Perge Coins obverse die by era year (Years 1–33)

From a clear peak in years 26–29, representation of coins per die plummets in year 30. In fact, the number of obverse dies remains fairly constant across this period (Figure 2), yet many more coins survive today from this four year period leading up to year 29.[24]

In fact, on the basis of Figures 8 and 9 in the Appendix to this paper, we can put this rather more forcefully. In the 17 hoards tabulated there, deposited between the 190s and the 140s BC, not a single coin of year 30 of Perge has been recorded. Yet Colin has recorded the same number of obverse dies for this year as for year 29.[25] The absence of year 30 not only from the hoards in Table 4, but also from

24. The relative scarcity of surviving specimens of years 30 and 31 had been apparent to Seyrig (1963), p. 48 and Boehringer (1972), p. 54. The significance in terms of the representation of numbers of dies was later pointed out by Boehringer (1999), p. 71, on the basis of Colin's die study: 'Die Zahl der für die 3 Jahre KΘ-ΛA = 29–31 geschnittenen Vorderseiten-Stempel blieb mit 2 pro Jahrgang konstant, ein gleichmäßiger Prägeausstoß war also zumindest beabsichtigt.'

25. Two dies from two specimens for year 30. Both coins are in the ANS collection: 1952.44.35 and 1956.108.5. The former coin was bought in the same year and from the same dealer (Poladian) as were the ANS coins from the Tell Kotchek hoard. However, no

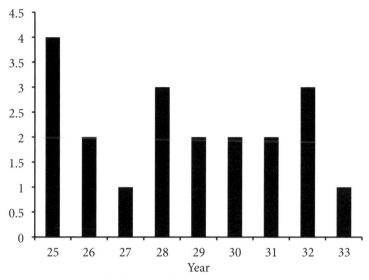

Figure 2. Recorded obverse dies per year at Perge (Years 25–33)

the large group of hoards that postdates the 190s (Appendix, Figure 9), makes it absolutely clear that for some reason the circulation of Pergaean Alexanders was dramatically curtailed in this year. In the absence of a die study, the picture for Aspendos cannot be painted with such clarity. Nonetheless, Figure 10 in the Appendix does suggest a comparable spike in the presence of issues of year 17–20 in the Table 3 hoards, and a tailing-off in year 20. Figure 11 for the later hoards also produces a spike in year 19 and a dip in years 20–21 before Aspendian issues appear again in significant quantities from year 22 onwards.

The representation of Alexanders of Aradus in the hoards of Table 4 also requires some commentary. It is no less uniform than that of the Pamphylian mints, containing, with the exception of the Pisidian hoard (1411), dates ranging from years 61–69 (199/8–191/0 BC), with a clear concentration in year 65 = 195/4 BC (4 hoards). The ranges for Perge and Aspendos are also of 9–10 years: 20–29 and 18–20 respectively.[26] We must ask, therefore, whether the same phenomenon may underlie this Aradian representation as has been hypothesised above for the Pamphylian: an unusually large release of Aradian Alexanders into circulation in the period leading up to year 65 (195/4 BC).

provenance is recorded with the Pergaean year 30, and this year is not mentioned in Seyrig's listing of the hoard.

26. Cuenca (8.375) is a clear outlier with year 3 only of Aspendos.

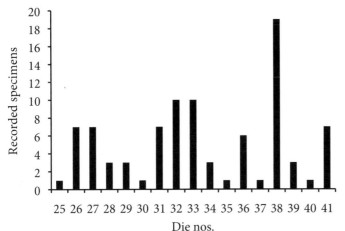

Figure 3. Recorded coins per die at Aradus (206/5–191/0 BC)

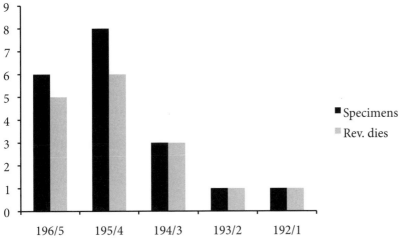

Figure 4. Recorded Aradian Alexanders struck from D38, by year

A summary of the representation of known coins per die recorded in Duyrat's (2005) study of the Aradian mint provides an interesting point of comparison with the Pergaean evidence. The continued use of dies over a number of years makes the picture slightly more complex, but a familiar pattern emerges (Figure 3).

There is a smaller spike for Dies 31–33, which were used in years 200–199 BC, and a large spike for Die 38, in use through the years 196–192. A closer look at the activity of this last die shows two disparities (Figure 4). Not only are a greater number of specimens known for years 196/5 and 195/4 BC, but also the ratio of

observed specimens to reverse dies is higher for these two years than later. Ir-
respective of the pattern of production at Aradus, this evidence suggests that a
proportionally high number of Aradian coins of these two years survive today. As
with the case of the Pamphylian issues, it appears that there was an unusual release
of Aradian coinage culminating in year 195/4 BC. We must, therefore, consider the
possibility that these similar phenomena might be contemporary. If so, then year
65 at Aradus (195/4 BC), equates with year 29 and 19 at Perge and Aspendos. This
would suggest start dates for the two Pamphylian eras of c. 223 and 213 respectively. In this case, the reconstruction on the basis of Table 4 fits perfectly the range
for Perge of 224–223 that we have suggested above on the basis of Tables 2 and 3.

　　If this picture of the circulation history of the Pamphylian and Aradian mints
is correct, then it has important consequences for the dating of the hoards in Table
4. With the exception of the hoards found within close proximity of one or another of these areas (essentially Syria [2.81] and Kosseir [1537], both probably from
the hinterland of Aradus), as already noted above, we can no longer assume that
these issues provide precise dates of deposit as, for example, Boehringer did with
the Mektepini (1410) and Sardis Pot (1318) hoards.[27] Rather, the Pamphylian and
Aradian issues included provide only a *terminus post quem*. With this in mind, it
is worth taking a brief look at the hoards in Table 4 to see the effects for the dates
generally assigned to them, and to ask what evidence remains for their chronology.
Clearly, a key element is now the Seleucid content, our understanding of which has
been placed on a new footing by the recent work of Houghton and Lorber, and specifically the issues of Antioch, for the chronology of which, as we have seen above,
significant new evidence has become available. The chronology of this mint has
now become our best indicator of both the relative and the absolute chronologies
of a subset of the Table 3 hoards, and presents the following picture (Table 5):

Table 5. Relative chronology of some hoards of the 190s

| Mektepini (1410)   | SC 1043 (203–198); 1063 |
|--------------------|--------------------------|
| Sardis pot (1318)  | SC 1044 (198–187); 1063 |
| Pisidia (1411)     | SC 1044 (198–187); 1063 |
| Ayaz-In (1413)     | SC 1045 (198–187)        |
| Unknown 2000       | SC 1046 (198–187)        |

The evidence is first and foremost suggestive of a relative chronology, but also
of differences of circumstances of deposit for at least some of these hoards. Of
particular interest is the Mektepini hoard (1410), the date of which, generally assumed to be c. 190 BC, has become canonical in the chronology of early 2nd century coinages. The Seleucid material in this hoard strongly suggests that it must be

27. Boehringer (1972), p. 59.

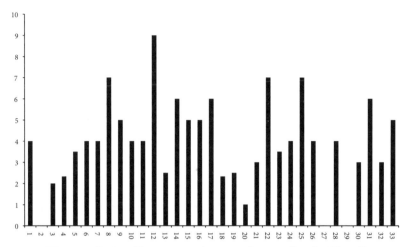

Figure 5. Ratio of known specimens to known dies for Phaselis

detached in time from the Ayaz-In hoard (1413), also found in Phrygia, and must be dated somewhat earlier. The Antiochene content, which stops with Series 2 (203–198 BC), must make it unlikely that the hoard can be very much later than its latest coin of Perge (year 29 = 195/4 BC, assuming a start date of 223/2). This chronology would suggest that the hoard may have been buried in the context of the early years of Antiochus' invasion of western Asia Minor, which began in 198 or 197. The Ayaz-In hoard, on the other hand, which contains issues of Antioch series 4, may well belong to the period around the Seleucid defeat at Magnesia in 190 BC. This overall picture is reinforced by the hoard representation of the Ɑ mint (SC 1063). Specimens are known only from Oylum Höyüğü (9.501), Mektepini (1410), Sardis pot (1318) and Pisidia (1411), which seem to span the period c. 205–195 BC, where they accompany SC 1042–1044. SC 1063 is absent from Ayaz-In.

If this reconstruction is correct, it has important consequences for our understanding of the dated coinage of Phaselis. As we have already noted, the era of Phaselis has proven in the past somewhat trickier to pin down than those of Perge and Aspendos. The assumption, based on the limited hoard evidence, has generally been that it began around three years after that of Perge.[28] With the advantage of McIntyre's forthcoming disentanglement of the two separate series (and eras) of the coinages previously attributed to Phaselis, it is possible to return to Heipp-

---

28. Boehringer (1972), pp. 60–61 thought the two eras contemporary, on the basis of their identical durations (33 years) and the assumption that the missing year 29 at Phaselis coincided with 190/89 BC. Price (1991), p. 348, interpreted the hoard evidence to suggest that Phaselis' era started approximately 3 years later than that of Perge.

Tamer's (1993) die study and construct a figure similar to that offered above for Perge, for the ratio of the number of surviving coins of Phaselis to the number of recorded dies (Figure 5).

There is little evidence for a period of overrepresentation as there is with Perge and Aradus. From this we may confirm the conclusion that the pattern of circulation of the Phaselite issues was different from that of their Pergaean counterparts. As we have noted above, such a difference was also suggested by the hoards of the period covered by Table 3 (c. 210–200 BC). This difference will be important to bear in mind when it comes to considering the historical circumstances of these issues. More specifically, the apparent lack of skew in the distribution in the coins of Phaselis renders them potentially more useful in the derivation of relative chronology for the hoards in which they occur. Whereas the Pergaean (and Aspendian) contents are dominated by year 29 (and 20/19), the Phaselite is more likely to reflect a regular progression into circulation.

With this in mind we may turn back to our group of hoards from the 190s and compare their Phaselite content:

Table 6. Phaselis in some hoards of the 190s

| Hoard | Last issue of Phaselis |
|---|---|
| Mektepini (1410) | 18 |
| Sardis pot (1318) | 5 |
| Pisidia (1411) | 25 |
| Ayaz-In (1413) | 26 |
| Unknown 2000 | 24 |

The evidence is thin, but seems to support the case for viewing Mektepini as earlier than the Pisidia or Ayaz-In hoards.

In conclusion, one should note a further corollary of this apparent difference in circulation pattern between Perge and Phaselis. The Mektepini hoard, which we have suggested was deposited in the environs of 196 or 195 contained Perge of year 29 and Phaselis 18. This may suggest that the Phaselis issue was some 10 years behind that of Perge. This would (in part) help to explain the absence of Phaselis from the hoards of Table 3, deposited c. 210–203 BC.

## PART II. THE HISTORICAL BACKGROUND

In the remainder of this paper I shall explore the ramifications of the higher chronology for the eras of Perge and Aspendos and the lower chronology for the era of Phaselis for the possible historical circumstances of the production and apparently uneven circulation of the Pamphylian Alexanders. First we may begin by applying the absolute chronology proposed above to the various eras with which we have been concerned. As we have seen above, on the basis of Tables 2 and 3, 224–223

Table 7: Absolute Dates and Civic Eras

| Year | Perge | Aspendos | Phaselis | Sillyon | Aradus |
|---|---|---|---|---|---|
| 223/2 | 1 | | | | 37 |
| 222/1 | 2 | | | | 38 |
| 221/0 | | | | 3 | 39 |
| 220/19 | 4 | | | 4 | 40 |
| 219/8 | | | | 5 | 41 |
| 218/7 | | | | 6 | 42 |
| 217/6 | 7 | | | | 43 |
| 216/5 | 8 | | | | 44 |
| 215/4 | 9 | | | | 45 |
| 214/3 | 10 | | | | 46 |
| 213/2 | 11 | 1 | 1 | 11 | 47 |
| 212/1 | 12 | 2 | 2 | | 48 |
| 211/0 | 13 | 3 | 3 | | 49 |
| 210/09 | 14 | 4 | 4 | | 50 |
| 209/8 | 15 | 5 | 5 | | 51 |
| 208/7 | 16 | 6 | 6 | | 52 |
| 207/6 | 17 | 7 | 7 | | 53 |
| 206/5 | 18 | 8 | 8 | | 54 |
| 205/4 | 19 | 9 | 9 | | 55 |
| 204/3 | 20 | 10 | 10 | | 56 |
| 203/2 | 21 | 11 | 11 | | 57 |
| 202/1 | 22 | 12 | 12 | | 58 |
| 201/0 | 23 | | 13 | | 59 |
| 200/199 | 24 | 14 | 14 | | 60 |
| 199/8 | 25 | 15 | 15 | | 61 |
| 198/7 | 26 | 16 | 16 | | 62 |
| 197/6 | 27 | 17 | 17 | | 63 |
| 196/5 | 28 | 18 | 18 | | 64 |
| 195/4 | 29 | 19 | 19 | | 65 |
| 194/3 | 30 | 20 | 20 | | 66 |
| 193/2 | 31 | 21 | 21 | | 67 |
| 192/1 | 32 | 22 | 22 | | 68 |
| 191/0 | 33 | 23 | 23 | | 69 |
| 190/89 | | 24 | 24 | | 70 |
| 189/8 | | 25 | 25 | | 71 |
| 188/7 | | 26 | 26 | | 72 |
| 187/6 | | 27 | 27 | | 73 |
| 186/5 | | 28 | 28 | | 74 |
| 185/4 | | 29 | | | 75 |
| 184/3 | | | 30 | | 76 |
| 183/2 | | | 31 | | 77 |
| 182/1 | | | 32 | | 78 |
| 181/0 | | | 33 | | 79 |

seems the likeliest range for Perge year 1, and on the basis of Table 4, 223 seems the more likely. Strong circumstantial support for this year will be offered below. In Table 7, therefore, 223/2 has been proposed as the start date for Perge, and the eras of Aspendos and Phaselis are assumed to start 10 years later.

*(a) The beginning of Pergaean coinage c. 223 BC and the campaign of Seleucus III*

In the early summer of 223 BC Seleucus III set out from Syria on an expedition against, according to Polybius, the Pergamene king Attalus I, who had been help-ing himself to Seleucid territory in Asia Minor. He crossed the Taurus and reached as far as Phrygia, before he was treacherously poisoned by two of his courtiers, Galatians named Apatourios and Nicanor, perhaps in 222 BC.[29] The meager con-tent of the literary sources for this campaign may be supplemented slightly by the numismatic evidence. In addition to the standard array of mints that struck for Seleucus III In Syria, Mesopotamia, Media and Susiana, three extraordinary groups of coinage have been connected by various commentators with Seleucus' ambitions in Asia Minor.

First there is the remarkable, and apparently co-ordinated group of dated coin-ages produced at the Phoenician mints of Gabala, Carne, Marathus, Simyra (Plate 6, nos. 8–11) and perhaps Aradus, all struck in the year 225/4. The first three of these mints, and perhaps Aradus, struck with the types of Alexander the Great (*SC* I. 927–931 = Price 3433, 3431–3432, 3453 and 3380); Simyra alone produced coin of Seleucid type (*SC* I. 931).[30] As Duyrat (2002) has now shown, these specific coin-ages of 225/4 are to be set against a broader background of co-ordinated monetary production in smaller denominations (both silver and bronze) within the Aradian Peraea in the 220s BC.[31] She hypothesises that a military build-up may explain both the tetradrachm issues (soldiers' pay) and the smaller denominations (for a corresponding increase in the frequency of 'day-to-day' transactions). Following

29. Cf. Plb. 4.48.8 and Appian Syr. 66. A summary of the story as told by Porphyry of Tyre survives in the Armenian translation of Eusebius (*FGrHist* 260 F32.9 = Eusebius 1. 253 Schoene) and Jerome's commentary on Daniel (*FGrHist* 260 F44). For the chronology see Schmitt (1964), pp. 2–3. Seleucus' own campaign had probably been preceded by an unsuc-cessful one in the previous year, perhaps under the command of Andromachus, father of Achaeus. See Ma (1999), p. 55 with n. 8; Allen (1983), pp. 35–36. For the death of Seleucus in 222 see *SC* II.1, p. 682.

30. The evidence has now been collected in detail by Duyrat (2005) for Aradus and (2002) for the other mints. She has been unable ([2005], p. 40 with n. 66) to confirm the existence of the Aradian issue, which was originally recorded by Müller and was included by Price and in *SC*. Hoover (2006), p. 46 notes that it is possible that that these issues were instigated by Seleucus II who, as Babylonian sources now suggest, lived until December or January 225/4.

31. Hoover (2006) has subsequently argued for the attribution of additional Seleucid bronze coinage of the Peraea (*SC* I. 72–73) to this period.

Seyrig, Duyrat suggests that the circumstance of this extraordinary production was the preparation for a campaign against the Ptolemaic possessions in southern Phoenicia but rightly expresses caution, given that there exists no evidence for this expedition having taken place.[32] Price, on the other hand, in discussing the Alexander issues, has associated them with preparations for the more firmly attested campaign to Asia Minor in 223, connecting them with the simultaneous elevated period of production at the Antioch mint that Newell similarly connected with this campaign.[33] In fact this would also seem to be the more natural reading of Jerome's summary of events than that proposed by Seyrig. The passage reads as follows:

> Post fugam et mortem Seleuci Callinici duo filii eius Seleucus cognomento Ceraunus et Antiochus qui appellatus est Magnus, provocati spe victoriae et ultione parentis, exercitu congregato adversus Ptolemaeum Philopatorem aram corripiunt. Cumque Seleucus maior frater tertio anno imperii esset occisus in Phrygia per dolum Nicanoris et Apaturii…. (*FGrHist* 260 F44)

The campaign on which Seleucus III died in Asia Minor seems here to follow logically from the decision to wage war on Ptolemy, and if the coinage of the Phoenician mints is to be connected with this passage, as Seyrig suggested, then it was perhaps intended to fund the naval element of Seleucus' campaign. This is an attractive suggestion, particularly since at this point the alternative Seleucid naval base of Laodicea was still in Ptolemaic hands. If correct, it strongly suggests that Seleucus' strategy consisted not just of a land campaign, but also of naval expedition, to which the Phoenician cities contributed, and for which they struck coin.[34] If so, in this sense, Seleucus' campaign was a forerunner of Antiochus III's similar land and sea campaign of 197 BC.

   The second coinage to be connected with the campaign of 223 is of Seleucid types, and with control marks ordinarily characteristic of Antioch (*SC* I. 915, Plate

---

32. Duyrat (2002), pp. 54–6. Seyrig (1971), pp. 7–11, relying upon Porphyry as transmitted by Jerome, *FGrHist* 260 F44 (see below).

33. Price (1991), p. 432, following Newell (1941), p. 132 who points out a remarkably ample bronze coinage for Antioch. Note also *SC* I.1, p. 327 on the exceptional gold octadrachms of the mint of Antioch, of which the two extant specimens have Phrygian find-spots, and Le Rider (1999), p. 103 on the increased production of silver at Antioch under Seleucus III compared with that of Seleucus II.

34. Houghton (1999), p. 181 has pointed out that earlier, in the 240s BC, the beginning of the production of Aradian Alexanders coincides with the cessation of production at the Seleucid mint of Laodicea (due the capture of the latter city by Ptolemy III). Cf. Duyrat (2005), pp. 231–232 on the Aradian issue: 'Celles-ci durent le même nombre d'années que la troisième guerre de Syrie et pouvaient donc bien être des dépenses militaires'. See also Duyrat (2003), pp. 30–32 and 37–38: 'on peut meme se demander si la réouverture de l'atelier aradien n'est pas le fruit d'une tractation entre la cité et le souverain' (p. 31).

6, no. 12). However the curious style of these pieces led Mørkholm to suggest that this coinage was struck by mint personnel transferred from Antioch, perhaps in a city in Phrygia. He has been followed in this hypothesis by the authors of SC.[35]

The third coinage that appears to be linked to Seleucus' campaign consists of a small pair of issues associated by the appearance of a forepart of a running horse as a control mark (SC I. 916.1–2, Plate 6, no. 13). The two issues were attributed by Newell to Seleucia on the Calycadnus, on the basis of the existence of a first century autonomous bronze coinage of this city that also bears a horse forepart (as SNG Levante 690ff.). On the other hand, Houghton's assembly of the evidence for the activity of this mint from the reign of Antiochus III to that of Seleucus VI has demonstrated that at other times the Seleucid mint at this city consistently used a reed-like plant as its symbol, and he has questioned the attribution of the horse-forepart issues to Seleucia.[36] The authors of SC have cautiously preserved the attribution, but it seems most unlikely that the mint should have used two different mint symbols in adjacent reigns, and the civic bronzes adduced by Newell must be at least a century later in date than the coins in the name of Seleucus III. In fact another obvious candidate now exists for the mint, thanks to the work of Ashton and McIntyre to clarify the nature of a small series of Alexanders of a similar period, which also bear the mint mark of the forepart of a running horse. These coins, all struck from a single obverse die, but with a number of different reverses bear in addition to the horse a letter T and, since the first example was published, have been firmly attributed to Termessos in Pisidia (Price 2986, Plate 5, no. 6).[37] Although originally believed to be marked with dates of a civic era, McIntyre has now demonstrated clearly that it is not, and we must fall back on hoard evidence for its chronology. Examples are recorded from the Gordion V and I hoards (for which dates of c. 217–210 and 210–205 have been suggested above), and from the Asia Minor 1963 hoard (IGCH 1426, deposited c. 215–210), which is to say that they predate the appearance of the neighboring Pamphylian Alexanders in the hoard record, and may have been struck not long after the demise of Seleucus III. Termessos must, therefore, be a strong candidate for the mint of the issues of Seleucus with horse forepart (SC I. 916), as well as for those later struck in the name of Antiochus III (SC I. 1016, Plate 6, no. 14).[38]

The reattribution of this Seleucid issue to Termessos, if correct, would contribute a significant piece of evidence for the route taken on Seleucus' expedition

35. Mørkholm (1969), pp. 14–15; cf. SC I.1, p. 331 and Ma (1999), p. 55.

36. Houghton (1989) and CSE I., p. 42 n.1.

37. For a full collection of the evidence and discussion of earlier bibliography, see Ashton (2005) and McIntyre (2006).

38. See SC I.1, p. 386, suggesting a date in the last decade of the third century for the coins of Antiochus, on the basis of portrait style.

in 223 BC. From Syria there were two obvious approaches to Phrygia. One ran overland through the Syrian Gates, across flat Cilicia then via the Cilician Gates through Lycaonia to Laodicea ad Lycum.[39] The other route, both shorter and faster heading westwards, was to take ship as far as Pamphylia and then go inland N.W. either by the route that would later be taken by the road of Manlius Aquillius, also emerging in Phrygia at Laodicea, or via Termessos and Kibyra, once more arriving at Laodicea, the route taken (in reverse) by Cn. Manlius Vulso in 188 BC.[40] This latter route, it seems, was also that taken by Seleucus.

Two objections may be raised to this reconstruction. First, the region of Pamphylia is generally assumed to have been Ptolemaic at this period. Second, it may be objected that Seleucus could not have undertaken such a transhipment without the cooperation of at least one Pamphylian city. To the first, response is easy: we have no evidence for the status of Pamphylia in the first half of the 220s BC. 222 BC, or shortly thereafter, is often assumed as the date of the Ptolemaic loss, since that is the date of Ptolemy Euergetes' death. But there is no compelling logic to this assumption. We may equally assume that Ptolemaic garrisons were withdrawn from the area earlier, or that Seleucus III's expedition itself brought an end to Ptolemaic rule over the region. The latter, as we have seen, is one possible conclusion to be drawn from Porphyry's account. Certainly it is clear that by 218 BC Achaeus could act in the area unopposed, and the cities of Perge, Aspendos and Side could all behave as autonomous entities.[41] As has long been noted, Antiochus III's *paraplus* of 197 BC involved no conquests in Pamphylia, suggesting that there were no Ptolemaic possessions left in the area by that time.[42]

To address the second objection, we must turn specifically to Perge. When, in 218 BC, Achaeus' general Garsyeris was sent with an army to relieve the siege of Pednelissos, he established his base in the territory of Perge. It was from here that he sent out ambassadors to Pisidia and Pamphylia. Its centrality within the Pamphylian plain, status as a major port and closest proximity of all the Pamphylian cities to the route north to Phrygia, made Perge an obvious choice. There can be little doubt that it could be regarded as a friendly city. These same factors would have made it an obvious choice of entrepôt for Seleucus III.[43]

39. The 'Lycaonian road:' Mitchell (2008), 176 and 188–189 and Syme (1995), p. 20.

40. For the route of the Aquillian road see Mitchell (1994), pp. 132–133 with fig. 2. For Manlius Vulso, see Grainger (1995), pp. 34–35.

41. αὐτὸς (Garsyeris) δὲ μετὰ τῆς στρατιᾶς εἰς Πέργην κατάρας ἐντεῦθεν ἐποιεῖτο τὰς διαπρεσβείας πρός τε τοὺς ἄλλους τοὺς τὴν Πισιδικὴν κατοικοῦντας καὶ πρὸς τὴν Παμφυλίαν, ὑποδεικνύων μὲν τὸ τῶν Σελγέων βάρος, παρακαλῶν δὲ πάντας πρὸς τὴν Ἀχαιοῦ συμμαχίαν καὶ πρὸς τὴν βοήθειαν τοῖς Πεδνηλισσεῦσιν (Plb. 5.72.9–10).

42. Schmitt (1964), p. 279; Ma (1999), pp. 60–61, n. 31.

43. Note also that Perge was the only Pamphylian city to maintain a Seleucid garrison in 188 BC: Livy 38.37.9: *inde ad Pergam ducit* (Manlius Vulso), *quae una in iis locis regio*

But most important of all, there is now, on the reconstruction offered in Part I of this paper, clear numismatic evidence for a change in the status of Perge around 223 BC, in the form of the introduction of a civic era, and the initiation of an Alexander coinage. It is worth dwelling a moment on the existence of this era, since amid the various debates that have taken place regarding its chronology, the extraordinary fact of its existence at all has tended to go unremarked. Within Asia Minor, it is the first of its kind, an innovation in the administration of coinage. Perge had never used such a dating system before,[44] nor had any other mint of posthumous Alexander coinage anywhere, with the single and obvious exception of the Phoenician mints. It is, in fact, a remarkable coincidence that the citizens of Perge chose to begin the production of such a dated Alexander coinage within a year of a similar initiative at a series of Phoenician mints, and that these Phoenician mints in the east and Perge in the west stand at either end of the sea route that Seleucus III seems to have taken in his expedition of 223 BC. It is unlikely that these two phenomena in Phoenicia and Pamphylia are unconnected, and we may perhaps begin to consider interpreting the Pergaean coinage in the same way as has been suggested for the Phoenician: a coinage of 'civic' appearance occasioned by Seleucid military needs, the result of a contract between king and city.

*(b) The Coinage of Sillyon*

As Boehringer has pointed out, the sole piece of hoard evidence for the dating of the era of Sillyon is a coin of year 11 in the Gordion I (1406) hoard (see above, Table 3). This may suggest that the era of Sillyon began around the same time as that of Perge.[45] If this is the case—caution is required here given the poverty of the hoard evidence—all that has been suggested above regarding the circumstances of the issue of first Pergaean coinage may also be applied to that of Sillyon. We may add the further observation that for Sillyon, this short Alexander coinage is the first and only silver coinage of the city. Silver coinage was clearly not the norm at Sillyon, and we are justified in seeking exceptional circumstances or external pressure behind the issue of these Alexanders. Seleucid military activity in the region is a plausible explanation.

*(c) The recommencement of Pergaean coinage in 218 or 217 and the Campaign of Achaeus*

Following the expedition of Seleucus III and his death in the late summer of 223, we

*tenebatur praesidio.*

44. The earlier silver coinage of Artemis Pergaia had used control letters running from B-I (with gaps), but these were all struck from a single obverse die, and so it seems unlikely that these letters could represent dates. Colin (1996), p. 37 (Series 1.1, Emissions 11–14).

45. Boehringer (1972), p. 61. Cf. Price (1991), pp. 347 and 366.

hear nothing further in the literary sources of Pamphylia until the involvement of Achaeus and his general Garsyeris there in 218 BC. It is plain from Polybius' account that the majority of Pamphylian cities threw in their lot with Achaeus, with the major exception of Side.[46] Interestingly, on the chronology of the coinage suggested here, it is perhaps in 217 BC, after Garsyeris' troops arrived in the region of Perge that the Pergaean Alexander coinage started up again (in year 7) after a two-year gap.

### (d) The beginning of Aspendian (and Phaselite) coinage in 213

Again, we hear nothing more about Pamphylia for a number of years. However, as we have already noted, Antiochus III's campaign of 197 BC involved no activity in Pamphylia, and from this it has generally been assumed that Pamphylia was back in Seleucid hands before this time. The obvious circumstance for the return of the region to Seleucid control is the capture and execution of Achaeus at Sardis, probably in the autumn or winter of 214/3.[47] Once more we note an interesting coincidence in the chronology of the coinage. It is from the following year that the city of Aspendos seems to have begun to count its era, and to have begun to strike its Alexander coinage. The autonomy that the existence of this era suggests at Aspendos is perhaps evidence for a generous settlement of the region by the victorious Antiochus.

If it is correct to suggest that Phaselis began to count its era of autonomy from this same year, then this may also be a sign of a shifting balance of power in the region, with the growing strength of the Seleucid kingdom in Asia Minor, and a readjustment in the administration of Ptolemaic Lycia. Seleucid support may have actively pulled the Phaselites towards Pamphylia at this time, and the formation at around the same period of the Lycian League,[48] which the Phaselites did not initially join, may have pushed them in the same direction.

### (e) The 'Overrepresentation' of Pergaean Coinage

The phenomenon of overrepresentation of certain years of Pergaean Alexanders among records of surviving specimens has been discussed above. It remains to see what historical background we can suggest for this phenomenon. Colin records 73 obverse dies from 361 specimens for the whole of the coinage, an overall $n:d$ ratio of 4.95:1.[49] In just five of the recorded years the ratio rises above 9:1: years 18, 21, 26, 27 and 29 (Figure 6). These equate to 206/5, 203/2, 198/7–197/6 and 195/4.

---

46. Plb. 5.73.4: Σιδῆται δὲ τὰ μὲν στοχαζόμενοι τῆς πρὸς Ἀντίοχον εὐνοίας, τὸ δὲ πλεῖον διὰ τὸ πρὸς Ἀσπενδίους μῖσος, οὐ μετέσχον τῆς βοηθείας.

47. Ma (1999), pp. 60–61.

48. The earliest evidence for the existence of the league seems now to belong to 212/11 BC: see Domingo Gygax (2001), p. 24 n. 21.

49. Colin (1996), summary on p. 99.

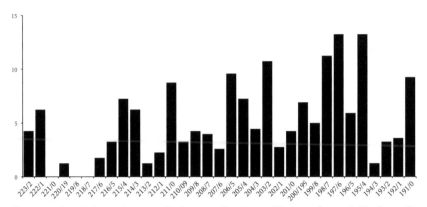

Figure 6. Surviving coins per die by year for Perge (Figures from Colin [1996])

The last of these years, year 29, has been discussed at length above, but should not be viewed in isolation: years 26–27 are similarly well represented, and the intervening year 28 is also represented above average.

The obvious background to this cluster of years spanning the period 198/7–195/4 is the invasion of Asia Minor by Antiochus the Great, which was certainly under way in 197 and 196 BC, but was conceivably preceded (as was the case with Seleucus III's campaign) by military activity led by subordinates, in 198 BC.[50] The abnormal number of coins which seem to have left Pamphylia and to have been hoarded elsewhere is to be explained, it seems, by the abnormally high level of transit of the Seleucid military through the region during these years. As we have seen above, a similar instance of overrepresentation of Aradian Alexanders occurred in years 196/5 and 195/4 BC. Just as the Aradian Peraea may be connected to Pamphylia in the context of Seleucus' expedition of 223 (section [a] above), so it appears to be connected again in the mid 190s. Presumably it was once more the position of the two areas at either end of a heavily used naval route from Syria to Asia Minor that created this similarity.

A similar case might be made for the other spike in the figure between years 18 and 21 (206/5–203/2). Again this exodus of Pamphylian coinage may have been due to heightened Seleucid military activity in S.W. Asia Minor around 203 BC.[51] Finally, we might note another, smaller spike in years 9 and 10 (c. 215/4–214/3). This, perhaps, is to be connected with the campaign of Antiochus to reclaim Asia from Achaeus: Antiochus crossed the Taurus in the summer of 216.[52]

50. For discussion of the probable Seleucid military activity against the Attalid kingdom in 198 BC (Livy 32.8.9–10), see Schmitt (1964), pp. 269–270.

51. See Ma (1999), pp. 65–70 for a discussion of the evidence.

52. Plb. 5.107.4. Schmitt (1964), p. 264.

## (f) The End of Pergaean Coinage, c. 191/0 BC

On the chronology proposed here, the Pergaean Alexander coinage ended in 191/0 BC. Why might this have been? And did the end of coinage also coincide with the end of the era? It has been suggested above that the coinage and the era of Perge began with the arrival of Seleucus III's expedition in 223 BC. The era must be one of freedom, since otherwise the city would have used the Seleucid era. Therefore it follows that the city was free, but closely allied to the Seleucid kingdom (and, for a while, to Achaeus). It has also been suggested above that the Alexander coinage was connected with Seleucid military needs. It was perhaps produced for the king in the 'civic' mint. If these suggestions are correct, the cessation of coinage in 191/0 would imply the cessation of military need or the cessation of the supply of Seleucid silver to the civic mint. The cessation of the era, if it did cease, would imply a change in the status of the city.

The broader historical circumstances of these years are well known. In 192 the focus of Antiochus III's activity shifted from Asia and Thrace to mainland Greece, where he clashed with Rome. 191 BC saw a major defeat at Thermopylae and Antiochus' withdrawal to Asia Minor. In late 190 occurred the further critical defeat at Magnesia, and the beginning of the discussion with Rome of the terms by which Antiochus would vacate western Asia Minor. By early in the year 190/89, therefore, Antiochus was preparing to withdraw his troops from west of the Taurus and to begin the payment of indemnities to Rome and Eumenes II. Pamphylia, moreover, was rapidly becoming the focus of dispute between the Seleucid king and the Attalid (Livy 38.39.17). These, surely, are the cirumstances in which was installed at Perge the garrison of which we hear in 188 BC (Livy 38.37.9). The battle of Magnesia had brought to an end the period of Seleucid sponsored freedom of Perge and, with or without the evidence of the coinage, this is when we might expect the era of freedom to have ended. On the chronology proposed for this era above, the Battle of Magnesia would have occurred, at the latest, early in year 34. No coinage of this year has been recorded. If this correlation is correct then it strongly suggests that the era began in 223/2 and ended in 191/0.

## (g) The Continuation of Aspendian Coinage after 188 BC.

While the coinage of Perge and perhaps also the Pergaean era ceased c. 191/0, the coinage and era of Aspendos carried on for another six years until c. 185/4 BC. An obvious reason for this continuation would be a difference in status of Aspendos in these years compared with Perge. As Livy clearly tells us, Perge was the only city in Pamphylia with a Seleucid garrison in 188 BC.[53] In fact, Aspendos had negotiated its own settlement with Rome in the previous year (Livy 38.15.6). Aspendian

---

53. Livy: 38.37.9 (above n. 43).

freedom had thus been preserved through the precarious period of 190–188 BC and continued after the Peace of Apamea. If the Aspendian Alexanders had in part been a proxy-Seleucid coinage before 189, then the city's coinage thereafter must be regarded as true civic coinage. Andrew McIntyre alerts me to a curious feature of the Aspendian Alexander coinage that may indeed indicate a change in nature of the coinage at precisely this time: in year 24 (190/89 BC), the mint of Aspendos began to place symbols on its Alexanders in addition to a date. Year 24 has an an eagle (Price 2903, Plate 7, no. 15), year 25 a wreath (Price 2905), year 26 a spearhead (Price 2907), year 27 a cornucopia (Price 2908–2909), year 28 a sling (Price 2911), and year 29 a horse-forepart (Price 2912).

The continuation of the Aspendian era may thus be explained in terms of the status of the city, but why did the coinage stop in 185/4 BC? No clear answer emerges from the history of Aspendos, since we know nothing of it in these years. It is tempting to question whether the cessation of the Aspendian Alexanders at this period has anything to do with the new monetary regime within the Pergamene kingdom. This is not the place to enter into the question of the date of the introduction of the cistophoric system. However, if, as has been argued by Bauslaugh and Ashton, this introduction is to be dated to some time before 181 BC,[54] then conceivably it was the appearance of this new, lower-weight coinage that led to the demise of the outmoded, heavier Alexander coinage in Pamphylia.

### (h) The Alexanders of Phaselis

The Alexander coinage of Phaselis, it has been noted above, behaved differently in circulation to the Alexanders of Perge and Aspendos. In the last decade of the third century, it does not appear in the hoards where the other mints are found (Table 3). It also lacks the pattern of 'overrepresentation' found for Perge and perhaps Aspendos (Figure 6 and cf. Figures 10–11). To these two anomalies we can add a third, the difference in pattern of cistophoric countermarking on the Phaselite Alexanders (Figure 7).[55]

If, as Bauslaugh suggests, the countermarks were applied to coin submitted by the Seleucid kingdom as indemnity to Eumenes, this evidence also seems to

54. Before 181 BC: Ashton (1994). 188–183 BC (cistophoric countermarking) and 183–180 BC (cistophori): Bauslaugh (1990).

55. Numbers are based on the catalogue of Bauslaugh (1990) with the addition of the following specimens: Ma'aret (Mattingly [1993]) no. 336 (Perge yr. 22, Sardis); Gaziantep (Augé et al. [1997]) no. 114 (Aspendos yr. 26, Apamea); CNG 72 (2006) 370 (Perge yr. 23, Tralles); SNG Munich 664 (Aspendos yr. 11, Apamea); Heipp-Tamer (1993), no. 253 (Phaselis yr. 14, Pergamum); Unknown findspot 1991 (Metcalf [1994])), nos. 139 (Phaselis yr. 8, uncertain), 158 (Phaselis yr. 14, Pergamum), 190 (Aspendus yr. 3, Sardis), 224 (Aspendos yr. 19, Synnada), 264 (Aspendos yr. 23, Sardis).

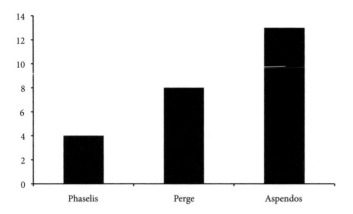

Figure 7. Cistophoric countermarks on Pamphylian Alexanders

suggest that the issues of Phaselis did not behave in the same 'Seleucid' fashion as those of neighbouring Perge and Aspendos.

The Phaselite issues, on the chronology proposed above, continued in production slightly longer than those of Aspendos. However, we may perhaps seek a similar explanation for their termination c. 181/0 BC: the rise of the cistophoric standard to the north, and the plinthophoric standard in Lycia, now under Rhodian control. Phaselis' subsequent issues of silver coinage seem largely to have been accommodated to the plinthophoric standard.[56]

*(i) The Coinage of Side*

Detailed discussion of the coinage of Side falls outside the scope of this article. However, the history of this city is closely tied to that of Perge and Aspendos during the period under consideration, and it is important not to allow the difference in appearance of the contemporary Sidetan coinage to compartmentalize our interpretation of it.

Side did, in fact, produce a posthumous Alexander coinage of the late third century, although it is known from just a single specimen and bears no date (Plate 7, no. 16).[57] From fabric and style, which is, as Seyrig noted, more closely akin to Ionian than Pamphylian issues, there can be little doubt that Price's date of *c.* 210

---

56. For the 'pseudo-League' issues of the city see Troxell (1982), pp. 65–68. The epichoric type coinage of tetradrachms and didrachms seems to have been struck to the same standard: Heipp-Tamer (1993) Series 10, emissions 2 and 3. As Heipp-Tamer notes, the two denominations can also be regarded and 16 and 8 obol coins on the Attic standard.

57. ANS 1944.100.33405 (Price 2975), first published by Seyrig (1963), p. 57.

BC for the piece is approximately correct.[58] It seems, then, that Side may have made its brief foray into Alexander coinage at around the same time as the Aspendians were beginning theirs. Alone of the Pamphylian cities, as we have seen, Side remained loyal to the Seleucid king during the period of Achaeus' secession.[59] Perhaps the Sidetan Alexanders are linked to Antiochus' reconquest of Pamphylia from Achaeus. In the absence of more specimens and hoard evidence for chronology, only speculation is possible.

Of greater size, and much better documented in the hoard record, is the coinage of Side generally regarded as being of autonomous type (Plate 7, no. 17). On the obverse this bears the helmeted head of Athena exactly as she had appeared on the gold coinage of Alexander the Great. On the reverse, again borrowed (though more freely) from Alexander's gold, was the standing figure of Nike, holding a wreath. The coins bear no ethnic. The mint is identified rather, in a manner reminiscent of Seleucid royal issues in western Asia Minor, by the appearance of a symbol drawn from the iconography of the civic mint, in this case a pomegranate in left field. The hoard evidence is clear: their production began within the last five years of the third century BC.[60]

It has been suggested above, in the cases of both Perge and Aspendos, that the beginning of their Alexander coinage may be linked to Seleucid military activity that involved the region of Pamphylia, first in c. 223 BC, second in 213 BC, and that both coinages may, to a degree, be regarded as Seleucid proxy coinages, struck perhaps with Seleucid silver in a civic mint within a free city. Could the same be true of the Sidetan coinage? The chronology fits well with the renewed interest of Antiochus III in Asia Minor, following his return from the east in 204 BC. In 203 BC Antiochus himself was in Asia Minor; his presence was felt in Ionia and Caria.[61] Moreover, it was at precisely this time, as inscriptions from Asia Minor attest, that Antiochus took Alexander's title of *Megas* ('the Great').[62] Could the autonomous coinage of Side be, in origin, another Seleucid proxy coinage? The chronology, iconography and lack of ethnic all support the suggestion that this was a Seleucid inspired coinage, and one further piece of evidence may be relevant. Two gold issues of Antiochus are known with the types of Alexander, but in the name of Antiochus (*SC* I. 1014–1015, Plate 7, nos. 18–19). As one of their controls they bear the letters *FA*, which are almost certainly to be read as first two letters

---

58. The control letters AΦ that appear on the ANS coin also occur on an issue of autonomous type, which may suggest that the two coinages are chronologically adjacent. See Price (1991), p. 363.

59. Plb. 5.73.4 (above n. 46).

60. For recent tabulation of the hoard evidence see Meadows (2006), pp. 155–156.

61. Ma (1999), p. 66.

62. Ma (1999), pp. 272–276 summarizes the evidence and the previous debate.

of the Aspendos' name. Seyrig was inclined to date these coins to the campaign of Antiochus in 203 BC, although his arguments for doing so no longer stand up to scrutiny.[63] Nonetheless, the choice of types at a mint very close to Side is a coincidence, and it is tempting to connect both coinages, Aspendian gold and Sidetan silver, with Antiochus' newly adopted persona, and his arrival in the region in 203 BC.[64]

### III. Conclusion

I have suggested (Part I) on the basis of the hoard evidence that the era of Perge began in either 224/3 or, more probably, 223/2 BC. By inference from historical circumstances for the likely start date (Part IIa) and end date (IIf) of the era of freedom of Perge, I have further noted the likelihood that this era and the coinage are coterminous and run from 223/2 to 191/0.

It has been observed by others (above n. 6) on the basis of hoard and die evidence that the era of Aspendos started ten years later than that of Perge. I have suggested on historical grounds that this era is likely to have begun in 213/2. Aspendos' coinage, though not necessarily its era of freedom, ended therefore in 185/4.

For Phaselis, on the basis of the hoard evidence, I have suggested a similar start date for the era and coinage to that of Aspendos, and have associated this beginning with a reorganization of the Ptolemaic province of Lycia and the Seleucid espousal of the freedom of Pamphylia at this period.

For the Alexanders of Perge, Aspendos and Sillyon (though not for those of Phaselis which exhibit a different circulation pattern), as well as for the Alexanders and autonomous coinage of Side, I have suggested that we should perhaps view these coinages not as straightforward civic issues, but rather as 'proxy-Seleucid' issues. These were perhaps produced partly with Seleucid silver at a civically controlled mint. Their nature perhaps accounts for the appearance of these coinages, and only these coinages with cistophoric countermarks. In original function, I have suggested a similarity between the Pamphylian Alexanders and the Alexanders of the Aradian Peraea and posited a connection between the issue of these coinages both in c. 223/2 and c. 197–195 BC during periods of heightened Seleucid military activity in Asia Minor.

The new chronology that I have proposed for the Pamphylian eras, combined with Le Rider's suggested lower dating for the Seleucid mint of Antioch under Antiochus III, has allowed the reconsideration of the deposit dates of a number

---

63. Seyrig (1963), pp. 52–56. On the fragility of Seyrig's argument, based on the suggestion that the pieces were struck, along with a gold Philip, at the time of the Syro-Macedonian pact with Philip V, see SC I., p. 386.

64. It is perhaps to these circumstances too that we may attribute Antiochus' brief issue at Termessos (SC I. 1016), if indeed it belongs there (above n. 38)

of hoards. Perhaps the most significant among these is the case of the Mektepini hoard, where the raising of the date of burial from c. 190 to c. 195 BC, will have an impact on the chronologies of a significant number of other coinages.

## References

Allen, R. E. 1983. *The Attalid kingdom: a constitutional history.* Oxford.

Ashton, R. H. J. 1994. The Attalid poll tax. *Zeitschrift für Papyrologie und Epigraphik* 104: 57–60.

———. 2005. The coinage of Oinoanda. *Numismatic Chronicle* 165: 65–84.

Augé, Ch., A. Davesne, R. Ergeç. 1997. Le début des tétradrachmes d'Athènes du "nouveau style:" un trésor trouvé près de Gaziantep en 1994 45. *Anatolia Antiqua* 5: 45–82

Bauslaugh, R. 1979. The posthumous Alexander coinage of Chios. *American Numismatic Society Museum Notes* 24: 1–45.

———. 1990. Cistophoric countermarks and the monetary system of Eumenes II. *Numismatic Chronicle* 150: 39–65.

Boehringer, C. 1972. *Zur Chronologie mittelhellenistischer Münzserien 220–160 v. Chr.* Deutsches Archäologisches Institut. Antike Münzen und Geschnittene Steine Bd. V. Berlin.

———.1999. Beobachtungen und Überlegungen zu den Ären der Pamphylischen Alexandreier. In *Travaux de Numismatique Grecque Offerts a Georges Le Rider,* M. Amandry and S. Hurter, eds., 65–75. London.

Colin, H. J. 1996. *Die Münzen von Perge in Pamphylien aus hellenistischer Zeit.* Tyll Kroha.

Domingo Gygax, M. 2001. *Untersuchungen zu den Lykischen Gemeinwesen in Klassischer und Hellenistischer Zeit.* Bonn.

Duyrat, F. 2002. Les ateliers monétaires de Phénicie de Nord à l'époque hellénistique. In *Les Monnayages Syriens: quel apport pour l'histoire du Proche-Orient hellénistique et romain? Actes de la table ronde de Damas, 10–12 novembre 1999,* C. Augé et al., eds., 21–69. Beirut.

———. 2003. La politique monétaire d'Arados: les Alexandres. In *La Syrie Hellénistique,* M. Sartre, ed., *Topoi Suppl.* 4: 25–52.

———. 2005. *Arados hellénistique: étude historique et monétaire.* Beirut.

Grainger, J. D. 1995. The campaign of Cn. Manlius Vulso in Asia Minor. *Anatolian Studies* 45: 23–42.

Heipp-Tamer, C. 1993. *Die Münzprägung der Lykischen Stadt Phaselis in Griechischer Zeit.* Saarbrücken.

Hoover, O. 2006. A second look at the Aradian bronze coinage attributed to Seleucus I, SC 72–73. *American Journal of Numismatics* 18: 43–50.

Houghton, A. 1989. The royal Seleucid mint of Seleuceia on the Calycadnus. In *Kraay-Mørkholm essays. Numismatic studies in memory of C.M. Kraay and O. Mørkholm*, G. Le Rider et al., eds., 77–98. Louvain.

———. 1999. The early Seleucid mint of Laodicea ad Mare (c. 300–246 BC). In *Travaux de Numismatique Grecque offerts a Georges Le Rider*, M. Amandry and S. Hurter, eds. 169–184. London.

Kinns, P. 1999. The attic weight drachms of Ephesus: a preliminary study in the light of recent hoards. *Numismatic Chronicle* 159: 47–97.

Kleiner, F. S. 1971. The Alexander Tetradrachms of Pergamum and Rhodes. *American Numismatic Society Museum Notes* 17: 95–125.

Le Rider, G. 1972. Les tetradrachmes pamphyliens de la fin du IIIe siècle et du début du IIe siècle avant notre ère. *Revue Numismatique* 14: 253–259.

———. 1998. Un Trésor hellénistique de monnaies d'argent trouvé en Syrie en 1971 (*CH* II, 81). *Syria* 75: 89–96.

———. 1999. *Antioche de Syrie sous les Séleucides: corpus des monnaies d'or et d'argent. I, de Séleucos I à Antiochos V, c. 300–161*. Paris.

Lorber and Houghton. 2009. Antiochus III Hoard. *American Journal of Numismatics* 21: 89–103.

Ma, J. T. 1999. *Antiochus III and the Cities of Western Asia Minor*. Oxford.

McIntyre, A. P. 2006. The Alexander tetradrachms of Termessos Major. *Numismatic Chronicle* 166: 27–30.

———. 2007. The eras of the Alexanders of Aspendos and Perge. *Numismatic Chronicle* 167: 93–98.

Mattingly, H. B. 1993. The Ma'Aret En-Nu'man hoard, 1980. In *Essays in honour of Robert Carson and Kenneth Jenkins*, A. Burnett and R. Bland, eds., 69–86. London.

Meadows, A. R. 2006. Side, Amyntas and the Pamphylian plain. In *Agoranomia: Studies in Money and Exchange presented to Jack Kroll*, P. van Alfen ed., 151–175. New York.

———, and C.C. Lorber. Forthcoming. The commerce 2002 ('Achaeus') Hoard. *Coin Hoards* 10.

S. Mitchell. 1994. Three Cities in Pisidia. *Anatolian Studies* 44: 129–48

———. 2008. Geography, politics and imperialism in the Asian customs law. In *The Customs Law of Asia*, M. Cottier et al. eds., 165–201. Oxford.

Mørkholm, O. 1969. Some Seleucid coins from the mint of Sardis. *Nordisk Numismatisk Årsskrift* 1969: 5–20

———. 1978. The era of the Pamphylian Alexanders. *American Numismatic Society Museum Notes* 23: 69–75.

Newell, E. T. 1941. *The coinage of the western Seleucid mints from Seleucus I to Antiochus III*. New York.

Özgen, E., and A. Davesne. 1994. Le trésor de Oylum Höyügü. In *Trésors et Circulation Monétaire en Anatolie antique,* M. Amandry and G. le Rider, eds., 45–49. Paris.

Price, M. J. 1991. *The coinage in the name of Alexander the Great and Philip Arrhidaeus. A British Museum Catalogue.* London/Zurich.

Schmitt, H. H. 1964. *Untersuchungen zur Geschichte Antiochos des Grossen und seiner Zeit.* Historia Einzelschriften 6. Wiesbaden.

Seyrig, H. 1963. Monnaies hellénistiques. I–X. *Revue Numismatique* 5: 7–64.

———. 1971. Monnaies hellénistiques, XVIII–XXI. *Revue Numismatique* 13: 8–25.

———. 1973. *Trésors du Levant anciens et nouveaux.* Paris.

Syme, R. 1995. *Anatolica. Studies in Strabo.* Oxford.

Troxell, H. 1982. *The coinage of the Lycian league.* American Numismatic Society Numismatic Notes and Monographs 162. New York.

Villaronga, L. 1984. Tresor de la segona guerra púnica de la Província de "Cuenca." *Numismatica e Antichità Classiche* 13: 127–137.

## KEY TO PLATES

1. Silver tetradrachm of Phaselis (Yr. 11 ): ANS 1951.35.37 (Newell, from the Tell Kotchek hoard, *IGCH* 1773)

2. Silver tetradrachm of Aspendus (Yr. 17 ): ANS 1944.100.32296 (Newell, from the Ain Tab hoard, *IGCH* 1542)

3. Silver tetradrachm of Perge (Yr. 20 ): ANS 1951.90.30 (from the Propontis hoard, *IGCH* 888)

4. Silver tetradrachm of Sillyon (Yr. 11 ): ANS 1964.93.2 (A. Kreisberg gift)

5. Silver tetradrachm of 'Magydos' (Yr. 14): ANS 1951.90.28 (from the Propontis hoard, *IGCH* 888)

6. Silver tetradrachm of Termessos: ANS 1965.56.2

7. Silver tetradrachm of uncertain mint (Yr. 2): ANS 1952.44.17

8. Silver tetradrachm of Gabala (Yr. 35): Utrecht

9. Silver tetradrachm of Carne (Yr. 35): Paris

10. Silver drachm of Marathus (Yr. 35): Paris (Seyrig)

11. Silver tetradrachm of Simyra (Yr. 35), reign of Seleucus III: *CSE* I. 687

12. Silver tetradrachm of Seleucus III, uncertain mint in Phrygia? (from the Asia Minor, 1963 hoard, *IGCH* 1411)

13. Silver tetradrachm of Seleucus III, mint of Termessos: Paris (De Luynes 3290)

14. Silver tetradrachm of Antiochus III, mint of Termessos: Paris (Valton 487)

15. Silver tetradrachm of Aspendus (Yr. 24 ): ANS 1944.100.32326 (Newell, from the Ain Tab hoard, *IGCH* 1542)

16. Silver tetradrachm of Side: ANS 1944.100.33405 (Newell)
17. Silver tetradrachm of Side: ANS 1944.100.50909 (Newell)
18. Gold stater of Antiochus III, mint of Aspendos: Paris (De Luynes 3270)
19. Gold half-stater of Antiochus III, mint of Aspendos: Paris

APPENDIX

NUMBERS OF PAMPHYLIAN ALEXANDERS RECORDED IN

SECOND-CENTURY BC HOARDS

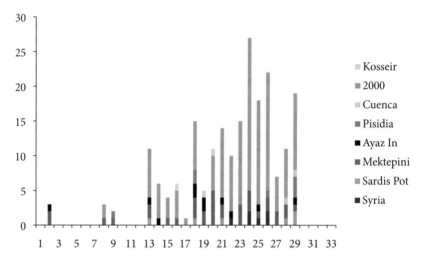

Figure 8. Coins of Perge present in hoards buried during the probable period of striking

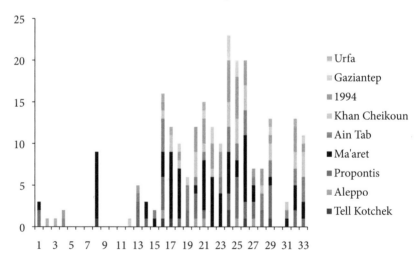

Figure 9. Coins of Perge present in hoards buried after the probable period of striking

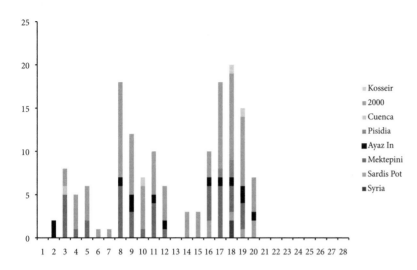

Figure 10. Coins of Aspendos present in hoards buried during the probable period of striking

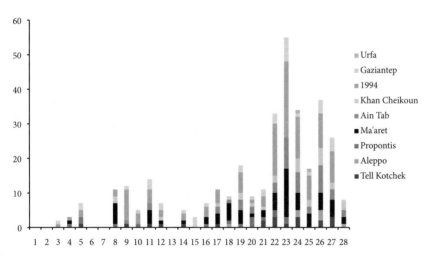

Figure 11. Coins of Aspendos present in hoards buried after the probable period of striking

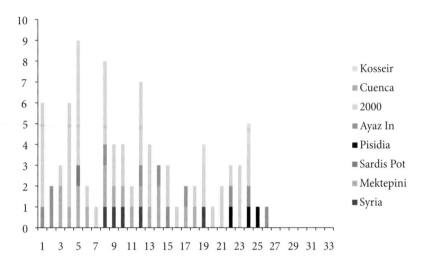

Figure 12. Coins of Phaselis present in hoards buried during the probable period of striking

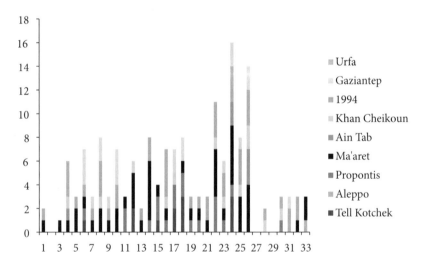

Figure 13. Coins of Phaselis present in hoards buried after the probable period of striking

*AJN* Second Series 21 (2009) pp. 89–104
© 2009 The American Numismatic Society

# Antiochus III Hoard

PLATES 8–13                    CATHARINE LORBER AND ARTHUR HOUGHTON

> A Hellenistic tetradrachm hoard recorded from commerce has brought to light a new Antigonid variety as well as a tetradrachm of Antiochus III that raises questions about the treatment of Uncertain Mint 68 (part of Newell's Nisibis) in *Seleucid Coins*, Part 1.

A Hellenistic hoard of 77 tetradrachms appeared in commerce in 2005.[1]
Deposit: 196 BC or shortly after
Contents: 77 tetradrachms
Alexander III (10): Pella (2), Cyme, Magnesia, Miletus (3), Mylasa, Rhodes, unidentifiable
Antigonus Gonatas or Antigonus Doson: new variety
Antigonus Doson (4)
Lysimachus (14): Pella, Amphipolis (2), Byzantium (3), Calchedon, Cius (2), Cyzicus, Lampascus, unattributed (3)
Attalids (8)
Perge
Antiochus I (6): Seleucia on the Tigris (5), Ecbatana
Antiochus II (8): Lysimachia, Seleucia on the Tigris (5), Susa, unattributed

---

1. The hoard was recorded by Arthur Houghton. The authors have profited from preliminary work on this hoard by Richard P. Miller, from discussions with Andrew R. Meadows, and from an unpublished manuscript of Ute Wartenberg Kagan treating the unique tetradrachm of Antigonus in the hoard.

issue perhaps of Asia Minor
"Antiochus Soter" issue
Antiochus Hierax (2), Abydus or imitation, Ilium
Seleucus III (4): Antioch (3), Seleucia on the Tigris
Antiochus III (18): Lysimachia, Antioch (4), Uncertain Mint 67, "Rose"
Mint (4), Nisibis, Uncertain Mint 68, Seleucia on the Tigris (2), Susa (3)

## DATE OF DEPOSIT

The probable closing coin of the hoard is no. 60 (see Appendix), a mint state tetradrachm of Antiochus III of the Lysimachia mint, datable to the year 196 BC or shortly afterward (on the mint, see Le Rider 1988). In 196 Antiochus III occupied the abandoned site of Lysimachia, recently destroyed by Thracian raiders. The Seleucid king refounded and rebuilt the city, bringing back former residents from exile and from slavery and drawing in new colonists as well. His coinage at Lysimachia comprises a single tetradrachm variety, known in just four examples, all from the same die pair. To all appearances this was an issue of prestige, advertising his benefactions; it was hardly adequate to finance the reconstruction of Lysimachia, even though Antiochus' military provided the labor. No. 60 is the only one of the four extant specimens of its emission for which we possess a hoard provenance.

Ostensibly equally late is no. 71, another tetradrachm of Antiochus III. In *Seleucid Coins* it is dated from c. 197 on the basis of its portrait type. It belongs to the coinage originally attributed to Nisibis by Newell (Newell 1941: 67–77). Newell's Series III underwent a provisional reorganization in *Seleucid Coins,* where it was reattributed to Uncertain Mint 68 in northern Mesopotamia and divided by portrait type into two series considered to be chronologically successive despite some shared controls (Houghton and Lorber 2002: 429–432). This analysis does not fit entirely comfortably within the iconographic program postulated in *Seleucid Coins* and used to classify the portrait coins of Antiochus III (Houghton and Lorber 2002: 357–360). The earlier portrait type of Uncertain Mint 68 has all the features of Type B, dated c. 211–205/4. But we drew a connection between the opening of Uncertain Mint 68 and the financing of the Asia Minor campaigns of the 190s and interpreted the portrait as a local variant of the later Type D so that it could be dated c. 197–c. 192/90.

The fragile nature of these hypotheses is obvious and evidence is mounting against them. In the first place, no. 71 is not a mint state coin; it shows a degree of wear that is difficult to reconcile with a date of issue just a year or less before the deposit of our hoard. Of particular importance is the appearance of a tetradrachm with an elderly Type E portrait, dated c. 192/90–187 in *Seleucid Coins*, in another Seleucid hoard recorded from commerce, the so-called Achaeus hoard of 2002

(Houghton, Lorber, and Hoover 2008: 693, Ad225). In commentary on that hoard Andrew Meadows has derived a probable date of deposit of c. 204–199 from analysis of the non-Seleucid contents (Meadows and Lorber forthcoming). The serious discrepancy between his date for the hoard and the supposed date of the tetradrachm of Uncertain Mint 68 points to problems with the chronology proposed in *Seleucid Coins*. For further discussion of Uncertain Mint 68, see commentary on no. 72 below.

### REGION OF HOARD FORMATION

The absence of coins of Seleucus II and the presence of two tetradrachms of Antiochus Hierax suggest that our hoard was formed in northwest Asia Minor. That the closing coin is a tetradrachm of Lysimachia tends to confirm the assumption. The presence of a second specimen from this mint, struck under Antiochus II, is noteworthy but not diagnostic: his Lysimachia tetradrachms have occurred in hoards from northwestern Asia Minor to Mesopotamia (Northwestern Asia Minor, 1929 (*IGCH* 1370); Mektepini (*IGCH* 1410); Meydancikkale (*CH* 8.308); Syria, 1959 (*IGCH* 1535); and Tell Halaf (*IGCH* 1763 = *CH* 8.302), see Houghton and Lorber 2002, vol. 2: 174–175). The rest of the Seleucid component does not strongly indicate an origin in northwest Asia Minor but the non-Seleucid contents are more supportive. Of the ten tetradrachms of Alexander type, seven are of mints in western Asia Minor, ranging from Cyme in the north to Rhodes in the south. Completely lacking are the Pamphylian Alexanders normally found in hoards deposited in or after the late third century (although a tetradrachm of Perge with civic types is included). The component of Lysimachi reinforces our impression that the hoard was formed in northwest Asia Minor: of eleven attributable tetradrachms, eight are of the mints of Byzantium, Calchedon, Cius, Cyzicus, and Lampsacus. Finally, the eight Attalid tetradrachms account for slightly more than 10% of the hoard. If we divide the mints by region, the Antiochus III hoard presents the following profile:

| Region | Hoard coins | N° | % |
| --- | --- | --- | --- |
| Macedonia | 1–3, 11–18 | 11 | 14.3 |
| Northwest Asia Minor | 4, 19–26, 30–37, 45, 54–55, 60 | 21 | 27.3 |
| Western Asia Minor | 5–10 | 6 | 7.8 |
| Southern Asia Minor | 38 | 1 | 1.3 |
| Syria | 53, 56–58, 61–64 | 8 | 10.4 |
| Mesopotamia | 65–72 | 8 | 10.4 |
| Seleucid East | 39–44, 46–51, 59, 73–75 | 18 | 23.4 |
| Unattributed | 27–29, 52 | 4 | 5.2 |
| Totals | | 77 | 100.1 |

Coins from the Seleucid east represent the second largest share after those from northwest Asia Minor. Mainly these are tetradrachms from Seleucia on the Tigris, the most prolific Seleucid mint under Antiochus I and II. We assume that for the most part the movement of these coins can be attributed to Seleucid military campaigns, in particular the war against Bithynia following the succession of Antiochus I, Soter's Galatian war, the Black Sea and Thracian operations of Antiochus II in the Second Syrian War, and the invasions of Thrace by Antiochus III in 196 and 195. However, it is instructive to compare other third-century and early second-century silver hoards from this region:

1. Northwest Asia Minor, c. 1970 (*IGCH* 1368; Houghton and Lorber 2002, vol. 2: 78)
2. Kirazli, near Amasya, Pontus, 1939 (*IGCH* 1369 = *CH* 8.324; Houghton and Lorber 2002, vol. 2: 81–82)
3. Asia Minor, c. 1925 (*IGCH* 1448; Houghton and Lorber 2002, vol. 2: 82)
4. Northwestern Asia Minor, 1929 (*IGCH* 1370; Houghton and Lorber 2002, vol. 2: 83)
5. Asia Minor, 1972 (*CH* 1.73; Houghton and Lorber 2002, vol. 2: 83–84)
6. Troas or Mysia, 1947 or earlier (*IGCH* 1301; Houghton and Lorber 2002, vol. 2: 85)
7. Edremit, Mysia, 1954 (*IGCH* 1302; Houghton and Lorber 2002, vol. 2: 85)
8. Pergamene Asklepieion, Mysia, 1960 (*IGCH* 1303; Houghton and Lorber 2002, vol. 2: 88–89)
9. Ilium, Troas, c. 1856 (*IGCH* 1316; Houghton and Lorber 2002, vol. 2: 93)
10. Asia Minor, c. 1947 (*IGCH* 1451; Houghton and Lorber 2002, vol. 2: 94)
11. Amasya, Pontus, c. 1860 (*IGCH* 1372; Houghton and Lorber 2002, vol. 2: 95)

Seleucid tetradrachms from eastern mints are well represented in hoards 1, 2, 5, and 10, but they are completely absent from nos. 3, 4, 6, and 7. It is perhaps significant that the latter group of hoards include no Seleucid rulers later than Antiochus Hierax, but we can offer no plausible explanation for the pattern.

## THE ALEXANDERS

Most of the Alexanders in our hoard are dated before 196 in the literature, based on their appearance in earlier hoards. No. 6, a tetradrachm of Miletus, belongs to a group that Price dated c. 210–c. 190, but its lower date should now be raised to a bit before 196. No. 10, a tetradrachm of Rhodes with the signature of Hephaestion, was dated c. 201–190 by Price, who cited the Mektepini hoard as his *terminus ante quem* (Price 1991: 317). R. H. J. Ashton discussed the problematic appearance of a specimen in the Diyarbekir hoard but confirmed that the Hephaestion issue belongs to the very late third century or first decade of the second (Ashton and Kinns

2004: 96–97). The specimen in the Antiochus III hoard shows virtually no wear, consistent with the currently accepted chronology. It was probably struck shortly before 196 and may imply a similar date for other Rhodian moneyers who are associated with Hephaestion by obverse die links.

The hoard includes several new varieties or variants. The tetradrachm of Cyme, no. 4, bears a normal ₳ monogram instead of the similar but more elaborate monograms of Price 1628 and 1629. No. 5, a tetradrachm of Magnesia, shares the controls of Price 2049, but its second monogram is situated not in the left field, but behind the rear leg of the throne. Nos. 7 and 8 exemplify our observation that new tetradrachm issues of Miletus seem to turn up in nearly every Hellenistic hoard of the third or second century.

## THE ANTIGONIDS

By far the most important Macedonian coin in our hoard is no. 11, a unique tetradrachm in the name of King Antigonus showing a laureate head of Zeus on the obverse. The reverse depicts Apollo seated left on a prow, examining his bow; this type is normally paired with a Poseidon obverse on common Macedonian tetradrachms assigned by most scholars to Antigonus III Doson. The letters TI appear below the prow on our coin. The same control also appears on Pan/Athena tetradrachms of Antigonus II Gonatas (Mathisen 1981: 111 n.47; Kremydi-Sicilianou 2000: no. 983); on rare drachms of Gonatas with the types Zeus/Athena (Merker 1960: 45; Kremydi-Sicilianou 2000: nos. 984–985); and on tetradrachms of the Poseidon/Apollo type, where the letters are associated with a star (Panagopoulou 2001: 320).[2] The drachms present an especially intriguing comparison, though not an exact parallel. On the drachms the head of Zeus is wreathed with oak and his brow bulges with an ominous scowl[3]; on the tetradrachm the god is laureate and his expression is serene, his features idealized. Yet in both cases the proportions are similar and the nose quite short; the two dies could be works of the same artist. In light of these artistic and control links, the new Zeus/Apollo tetradrachm might be attributed to Antigonus Gonatas, as an isolated special emission. A plausible occasion for the issue is the naval battle of Cos: after defeating the superior force of the Ptolemaic admiral Patroclus, Antigonus dedicated his flagship to Apollo (Athenaeus 5.209e). If the reverse type of the tetradrachm commemorates this dedication, the coin itself could be dated to the aftermath of the battle of Cos (fought sometime between 262 and 255). The Apollo on prow reverse

2. Panagopoulou also cites Zeus/Athena pentobols with TI.

3. Although the oak wreath was a well-known attribute of Zeus, it appears in a only a small minority of representations of the god. *LIMC* VIII/1, s.v. "Zeus," includes a section by S. Kremydi-Sicilianou listing coins that portray Zeus in an oak wreath; the examples are mainly from Epirus and Thessaly but also include a bronze of Philip V of Macedon.

type of Antigonus Doson, which differs in some details, would then represent a later revival of the design, perhaps motivated by its association with victory in Caria, a theme highly suitable for the coinage of Doson's Carian campaign.

In a recent article on Antigonid coinage, Katerina Panagopoulou proposed extensive reattributions (Panagopoulou 2001: 325–328). She submitted that the Pan tetradrachms of Antigonus Gonatas continued to be struck by his successors, and she dated the introduction of the Poseidon tetradrachms to the aftermath of the battle of Andros (246/5), so that her model assumes the parallel production of both Pans and Poseidons "at least until Doson." According to Panagopoulou, Pan tetradrachms marked with the letters TI were issued in her periods II (c. 252–246/5), III (c. 246/5–229), and IV (c. 229–221, i.e., the reign of Antigonus Doson). The Zeus drachms marked TI belong to period IV.[4] By implication, the new Zeus/Apollo tetradrachm would also fall in the reign of Doson.

The new tetradrachm shows slight but visible wear on the high points of Zeus' hair and beard, and Apollo's bow and left hand are eroded to the level of the prow. The coin is clearly earlier than the Poseidon varieties represented in our hoard and thus presents a challenge to Panagopoulou's arrangement, since she assigns these particular Poseidons to her period III. Unfortunately, wear comparison fails to clarify the regnal attribution of the Zeus tetradrachm according to the traditional chronology. The coin does not give the impression of being thirty or more years older than the Poseidon/Apollo tetradrachms in the hoard. Yet its wear may be excessive for an issue Antigonus Doson that can be no more than nine years older than the Poseidon tetradrachms. We offer the *caveat* that wear comparison can be misleading when based upon a single coin, especially when there is reason to believe that the coin in question is a special emission that might not have circulated according to the patterns of normal currency.

The absence of the common Pan tetradrachms may be quite significant. It represents another challenge to Panagopoulou's arrangement of the Antigonid coinage. It is also a clue to the attribution of the Zeus/Apollo tetradrachm. It would be highly unusual if the only issue of Gonatas in our hoard should be a unique variety never seen before. This consideration favors a provisional attribution of the coin to Antigonus Doson. Another possibility, once suggested by Ute Wartenberg-Kagan, is that the Zeus drachms might represent a posthumous coinage issued by Demetrius II, in which case the Zeus/Apollo tetradrachm itself could also be an issue of Demetrius II.

As our hoard does not support Panagopoulou's reattributions, we retain the traditional assignment of the Poseidon tetradrachms to Antigonus Doson. The

---

4. Panagopoulou's summary of her die study indicates that she recorded 33 of these drachms, a number that suggests a sizable if not sustained issue (Panagopoulou 2001: 332).

four examples in our hoard include two of the common variety with the mono-gram ✪. Three specimens of this issue occurred in the Seleucus III hoard, a trea-sure from the Upper Euphrates region whose closing coins were a large number of tetradrachms of Seleucus III belonging to his first issue at Antioch. These date the deposit of the Seleucus III hoard very securely to the first year of his reign, 225/4.[5] In consequence, Doson's most common tetradrachm issue can be dated to his early years and can be associated quite plausibly with his Carian campaign of 227–225. The two other tetradrachms of Doson in the Antiochus III hoard feature a second control alongside the common monogram. These varieties are rare and their absence from the Seleucus III hoard may (but does not necessarily) indicate that they belong to a later phase of Doson's coinage.

## THE LYSIMACHI

Four of the Lysimachi are lifetime issues of Macedonia and Lampsacus (nos. 16–18, 26). The tetradrachm of Cyzicus (no. 25) was represented in the Meydancikkale hoard and therefore must be dated before c. 240/35. The Lysimachi of Byzantium, Calchedon, and Cius will be the subject of a forthcoming book by Constantin Ma-rinescu. In the meantime we may note that no. 19 of Byzantium was represented in a recent Black Sea hoard with a closure c. 240; no. 20 of Byzantium and no. 23 of Cius were represented in the Meydancikkale hoard (c. 240/235); and no. 24 of Cius was represented in the Seleucus III hoard (225/4).

## THE SELEUCIDS

No. 72 of our hoard revealed a new portrait type of Uncertain Mint 68, apparently a local version of Type C, dated 205/4–197 in *Seleucid Coins* (Houghton, Lorber, and Hoover 2008, vol. 1: 692–693, note under Ad224). Features of the portrait that identify it as a probable Type C image include the curly hair, the hornlike lock of hair above the ear, the fillet border, and—to a lesser extent—the aquiline nose. The fabric, with moderately high relief on the obverse and low relief on the reverse, falls between the fabric of the tetradrachms retained at Nisibis and those reassigned to Uncertain Mint 68. In light of the preceding discussion of the chro-nology of the portrait types at this mint, the date of no. 72 should probably be narrowed, to 205/4 and shortly afterward, in order to allow for introduction of the elderly portrait type around 200. In commentary on this coin in the Addenda to *Seleucid Coins,* Part 2, we suggested that it might bridge the gap between Newell's Nisibis Series I–II, retained at Nisibis in *Seleucid Coins,* and his Series III, reattrib-uted to Uncertain Mint 68 (Houghton, Lorber, and Hoover 2008, vol. 1: 692). We

---

5. The reign of Seleucus III is dated 226–223 is most standard works of reference, but a new interpretation of Babylonian cuneiform documents points to a slight reduction in these dates, see Houghton, Lorber, and Hoover 2008, vol. 1: 657–658.

concluded that Newell was probably right to assign his three series to a single mint, but that the case for Nisibis is weak and a more westerly location in Mesopotamia would be more consistent with the dispersion of his Series III tetradrachms, some two thirds of whose provenances are from Asia Minor.

Here we suggest a different solution to the problem of Uncertain Mint 68: that the portraits of *SC* 1132 resemble Type B portraits because they really *are* Type B portraits, and that no. 72 of our hoard is a bridge between *SC* 1132 with its Type B portraits and *SC* 1133 with its elderly portraits. If this new interpretation is correct, it would imply that Uncertain Mint 68 began its operations in the period 211–205, after the Armenian victory of Antiochus III, and most likely in 211/10, when the king was still in Mesopotamia. Any later date would tend to place Uncertain Mint 68 further east, along the path of Antiochus' eastern anabasis, an alternative almost certainly excluded by the vertical die axes of its tetradrachms and by their western findspots. For *SC* 1132 we have the following provenances: the present hoard from northwest Asia Minor for no. 71; Mektepini (*IGCH* 1410) for *SC* 1132.2; Pamphylia or perhaps Cilicia, 2000 for *SC* 1132.4; Syria (perhaps Aradian Peraea), 1971 (*CH* 2.81) for *SC* 1132.6; and Urfa (*IGCH* 1772) for *SC* 1132.8.[6] The new chronology we propose would eliminate the possibility that Uncertain Mint 68 could be identified with Nisibis, because the latter mint also employed portrait types B and C on tetradrachms with a control sequence distinct from that of Uncertain Mint 68.

## REFERENCES

Ashton, R. H. J., and P. Kinns 2004. Opuscula Anatolica III: iii. Redating the earliest Alexander tetradrachms of Rhodes. *Numismatic Chronicle* 164: 71–107.

Davesne, A., and Le Rider, G. 1989. *Le Trésor de Meydancıkkale (Cilicie Trachée 1980)*. Gülnar II. Paris: Éditions Recherche sur les Civilisations.

Houghton, A., and C. Lorber 2002. *Seleucid Coins: A Comprehensive Catalogue.* Part I: *Seleucus I through Antiochus III.* New York/Lancaster: American Numismatic Society/Classical Numismatic Group.

Houghton, A., C. Lorber, and O. Hoover 2008. *Seleucid Coins: A Comprehensive Catalogue.* Part II: *Seleucus IV through Antiochus XIII.* New York/Lancaster: American Numismatic Society/Classical Numismatic Group.

6. For the first published description of the Pamphylia or perhaps Cilicia hoard of 2000, see Houghton and Lorber 2002, vol. 2: 94–95. This hoard will be published in full in *Coin Hoards 10* (forthcoming). For the Mektepini hoard, see Olcay and Seyrig 1965 and Houghton and Lorber 2002, vol. 2: 89–91; for Syria, 1971, see Le Rider 1998 and Houghton and Lorber 2002, vol. 2: 102–103; for Urfa, see Price 1969 and Houghton and Lorber 2002, vol. 2: 111–112.

Jameson, R. 1913. *Collection R. Jameson: Monnaies grecques antiques.* Vol. 1. Paris: Feuardent.

Kremydi-Sicilianou, S. 2000. *SNG Greece II. The Alpha Bank Collection Macedonia I: Alexander I–Perseus.* Athens: Alpha Bank.

Le Rider, G. 1988. L'atelier séleucide de Lysimachie. *Numismatica e Antichità Classiche* 17: 195–207.

———. 1998. Un trésor hellénistique de monnaies d'argent trouvé en Syrie en 1971 (*Coin Hoards* II, 81). *Syria* 75: 89–96.

Mathisen, R. M. 1981. Antigonus Gonatas and the silver coinages of Macedonia circa 280–270 B.C. *American Numismatic Society Museum Notes* 26 79–124.

Meadows, A. R., and C. Lorber. Forthcoming. The Achaeus hoard. In *Coin Hoards 10,* O. Hoover, ed. New York: American Numismatic Society.

Merker, I. L. 1960, The silver coinage of Antigonus Gonatas and Antigonus Doson. *American Numismatic Society Museum Notes* 9: 39–52.

Muller, L. 1858. *Die Münzen der Thracischen Königs Lysimachus.* Copenhagen: B. Luno.

Newell, E.T. 1941. *The Coinage of the Western Seleucid Mints.* Numismatic Studies 4. New York: American Numismatic Society.

Olcay, N., and H. Seyrig. 1965. *Le Trésor de Mektepini,* Trésors monétaires séleucides I. Paris: Librairie Orientaliste Paul Geuthner.

Panagopoulou, K. 2001. The Antigonids: patterns of a royal economy. In *Hellenistic Economies,* Z. H. Archibald, J. Davies, V. Gabrielson, and G. J. Oliver, eds. London/New York: Routledge.

Price, M. J. 1969. Greek coin hoards in the British Museum. *Numismatic Chronicle* 129: 10–14.

———. 1991. *The Coinage in the Name of Alexander the Great and Philip Arrhidaeus.* Zurich/London: Swiss Numismatic Society/British Museum.

SNG GB 5, Part 3. 1976. *Sylloge Nummorum Graecorum: Ashmolean Museum, Oxford. Part 3. Macedonia.* Oxford: Oxford University Press for the British Academy.

Thompson, M. 1968. *The mints of Lysimachus. In Essays in Greek Coinage Presented to Stanley Robinson,* C.M. Kraay and G.K. Jenkins, eds, pp. 163–82. Oxford: Clarendon.

Westermark, U. 1960. *Das Bildnis des Philetairos von Pergamon: Corpus der Münzprägung.* Stockholm/Göteborg/Uppsala: Almqvist & Wiksell.

# APPENDIX
# ANTIOCHUS III HOARD CATALOGUE

## Alexanders

*Pella*

*1. 16.68 g. Head of young Heracles r. in lion skin headdress / ΑΛΕΞΑΝΔΡΟΥ, Zeus enthroned l., holding eagle and sceptre, CRESTED HELMET in l. field, [monogram] under throne, [monogram] in ex. Price 1991: no. 624.

*2. As last, but CRESTED HELMET in l. field, [monogram] under throne, [monogram] in ex. with faint H to lower r. Price 1991: no. 629.

*Macedonia?*

3. FACING HELMET(?) in l. field, other details (if any) illegible.

*Cyme*

*4. 16.54 g. As last, but ONE-HANDLED CUP above [monogram] in l. field. Cf. Price 1991: no. 1628.

*Magnesia on the Meander*

*5. 16.51 g. As last, but HORSE HEAD L. above [monogram] in l. field, [monogram] in inner r. field behind sceptre, MEANDER in ex. Cf. Price 1991: no. 2049.

*Miletus*

6. As last, but STAR above LION L. above [monogram] in l. field, [monogram] under throne. Price 1991: no. 2175.

*7. 16.50 g. As last, but STAR above LION L. above [monogram] in l. field, [monogram] under throne, outer r. control (if any) off flan. Price 1991: —.

*8. 15.41 g. As last, but STAR above LION L. above [monogram] in l. field; in inner r. field unclear monogram ([monogram]?) above [monogram]. Price 1991: —.

*Mylasa or Kaunus*

*9. As last, but DOUBLE-BLADED AXE in l. field. Price 1991: no. 2074 (Miletus or Mylasa).

*Rhodes*

*10. As last, but ΗΦΑΙΣΤΙΩΝ above ROSE in l. field, PO under throne. Price 1991: no. 2522.

## Antigonus Gonatas or Antigonus Doson

*11. 16.78 g. Laureate head of Zeus r. / ΒΑΣΙΛΕΩΣ ΑΝΤΙΓΟΝΟΥ on prow of galley on which Apollo seated l., examining bow, TI below. Gemini II, 10 January 2006, lot 65 (this coin).

## Antigonus Doson

*12. Head of Poseidon r., wreathed with sea grass / ΒΑΣΙΛΕΩΣ ΑΝΤΙΓΟΝΟΥ on prow of galley on which Apollo seated l., examining bow, ⊠ below. SNG GB 5, Part 3: no. 3264.

13. As last.

*14. 17.12 g. As last, but ⊠ M below. Merker 1960: 49. Jameson 1913: no. 1008 (same dies). Olcay and Seyrig 1965: no. 699 (same obverse die). Gemini II, 10 January 2006, lot 66 (this coin).

*15. 17.05 g. As last, but ⊠  ⋈ below. Merker 1960: 49. Hess 153, 8 March 1983, lot 149 (same dies). Gemini II, 10 January 2006, lot 67 (this coin).

## Lysimachus

*Pella*

*16. Diademed head of the deified Alexander r., with horn of Ammon / ΒΑΣΙΛΕΩΣ ΛΥΣΙΜΑΧΟΥ, Athena enthroned l., holding Nike and resting elbow on round shield propped against throne, ⊢ in inner l. field. Thompson 1968: no. 247.

*Amphipolis*

*17. As last, but RACE TORCH in inner l. field, BEE in outer r. field. Thompson 1968: no. 187.

*18. As last, but ⋈ in inner l. field, ⋈ in outer r. field. Thompson 1968: no. 201.

*Byzantium*

*19. As last, but ⋈ in inner l. field, double spiral on throne.

*20. As last, but ⋈ in inner l. field, double spiral on throne. Davesne and Le Rider 1989: no. 2699 (same obverse die).

21. As last, but Ε in inner l. field, double spiral on throne.

*Calchedon*

*22. As last, but ⋈ in inner l. field, double spiral on throne, GRAIN STALK l. in ex.

*Cius*

*23. As last, but CLUB in outer l. field, 𝕄 in inner l. field, BOW IN GORYTUS and Ⅎ in ex. Davesne and Le Rider 1989: no. 2668.

*24. As last, but CLUB in outer l. field, 𝕙 in inner l. field, BOW IN GORYTUS and Ⅎ in ex. Müller 1858: no. 415.

*Cyzicus*

*25. As last, but 𝕏 in inner l. field, CRESCENT in inner r. field. Davesne and Le Rider 1989: no. 2713 (same dies).

*Lampsacus*

*26. As last, but HERM(?) in outer l. field, ≙ in inner l. field. Thompson 1968: no. 50.

*Unattributed*

*27. As last, but uncertain, squarish control (𝔸?) in inner l. field.

*28. As last, but MEANDER in ex., and no other visible controls.

29. As last, but corroded.

## Attalids

*30. Head of Philetaerus r., wearing taenia / ΦΙΛΕΤΑΙΡΟΥ, Athena enthroned l., resting hand on large round shield before her, IVY LEAF in inner l. field, BOW in outer r. field, ⋏ on throne. Westermark 1960 Group II.

*31. As last.

32. As last, but head of Philetaerus possibly laureate. Westermark 1960 Group II or III.

33. As last, but head of Philetaerus laureate. Westermark 1960 Group III.

*34. Laureate head of Philetaerus r./ ΦΙΛΕΤΑΙΡΟΥ, Athena enthroned l., crowning royal name, IVY LEAF inner l., other details unrecognizable. Westermark 1960 Group IV A.

35. As last, but IVY LEAF outer l., ⋏ inner l., BOW outer r. Westermark 1960 Group IV A.

36. As last, but GRAPES outer l., ⋏ inner l., BOW outer r. Westermark 1960 Group IV B or V.

37. As last, but BEE outer l., 𝕐 inner l., BOW outer r. Westermark 1960 Group VI A.

## Perge

*38. Laureate head of Artemis r., quiver over shoulder/ ΑΡΤΕΜΙΔΟΣ ΠΕΡΓΑΙΑΣ, Artemis standing l., crowning her epithet, stag l. at her feet, looking back at the goddess. Die break above head of stag obscuring possible control.

## Antiochus I

*Seleucia on the Tigris*

*39. 16.55 g. Diademed head of Antiochus I r. / ΒΑΣΙΛΕΩΣ ΑΝΤΙΟΧΟΥ, Apollo seated l. on omphalos, examining arrow and resting hand on grounded bow, Ⓐ in outer l. field, ᴴᴾ in outer r. field. Houghton and Lorber 2002: no. 379.3a.

*40. 15.73 g. As last.

41. As last, but Ⓐ in outer l. field, Ⓜ in outer r. field. Houghton and Lorber 2002: no. 379.3a.

*42. 16.02 g. As last, but Ⓐ in outer l. field, ℞ in outer r. field. Houghton and Lorber 2002: no. 379.3d.

*43. 16.54 g. As last, but Ⓜ in outer l. field, ⊠ in outer r. field. Houghton and Lorber 2002: no. 379.5a.

*Ecbatana*

*44. 16.32 g. As last, but Apollo holds three arrows, in inner l. field ⚼ above arrows and ΑΚ below his arm, before his legs FOREPART OF HORSE GRAZING L. Houghton and Lorber 2002: no. 409.2f.

## Antiochus II

*Lysimachia*

*45. Diademed head of Antiochus I r. / ΒΑΣΙΛΕΩΣ ΑΝΤΙΟΧΟΥ, Apollo seated l. on omphalos, examining arrow and resting hand on grounded bow, LION HEAD L. in inner l. field, Ⓜ in outer r. field. Houghton and Lorber 2002: no. 481.

*Seleucia on the Tigris*

*46. 16.76 g. As last, but Ⓜ in outer l. field, Ⓐ in outer r. field. Houghton and Lorber 2002: no. 587.1c.

*47. 16.33 g. As last.

*48. 15.94 g. As last.

*49. 16.86 g. As last, but Ⓜ in outer l. field, Ⓐ in outer r. field. Houghton and Lorber 2002: no. 587.4b.

50. As last, but controls illegible. *SC* 587.

*Susa*

*51. 16.12 g. Head of young Heracles r. in lion skin headdress / ΣΕΛΕΥΚΟΥ ΒΑΣΙΛΕΩΣ, Zeus enthroned l., holding eagle and sceptre, ℞ in l. field, ⚹ under throne. Houghton and Lorber 2002: no. 603.3c.

*Unattributed issue, perhaps of Asia Minor*

\*52. 16.65 g. Diademed head of Antiochus II r. / ΒΑΣΙΛΕΩΣ ΑΝΤΙΟΧΟΥ, Apollo seated l. on omphalos, examining arrow and resting hand on grounded bow. Houghton and Lorber 2002: no. 639.

## "Soter" Coinage

\*53. 16.02 g. Diademed head of Antiochus I r. / ΣΩΤΗΡΟΣ ΑΝΤΙΟΧΟΥ, Apollo seated l. on omphalos, examining arrow and resting hand on grounded bow. Houghton and Lorber 2002: no. 641.

## Antiochus Hierax

*Abydus, or barbarous imitation*

\*54. 16.41 g. Diademed head r., of barbarous style / ΒΑΣΙΛΕΩΣ ΑΝΤΙΟΧΟΥ, Apollo seated l. on omphalos, examining arrow and resting hand on grounded bow, CADUCEUS in inner l. field above arrow, ⋈ in inner l. field below arrow, EAGLE L. in exergue. Houghton and Lorber 2002: no. 845.

*Ilium*

\*55. 16.60 g. Diademed head of young king r. / ΒΑΣΙΛΕΩΣ ΑΝΤΙΟΧΟΥ, Apollo seated l. on omphalos, examining arrow and resting hand on grounded bow, OWL in ex. Houghton and Lorber 2002: no. 868.

## Seleucus III

*Antioch on the Orontes*

\*56. 16.77 g. Diademed head of Seleucus III r. / ΒΑΣΙΛΕΩΣ ΣΕΛΕΥΚΟΥ, Apollo seated l. on omphalos, examining arrow and resting hand on grounded bow, ⋢ in outer l. field, Ⴅ in outer r. field. Houghton and Lorber 2002: no. 921.1.
\*57. 16.46 g. As last.
\*58. 16.35 g. As last.

*Seleucia on the Tigris*

\*59. 16.20 g. As last, but with ⋈ in outer l. field, ⋈ᴾ in outer r. field. Houghton and Lorber 2002: no.939.2.

## Antiochus III

### *Lysimachia*

*60. Diademed head of Antiochus III r. (Type D) / ΒΑΣΙΛΕΩΣ ΑΝΤΙΟΧΟΥ, Apollo seated l. on omphalos, examining arrow and resting hand on grounded bow, THYRSUS in inner l. field above arrow, ⋈ in inner r. field, Œ Ν in ex. Houghton and Lorber 2002: no. 960.

### *Antioch on the Orontes*

61. As last, but Type Ai portrait, ⊥ in outer l. field. Houghton and Lorber 2002: no. 1041.1.

*62. 16.25 g. As last, but Type B portrait, Ⴤ above ⋔ in outer l. field, outer r. field off flan. Houghton and Lorber 2002: no.1043.6 or 7.

*63. 16.40 g. As last, but Type C portrait, Ⴤ in outer l. field. Houghton and Lorber 2002: no. 1044.1.

*64. As last, with Type C portrait, but TRIPOD in outer l. field. Houghton and Lorber 2002: no. 1044.2.

### *Uncertain Mint 67 in northern Mesopotamia, perhaps Carrhae*

*65. 17.00 g. As last, but Type B portrait, in outer l. field ⚡ placed sideways, reading downward. Houghton and Lorber 2002: no.1118.

### *"Rose" Mint, perhaps Edessa*

*66. 16.73 g. As last, but Type Aii portrait, ROSE in outer l. field, ⊕ in outer r. field. Houghton and Lorber 2002: no. 1121.2a.

*67. 16.89 g. As last, with Type Aii portrait, ROSE in outer l. field, but Ⲁ in outer r. field. Houghton and Lorber 2002: no. 1121.2c.

*68. 16.27 g. As last, with Type Aii portrait, Ⴤ in outer l. field, Ⲁ in outer r. field. Houghton and Lorber 2002: no. 1121.3a.

*69. 15.93 g. As last, but Type B portrait, ROSE in outer l. field, ⋏ in outer r. field. Houghton and Lorber 2002: no. 1122.1c.

### *Nisibis*

*70. 16.39 g. As last, but Type Ai portrait, Ⴤ in outer l. field, ΔΡ in outer r. field, ex. off flan. Houghton and Lorber 2002: no. 1128.3.

*Uncertain Mint 68, in northern Mesopotamia, perhaps Nisibis*

*71. 16.70 g. As last, with Type B? portrait, ⟨A⟩ in outer l. field. Houghton and Lorber 2002: no. 1132.1 (where the portrait is described as Type D).

*72. 16.26 g. As last, with Type C portrait, ΑΣ in outer l. field, ΣΩ in outer r. field. Houghton, Lorber, and Hoover 2008: no. II Addenda Ad224.

*Seleucia on the Tigris*

*73. 16.95 g. As last, with Type B portrait, ⟨⟩ in outer l. field, ⟨M⟩ in outer r. field, and ⟨⟩ in ex. Houghton and Lorber 2002: no. 1162.

*74. 16.32 g. As last, with Type B portrait, ⟨⟩ in outer l. field, ⟨M⟩ in outer r. field. Houghton and Lorber 2002: no. 1164.

*Susa*

*75. 16.75 g. As last, with Type Ai portrait, ⟨K⟩ above ⟨⟩ in outer l. field. Houghton and Lorber 2002: no. 1209.3.

*76. 16.98 g. As last, with Type Aii portrait, ⟨⟩ in outer l. field, ⟨K⟩ in outer r. field. Houghton, Lorber, and Hoover 2008: no. II Addenda Ad226.

*77. 16.92 g. As last, with Type B portrait, ⟨⟩ in outer l. field, ⟨K⟩ in outer r. field. Houghton and Lorber 2002: no. 1211.

*AJN* Second Series 21 (2009) pp. 105–121
© 2009 The American Numismatic Society

# The Metrology of Judaean Small Bronze Coins

DAVID HENDIN*

Based on the the weights of more than 10,000 bronze coins dating from 134 BC to AD 70, this study offers a comprehensive analysis of the weight standards for each series, and of the role of fudiciary coinage in ancient Judaea.

## INTRODUCTION

The denominations and weight standards of ancient Jewish bronze coins have previously been discussed. However, the samples used for study were often limited only to examples in the British Museum collection[1] or to samples from a specific hoard or site.[2] Further, average weights for Judaean small bronzes have generally been presented without statistical information beyond generic ranges and averages.

This is a metrological study of 10,312 Jewish bronze coins of 27 general types and various denominations. The majority of the coins were weighed by the author,

---

*DHendin@aol.com. The following standard abbreviations are used: *GBC*: Hendin, D. 2001. *Guide to Biblical coins, 4th edition.* New York: Amphora; *RPC* I: Burnett, A., Amandry, M., Ripolles, P. *Roman provincial coinage* I, London 1992; *SC* I: Houghton, A., Lorber, C. 2002. *Seleucid coins, a comprehensive catalog*, Part I, Vols I & II, NY: American Numismatic Society and Classical Numismatic Group; *SC* II: Houghton, A., Lorber, C., and Hoover, O. 2008. *Seleucid coins, a comprehensive catalog*, Part II, Vols. I & II, NY: American Numismatic Society and Classical Numismatic Group; *TJC*: Meshorer, Y. *A treasury of Jewish coins.* 2001. Jerusalem and New York: Yad Ben Zvi Press and Amphora.

1. Kindler (1967), 194.
2. Kindler (1954), 170–185; *TJC*, 72, n.35.

while other weights were obtained from published sources. The coins range in date from those of John Hyrcanus I (134–104 BC) to those struck during the Jewish War (AD 66–70). The specific types of coins studied were mainly dictated by supply: some coin types are so rare that it was difficult to collect enough samples for meaningful statistics. Our statistical analysis of the material (see Tables 1–4 below) provides averages and the average standard deviations for these groups, in order to provide a basis for future study and to make some observations.[3]

The actual names of the ancient Jewish bronze coin denominations are not known. For some 60 years it has been standard practice to refer to the most common denomination with the Hebrew word *prutah*,[4] (pl. *prutot*) but this word is known to us only from later rabbinic literature.[5] The contemporary writer Josephus, for example, does not mention bronze coins or any terminology associated with them. However, since the *Mishnah* was codified early in the third century AD, and was based upon discussions among the rabbinical sages during the mid-first and second centuries AD, we can assume that the use of the word *prutah* was current during the time the small Jewish bronze coins were minted, c. 134 BC–AD 70. The first *prutot* were the Jerusalem bronze lily/anchor coins issued under Antiochus VII/Hyrcanus I (Figure 1), which were equivalent to a Seleucid *chalkous*, and which aligned with the weight standard introduced by Alexander Balas (150–145 BC).[6] During the first century AD, a *prutah* was the price of one pomegranate.[7]

Also, the Greek word *lepton* (pl. *lepta*) is used in the New Testament to de-

---

3. 10,312 Judaean bronze coins were recorded for this study. From October 2008 to January 2009, more than 7,000 coins were weighed by the author from coins in his possession as well as from the Israel Museum in Jerusalem (courtesy of Haim Gitler), the Sofaer Collection at the American Numismatic Society, and the following dealers in Jerusalem: J. Zadok, Maxim Schick, J. Wazwaz, J. Abou Eid and Son, and S. Taha. Additional information regarding coin weights has been supplied by Yigael Ronen, Isadore Goldstein, Harlan J. Berk, and Cecelia Meir for coins in the Eretz Israel Museum in Tel Aviv. We also recorded data from the Gamla and Masada excavation reports, Agora Auctions I and II, Hill (1914), Baramki (1974), Meshorer (1981), Kaufman (1995, 2004), Houghton and Spaer (1998), Oliver (2007), V-Coins.com, and the Menorah Coin Project.org.

During data gathering care was taken to avoid duplication. Further, data collection was limited to a relatively short period, so coins disbursed would not enter the market and be repeated in the sample. We also eliminated coins that were broken, heavily worn, heavily encrusted, or not clear as to type.

4. According to Y. Meshorer (per. com.), Israeli numismatists have used the word *perutah* (by Israelis who emigrated from Europe) or *prutah* (by native Israelis) since at least the late 1950s. Klimowsky (1963, 68–69) was the first to explain the term in this context.

5. E.g., Mishnah *Kiddushin*, 1:1.

6. *SC* II, vol II, 41.

7. Sperber (1974), 104.

Figure A. *Prutot* (*GBC* 653)

scribe the smallest bronze coin in circulation during the time the gospels were composed (c. 1st c. AD), which was equal to half a Roman *quadrans*.[8] Kindler suggests that during the Hasmonean period Jewish bronze coinage consisted mainly of "the *dilepton*...commonly named *Perutah* (*sic*)."[9] Hence a *lepton* was equal to a half-*prutah*, and the *prutah* equaled two *lepta*, as mentioned in the Gospel of Mark (12:42).

For our purposes, the terms *prutah* and *lepton* are used for the sake of consistency and comparison. The *prutah* (and its half) and the *lepton* should not, then, be considered weights as such, but rather coin denominations, individual examples of which had greatly varying weights.

## GENERAL OBSERVATIONS ON JUDAEAN BRONZE COINAGE

The data discussed in more detail below (Tables 1–4) clearly show that Judaean bronze coins were manufactured *al marco* and not *al pezzo*. As Meshorer (1982, 59) observed: "[a]lthough it is likely that the mint masters knew the amount of coins to be produced from a specific amount of bronze, the exact quantity of the metal included in each coin would have been exceptionally difficult to control. It would not have been expedient to remove bronze from coins that were too heavy or to add bronze to the lighter issues." He also remarked (2001, 30) that the range of weights of the Jewish bronzes was so great that "[i]t is difficult to assume that these light coins were given the same value in the market as the heavier *prutot*."[10]

Our results, however, allow us to suggest that in Judaea, when coins were

8. In context (Gospel of Mark 12:42) *lepton* seems to be a coin rather than a denomination, which usage modern students have applied to the term. Although the word is used in the New Testament, it is never mentioned in the Talmud. The term *lepton* is further discussed in *RPC* I: 31.

9. Kindler (1967), 186.

10. Meshorer was specifically discussing the Jannaeus anchor/star-in-diadem coin (Figure 4; *TJC* K, *GBC* 469). From our data, however, it is clear that the same range existed for every issue that we have studied.

struck in the same metal, with the same or very similar designs, lacking indications on the coins to the contrary, they were intended to represent coins of the
same denomination. Even with small bronzes, differences of 1 or 2 or even 3 grams
would not have been of great concern between coins that shared types, since the
relative weights of the coins were of little consequence in circulation. For example,
Figure A shows three coins of the same types dated to the year 5 of Nero (*GBC* 653),
weighing (from left) 1.49, 2.43, and 3.67 g.—the lightest of which weighs only 40%
of the heaviest. It is almost impossible for a person using quick weighing by hand
to determine a difference between the weights of these three coins. This group is
only one of many examples of similar and even more drastic weight ranges within
a single type. Despite the great variance in weight, these coins were undoubtedly
the same denomination since type, not weight, was the determinant.[11] Indeed,
similar extreme variances in weight were noted in every group of similar types we
studied, wherein the heaviest coins weighed 2x to 4x those of the lightest.

Although we did not measure diameters, the range generally from nar-
rowest to widest for any given denomination is within approximately 2–4 mm.
While there is no doubt that in multiple-*prutah* and even half-*prutah* denominations the diameter relative to the *prutah* was, in addition to type, an indication
of denomination,[12] the diameter of the *prutot* themselves were subject to change
over time as the coins became smaller and lighter. We also noted the diameter of
a particular coin is not necessarily a reflection of its weight. From handling thousands of coins, it was observed that the largest variable regarding the weight of a
coin is most frequently the *thickness*, not the diameter, which was determined by
the molds in which the planchets were cast.[13]

While the data gathered indicate that even though the weights of any coin type
could vary dramatically, nevertheless the statistical analysis of the weights show
trends in both denomination and standards among coins issued under specific
political authorities.

11. Meshorer (*TJC*, 71) states that "[t]he decisive factors in determining the denominations in a series of coins are their relative weights and designs that appear on them." Here he
refers specifically to the four coins in the Herodian dated series. While the weights of these
denominations certainly overlap, one may be absolutely certain which coin is being dealt
with because the motifs are quite different.

12. Le Rider and de Callataÿ (2006) provide useful comparanda for these problems of
correlating the weights, diameters, and types with probable denominations in their survey
of both Seleucid bronzes (pp. 31–36) and Ptolemaic bronzes (pp. 38–42). Cf. *SC* II, vol. II,
Append. 2B.

13. Planchet strips were cast in chalk-stone molds (*TJC*, 50–51). The space for each
planchet was drilled, but the controls for measuring exact depth of the drilling were not accurate and some coins are more than double the thickness of others, with resultant increase
in weight.

## Hasmonean Coins

The first Hasmonean coins from the Jerusalem mint (Table 1) may be the lily/anchor issue with the name of Antiochus VII, struck in conjunction with Hyrcanus I (Figure 1). Our average weight for this series, 2.47 ± 0.03 g, is similar to coins classified by Houghton and Lorber as "denomination D," the probable equivalent to the *chalkous* denomination of Alexander Balas and the early Roman period.[14]

| Name | Sample Size | Avg. Wt. g | Range in g | Avg. Std. Deviation Calc. |
|---|---|---|---|---|
| Antiochus VII GBC 451; TJC (Fig. 1) | (162) | 2.47 ± 0.03 | (1.62–3.41) | .33547 / 12.72792 = 0.0264 |
| Yehohanan GBC 453–455, 459, 460; TJC A, B, D, E, F, G, I (Figs. 2, 2a–b) | (599) | 1.92 ± 0.01 | (1.12–3.06) | .33631 / 24.47448 = 0.0137 |
| Jannaeus GBC 467, 478; TJC N, T (Figs. 3, 3a) | (344) | 2.15 ± 0.02 | (1.04–3.50) | .44343 / 18.547237 = .0239 |
| Jannaeus GBC 469; TJC K (Fig. 4) | (523) | 1.71 ± 0.03 | (0.64–3.85) | .59961 / 22.86919 = .0262 |
| Jannaeus GBC 471; TJC L1, L2 (Fig. 5) | (200) | 1.20 ± 0.02 | (0.61–1.79) | .23919 / 14.142136 = .0169 |
| Jannaeus GBC 472; TJC L3–L17 (Fig. 6) | (1251) | 0.81 ± 0.01 | (0.20–1.70) | .24731 / 35.369478 = .0070 |
| Yehonatan GBC 473–475; TJC P, Q, R (Figs. 7, 7a–b) | (520) | 1.81 ± 0.02 | (0.96–3.57) | .37566 / 22.80351 = .0165 |
| Jannaeus GBC 476; TJC M (Fig. 8) | (196) | 4.10 ± 0.07 | (2.36–7.96) | .94631 / 14 = .0676 |
| Yntn GBC 479; TJC S (Fig. 9) | (432) | 2.00 ± 0.02 | (0.85–3.27) | .36689 / 20.784610 = .0177 |
| M. Antigonus GBC 481; TJC 36 (Fig. 10) | (171) | 14 ± 0.09 | (11.67–17.64) | 1.19389 / 13.076697 = .0913 |
| M. Antigonus GBC 482; TJC 37 (Fig. 11) | (106) | 7.19 ± 0.07 | (4.47–8.79) | .74409 / 10.29563 = .0723 |
| M. Antigonus GBC 483; TJC 40 (Fig. 12) | (144) | 1.68 ± 0.02 | (1.18–2.34) | .18976 / 12 = .0158 |

Table 1.Hasmonean Coins

14. *SC* I, vol II: 4.

Figures for Table 1

Figure 1. *GBC* 451

Figure 2. *GBC* 454

Figure 2a. *GBC* 455

Figure 2b. *GBC* 457

Figure 3. *GBC* 467

Figure 3a. *GBC* 478

Figure 4. *GBC* 469

Figure 5. *GBC* 471

Figure 6. *GBC* 472

Figure 7. *GBC* 473

Figure 7a. *GBC* 474

Figure 7b. *GBC* 475

Figure 8. *GBC* 476

Figure 9. *GBC* 479

Figure 10. *GBC* 481

Figure 11. *GBC* 482

Figure 12. *GBC* 483

Figures for Table 2

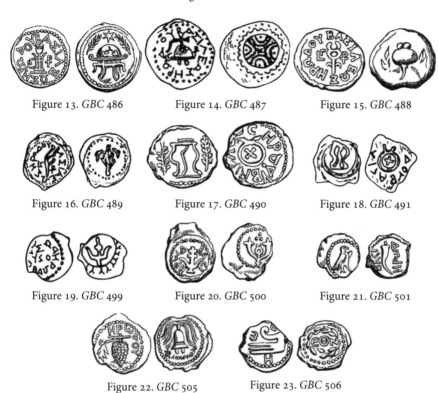

Figure 13. *GBC* 486

Figure 14. *GBC* 487

Figure 15. *GBC* 488

Figure 16. *GBC* 489

Figure 17. *GBC* 490

Figure 18. *GBC* 491

Figure 19. *GBC* 499

Figure 20. *GBC* 500

Figure 21. *GBC* 501

Figure 22. *GBC* 505

Figure 23. *GBC* 506

Figures for Table 3

Figure 24. *GBC* 635

Figure 24a. *GBC* 636

Figure 24b. *GBC* 637

Figure 24c. *GBC* 638

Figure 24d. *GBC* 639

Figure 24e. *GBC* 640

Figure 24f. *GBC* 641　　　Figure 24g. *GBC* 642　　　Figure 24h. *GBC* 643

Figure 24i. *GBC* 644　　　Figure 24j. *GBC* 645　　　Figure 24k. *GBC* 646

Figure 24l. *GBC* 647　　　Figure 24m. *GBC* 648　　　Figure 24n. *GBC* 649

Figure 24o. *GBC* 649a　　　Figure 24p. *GBC* 650　　　Figure 25. *GBC* 553

Figure 26a. *GBC* 651　　　　Figure 26. *GBC* 652

Figures for Table 4

Figure 27. *GBC* 661　　　　Figure 27a. *GBC* 664

The average weight drops 20 per cent to 1.92 ± 0.01 g for the coins with the title "High Priest" and name Yehohanan (Hyrcanus I) in paleo-Hebrew script (Figure 2). There is a drift down to 1.81 +/- 0.02 g for the similar coins struck by Jannaeus (Figure 7). But when Jannaeus' mint issued the first coins that mentioned his Hebrew name Yehonatan and the title "King" in both Greek and Hebrew (Figure 3, 3a), the average weight goes up 16 per cent to 2.15 ± 0.02 g. From that first royal coin onward, the weight of the *prutah* under Jannaeus falls to a low of 1.20 ± 0.02 g for the coins of Jannaeus dated year 25 in both Greek and Aramaic (Figure 5).

The succeeding series (Figure 6) are those referred to by Hill (1914: xcv) as "wretched" imitations of the Jannaeus coins. They may have been issued under Jannaeus, but due to the sheer volume produced, it seems possible that they were issued through the reigns of his widow Salome Alexandra (76–67 BC), and their sons Aristobulus II (67–63 BC) and Hyrcanus II (67 and 63–40 BC).[15]

The average weight of these poor anchor/star coins (Figure 6) is 0.81 ± 0.01 g, but it fluctuates dramatically from coins as light as 0.20 g to coins weighing 1.70 g (8.5x). These coins may well be degraded *prutot* and *not* half-*prutah* coins.[16] Hyrcanus I (*GBC* 458, 461) and Jannaeus (*GBC* 468) issued coins with different designs or inscriptions that were intended to be smaller denominations, probably half-*prutot*. Both types are so scarce we could not include them in this study.

The controversial coins with the *Yntn* inscription in paleo-Hebrew script weigh 2.00 ± 0.02 g (Figure 9). Hendin and Shachar have established that the overstruck series with the name *Yntn* are coins of Jannaeus and not, as previously believed coins of his widow Queen Salome Alexandra as regent for their sons Hyrcanus II and Aristobulus II.[17] In a recent metallurgical study focusing on cluster analysis of

15. If indeed no coins were issued in Judaea between the death of Jannaeus and the rule of Mattathias Antigonus (40–37 BC), there would have been a gap of 36 years without coins being struck by Jewish rulers, which seems like a very long period.

16. The Talmud recognizes some coins, possible these, as devalued *prutot* since it assigns the *prutah* a very small value indeed. The Talmud indicates that through the first century AD there were 768 *prutot* to the silver shekel (Baba Bathra 166b; 192, *prutot* equal one zuz or quarter-shekel). The smallest possible version of the *prutah* is apparently used in this calculation to insure that in any financial transactions that involved the Temple, which surely accounted for a large number of transactions in Judaea at the time, the value of the *prutah* was at the lowest rate possible vis-à-vis an actual silver equivalent in order not to deprive the Temple of its proper due. This reflects the early rabbinic principal of "Yafeh Koach Hekdesh," stating that the Temple must be the greater beneficiary of any transaction. The Talmud, of course, reflects discussions of Jewish life around the first and second centuries AD, yet the devalued *prutot* were issued between c. 76 and 40 BC. Bijovsky (2002, 202) notes, however, that these poor, small coins were actually used in the area for hundreds of years, up to at least the fifth century AD.

17. Hendin and Shachar (2009), 87–94. This conclusion is based upon the discovery of one of the overstruck *Yntn* coins (*GBC* 478) that has been again overstruck by an estab-

alloys, Krupp suggested that these *Yntn* coins may be from a different period than that of Jannaeus.[18] However, more certain chronological proof is provided by the overstruck coins than by the ambiguities inherent in Krupp's analysis.

Meshorer noted that in the modern period the value of lead has been about half that of copper. Assuming an analogous price differential in antiquity, and noting the lead coins of Jannaeus (Figure 8) appeared to be about double the weight of the comparable bronze coins (Figure 3), he suggested that "one can reasonably assume that the lead coins were *prutot*."[19] Our study confirms the weight difference: the weight of the lead anchor/Aramaic coins (4.10 ± 0.07 g) is around twice the weight of the heaviest bronze coins of Jannaeus, the anchor/lily coins and overstrikes of them (Figure 3a ; 2.15 ± 0.02 g). Even though there was a minor difference in types, one side of these lead coins (*GBC* 476) was directly patterned on the Jannaeus anchor/lily (*GBC* 467) type. The significant difference in the weight, but likely not the denomination of the coins, suggests that the commodity price of non-precious metals may have played a role in the creation of fiduciary coinage in certain circumstances.

Mattathias Antigonus' three denominations (Figs. 10–12) struck on double-thick planchets, can be broken clearly into the denominations of eight *prutot* (14.00 ± 0.09 g), four *prutot* (7.19 ± 0.07 g), and one *prutah* (1.68 ± 0.02 g). Meshorer noted that the weight of these particular coins "was not of fundamental significance."[20] This study reaffirms that when average weights are drastically different between coins clearly intended to represent separate denominations, weight fluctuations *within a specific denomination* are clearly not significant.

Mattathias Antigonus' *prutot* are *twice* the weight of the previous small *prutah* coins issued by Jannaeus or one of his successors (*GBC* 472), and may have been intended to fit proportionally with his new, larger denomination coins. Even though this was low value fiduciary coinage, there was some merit, even if mainly political, to coins with more heft; otherwise many more coins could have been manufactured from the same amount of bronze. It further seems likely that the innovative larger coins of Mattathias Antigonus are related to the principal denominations of the SC coinage of Antioch, which was struck on a standard of around 15 g, and these could be considered 8 *chalkoi* coins.[21]

---

lished Jannaeus type (*GBC* 469), thus proving the *Yntn* coin's earlier attribution.

18. Krupp (2007–08), 57–75.

19. *TJC*, 47.

20. *TJC*, 54.

21. *RPC* I: 33–34. Somewhat inexplicably, Meshorer (*TJC*, 54) suggests that these large denominations should be considered to be one *chalkous* denominations, but without further discussion.

| Name | Sample Size | Avg. Wt. g | Range in g | Avg. Std. Deviation Calc. |
|---|---|---|---|---|
| Herod I<br>GBC 486; TJC 44 (Fig. 13) | (354) | 6.93 ± 0.07 | (2.75–11.46) | 1.28202 / 18.81489 = .0681 |
| Herod I<br>GBC 487; TJC 45 (Fig. 14) | (130) | 4.45 ± 0.07 | (2.91–6.52) | .81476 / 11.40175 = .0715 |
| Herod I<br>GBC 488; TJC 46 (Fig. 15) | (76) | 3.12 ± 0.08 | (1.7–5.34) | .70509 / 8.717798 = .0809 |
| Herod I<br>GBC 489; TJC 47 (Fig. 16) | (73) | 2.50 ± 0.05 | (1.55–3.62) | .4035 / 8.54400 = .0472 |
| Herod I<br>GBC 490; TJC 49 (Fig. 17) | (194) | 2.94 ± 0.05 | (1.30–4.6) | .63719 / 13.92839 = .0457 |
| Herod I<br>GBC 491–4; TJC 50–54 (Fig. 18) | (153) | 1.48 ± 0.03 | (0.78–2.6) | .33279 / 12.36932 = .0269 |
| Herod I<br>GBC 499; TJC 61–64 (Fig. 19) | (298) | .94 ± 0.01 | (0.49–1.78) | .18902 / 17.262677 = .0109 |
| Herod I<br>GBC 500; TJC 59 (Fig. 20) | (480) | 1.42 ± 0.01 | (0.81–2.11) | .24499/21.90890 = .0112 |
| Herod I<br>GBC 501; TJC 66 (Fig. 21) | (278) | .86 ± 0.01 | (0.41–1.42) | 0.1924/16.67333 = .0115 |
| Archelaus<br>GBC 505; TJC 73–74 (Fig. 22) | (317) | 2.06 ± 0.02 | (0.70–3.37) | .44349 /17.804493 = .0249 |
| Archelaus<br>GBC 506; TJC 72 (Fig. 23) | (391) | 1.19 ± 0.01 | (0.44–2.1) | .29426 / 19.773719 = .0149 |

Table 2. Coins of Herod I and Herod Archelaus

## HEROD I AND HEROD ARCHELAUS

One surprising observation from this study is that the dated coins struck under Herod I may be based on a different denominational system than those of Mattathias Antigonus.[22] While the M. Antigonus coins are clearly 8/4/1 units, described here as *prutot*, the Herodian series is not only struck on a different weight standard, but

---

22. Meshorer (*TJC*, 59; 71–72) recognized a difference in weights, but dismissed it on the grounds that the difference was not significant. The systems of multiple denominations, however, show again that the weight of bronze coins in aggregate, rather than individually, was relevant.

also divided differently. The largest coin struck by Herod (6.93 ± 0.07 g) (Figure 13) is only half the weight of the Mattathias Antigonus coin (14.00 ± 0.09 g) struck at nearly the same time. While it is accepted that the coins of M. Antigonus are from the Jerusalem mint, Meshorer argues convincingly that the Herodian coins were struck at Samaria.[23] It is possible that the largest Herodian coins were intended as 4 *prutot*, since they are the weight of M. Antigonus' half denomination (*GBC* 482), it seems equally possible that Herod decided to set a new standard for his new reign.[24]

It is not likely that these changes of weight represented any devaluation, such as that discussed by Martin Price regarding bronze coinage in the Classical Greek world. Once people were willing to accept overvalued pieces of small bronze, size and weight simply became general indicators of their value at that particular time and place; size and weight therefore could be subject to change and the same denomination could be represented by coins of differing weights and sizes.[25] Herod may have been attempting to create more coinage with fewer raw materials, and also increase his profits from the creation of coinage.[26]

Meshorer suggested that the denominations of the Herodian series (Figures 13–16) were 8/4/2/1 *prutot*, which in spite of lighter weight still seems likely.[27] The "tripod table" series from the Jerusalem mint consists of a larger coin of 2.94 ± 0.05 g (Figure 17), most likely a double *prutah*, and a *prutah* (Figure 18) averaging 1.48 ± 0.3 g. There is also a series of rare coins in this series that were apparently meant to be half-*prutah* denominations (*GBC* 495–497). Due to the rarity of the smallest coins, they are not included in this analysis. However, they fit well as the smallest in a series of three denominations since there are obvious design differences and weight differences among them.

Herod's most common coin, the anchor/cornucopias with caduceus (Figure 20) weighs 1.42 ± 0.01 g and fits into the *prutah* series. Herod's well known eagle coin (the first Judaean coin portraying the image of a living creature) with a single cornucopia reverse (Figure 21), may well be a half denomination (as suggested by the single rather than double cornucopias), weighing 0.86 ± 0.01 g. We can sug-

23. Meshorer (*TJC*), 61–62.

24. Since the Herodian coinage, like the Hasmonean coinage before it, was both fiduciary and intended for local circulation, this is credible.

25. Price (1979), 358.

26. Price (1968) noted the possibility of producers issuing bronze coins for the sake of generating income. Certainly, with his wide range of expensive building projects, Herod needed to generate funds wherever he could.

27. Ariel (2006, 118) calls our attention to another possibility. He cites a series of four bronze denominations struck at Aigion, which Kroll was able to correlate with obols. The denominations were 1 hemiobol / 1/3 obol / ¼ obol / 1/6 obol; use of the name "obol" is not necessarily relevant, but the ratios 1/ ⅔ / ½ / ⅓ may suggest a "similar distant ancestor in common," according to Ariel.

| Name | Sample Size | Avg. Wt. | Range in g | Avg. Std. Deviation Calc. |
|---|---|---|---|---|
| Procur. pre Agr. I GBC 635–50; TJC 311–339 (Figs. 24, 24a–p) | (759) | 1.90 ± 0.01 | (0.83–2.85) | .33795 / 27.54995 = .0123 |
| Agrippa I GBC 553; TJC 120 (Fig. 25) | (428) | 2.33 ± 0.02 | (1.13–3.40) | .37602 / 20.68816 = .0182 |
| Procur. post Agr.I GBC 651–53; TJC 340–45 (Figs. 26, 26a) | (476) | 2.27 ± 0.02 | (1.15–3.66) | .42016 / 21.817424 = .0193 |

Table 3. Agrippa I and the Roman Administration of Judea

| Name | Sample Size | Avg. Wt. | Range in g | Avg. Std. Deviation Calc. |
|---|---|---|---|---|
| Jewish War GBC 461, 464; TJC 196–198, 204–206 (Figs. 27, 27a) | (1257) | 2.51 ± 0.02 | (0.93–4.24) | 0.63921 / 35.45420 = .0180 |

Table 4. The Jewish War

gest that the coins of Herod Archelaus (Figs. 22, 23) studied here are also probably *prutah* and half-*prutah* denominations respectively.

## AGRIPPA I AND THE ROMAN ADMINISTRATION OF JUDAEA

After Archelaus was banished, the government of Judaea was assigned to a series of Roman governors, the prefects or procurators, who ruled on behalf of Rome between AD 6 and 66, excepting the years of Agrippa I. The weights of the coins struck by the procurators between AD 6 and 37, during the reigns of Augustus and Tiberius, were slightly lower than the coins issued by Archelaus (1.90 ± 0.01 g). When Herod I's grandson Agrippa I (AD 37 to 44) took over for a brief interval, the average weight of the *prutah* jumped 18 per cent to 2.33 ± 0.02 g.[28] After Agrippa I's death, procuratorial rule returned to Judaea under Claudius and Nero, and they continued to strike coins of about the same weight as those of Agrippa I. The coins of Agrippa I and the procurators who followed him approach the weight of a Roman *quadrans* of the first century.[29]

28. These *prutot* are the coins Agrippa I struck in Jerusalem for circulation in the immediate area of Judaea, which was the part of his territory with a heavy Jewish population. While they are found in all parts of ancient Palestine and Transjordan, and also even as far away as the Acropolis in Athens, their main use was local. These coins differed from Agrippa I's other coinage since they did not carry either the names or the images of the Roman emperors; see *TJC*, 97–98.

29. Sutherland 1984: 3. The Augustan standard for the *quadrans* was about 3 g, but a

## The Jewish War

The political situation as well as the geography of the Jewish War encouraged the Jews to strike coins of their own. The average weight of the *prutot* (2.51 ± 0.02 g) of the second and third years (Figs. 27, 27a) of the war saw an increase of 10 per cent over the heaviest procuratorial coins. Perhaps the Jews purposely produced heavier bronze coins as a political statement. After 200 years of fluctuations in the weight of the *prutot* of Judaea, it is, however, interesting to note the coincidence that the bronzes of the Jewish War (2.51 ± 0.02 g) were struck at almost the exact weight as the first bronze coin of the Judaean series (*GBC* 451; Figure 1)(2.47 ± 0.03 g).[30]

## Conclusions

In general, this study has shown that while the average weights ("Avg. Wt. g" in the Tables) for the various issues fluctuate in a relatively insignificant manner (generally ± > 0.5 g), there is a significant range of weigh ("Range in g" in the Tables) within each denomination or series. This great variation in range proves that these coins were probably heavily overvalued relative to the intrinsic value of their metal content.[31] This fiduciarity in Judean bronzes had a number of ramifications.

During the Hellenistic period in Judaea, the issuance of coins was a royal prerogative, and the grant made to the Jews by Antiochus VII appears only to have been good for bronze coinage.[32] Silver coins were struck in ancient Judaea only during the two revolts against Rome, AD 66–70 and AD 132–135. Based on finds of coins dated from 132 BC to AD 135 in Judaea and the immediate region, it is clear that the bronze coins were widely used in daily transactions; silver coins were far less common. Thus locally issued bronze coinage played a key role in local economies and in the economic policies of the Jewish state. Significantly, the fiduciary nature of this bronze coinage also caught the attention of the Talmud, one of the most important cultural (and religious) documents we possess from roughly the same period as the coinage in this study.

The Talmud discusses, for example, whether bronze coins should be considered money or commodities when traded against silver coins. Typically, the au-

review of Flavian and Antonine examples listed at CoinArchives.com suggests it dropped slightly after the Julio-Claudians (Oliver Hoover, per. com.).

30. It is of course that the slight increase in weight was a political consideration making the local administration look better due to heavier coins; this must still be considered a political-economic consideration.

31. As Cathy Lorber noted (per. com.), the lack of weight control for bronze coins is one of our major clues that they were fiduciary currency. Also, as Le Rider and de Callataÿ (see n.12 above) note in their discussion of Seleucid and Ptolemaic bronzes, we cannot assume that all bronze coinage was significantly overvalued.

32. I Maccabees 16:6 for the grant, discussed further in *RPC* I, 1; *TJC*, 23, and *GBC*, 110.

thors of the Talmud weighed both sides of the argument: they are money because in areas where the bronzes were the common form of currency, they were more readily accepted and exchanged than silver coins; they are commodities because their greater acceptance increases their value.[33] Significantly the Talmud also refers to a specific small piece of bronze—a *protitot*—described as "uncoined metal which bear[s] no imprint."[34] This seems to be a clear reference to unstruck coin planchets, often found in Israel.[35] Again, the Talmud discusses these in the context of whether they should be exchanged as commodities or as money. The conclusion is that while unstruck planchets could have value, they were strictly to be defined as "goods" and not as "money." Also, when the Talmud states that something is worth less than a *prutah* it means that it has no commercial value at all.[36] Thus, there was clear awareness of the social convention of fiduciarity in these objects and the fact that the same bronze object could have a range of values depending on its use.

When we consider these Talmudic insights alongside the dramatic weight variations within individual series of Judaean coins observed in this study, the extreme low value of these small bronze coins becomes still more readily apparent. This, of course, served the needs of those conducting daily transactions. But the issuance of these bronzes likely also served the state as well. While all manufactured coins were fiduciary to some degree, bronze coinage "differed from that of coinages in the noble metals by the fact that the profit to the issuing authority was much greater, the bronze being used as a token coinage of very little intrinsic value." [37] The profit motive for striking coins thus joins both market and political issues in driving the desire for local rulers to obtain the right to strike their own coins.[38] Indeed, while the creation of Judaean bronze coinage certainly had economic elements, the need for Jews to establish and maintain an independent Jewish state at the time, suggests this coinage had a political significance nearly as great as its economic significance. Thus the ability to manufacture coins likely enriched the treasuries *and* underlined the political independence of the Hasmonean and Herodian rulers of Judaea, even though they were permitted only to issue bronze coins.

---

33. Baba Metziah 44b.
34. Baba Metziah 46a.
35. Among the 10,000 to 20,000 Judean bronzes the author cleans every year, roughly 0.2–0.5% of these are unstruck planchets.
36. The Talmud states that it is forbidden to steal even an amount less than a *prutah*, but if one does steal less than a *prutah* he cannot be subpoenaed to court. At the same time, he must answer to G-d even for such a tiny transgression. (Baba Metziah 55:1)
37. Mørkholm, O., Grierson, P., Westermark. 1991:6.
38. *Ibid.*

## ACKNOWLEDGEMENTS

Thanks to Yigael Ronen and Alexander Hendin for mathematical advice, Catherine Lorber, Oliver Hoover, Danny Syon, Donald T. Ariel, and Isadore Goldstein, with a special nod to Peter van Alfen, for numismatic and historical advice, and Ben Hendin and Robert Cohen for assisting with the charts and graphs. All opinions herein are those of the author.

## MATHEMATICAL METHODOLOGY

The average weights and the standard deviations were calculated according to standard mathematical formulas and facilitated by using the Maths Calculator at http://www.easycalculation.com/statistics/standar-deviation.php. The average standard deviation, also a standard mathematical formula, is calculated by dividing the standard deviation by the square root of the number of specimens in a particular sample.

## REFERENCES

Ariel, D. 2006. *A numismatic approach to the reign of Herod the Great.* Unpublished Ph.D. dissertation, Tel Aviv University.

Baramki, D. C. 1974. *The coin collection of the American University of Beirut Museum, Palestine and Phoenicia.* Beirut: American University of Beirut.

Bijovsky, G. 2002. Fifth-century C.E. currency in Palestine. *Israel Numismatic Journal*, 14: 196–210.

*RPC* I: Burnett, A., Amandry, M., Ripolles, P. *Roman provincial coinage* I, London 1992.

Hendin, D and Shachar, I. 2009. The identity of YNTN on Hasmonean overstruck coins and the chronology of the Alexander Jannaeus types. *Israel Numismatic Research* 3: 87–94.

Hendin, D. 2001. *Guide to Biblical coins, 4th edition.* New York: Amphora.

Hill, G. F. 1914. *A catalog of the Greek coins in the British Museum: Palestine.* London.

Hoover, O. 2007. *Coins of the Seleucid Empire from the collection of Arthur Houghton.* New York: American Numismatic Society.

Houghton, A. and A. Spaer. 1998. *Sylloge Nummorum Graecorum, Israel I.* 1998. London: Italo Vecchi Ltd.

*SC* I: Houghton, A., Lorber, C. 2002. *Seleucid coins, a comprehensive catalog*, Part I, Vols I & II, NY: American Numismatic Society and Classical Numismatic Group.

*SC* II: Houghton, A., Lorber, C., and Hoover, O. 2008. *Seleucid coins, a compre-

*hensive catalog*, Part II, Vols. I & II, NY: American Numismatic Society and Classical Numismatic Group.

Kaufman, J. C. 1995. *Unrecorded Hasmonean coins from the J. Ch. Kaufman collection*. Jerusalem: Israel Numismatic Society.

Kaufman, J. C. 2004. *Unrecorded Hasmonean coins from the J. Ch. Kaufman collection*, Part II. Jerusalem: Israel Numismatic Society.

Kindler, A. 1954. The Jaffa hoard of Alexander Jannaeus. *Israel Exploration Journal* 4 (3–4): 170–185.

Kindler, A. 1967. The monetary pattern and function of the Jewish coins. *Proceedings of the International Numismatic Convention 1963*. Jerusalem: Schocken: 180–203.

Klimowsky, E. W. 1963. Danka and *prutah*: the *prutah*. *Israel Numismatic Journal* 1, 4: 68–69.

Krupp, M. (2007–2008). A metallurgical examination of Hasmonean coins. *Israel Numismatic Journal* 16: 57–75.

Le Rider, G. and F. de Callataÿ. 2006. Les Séleucides et le Ptolémées: l'héritage monétaire et financier d'Alexandre le Grand. Paris: Rocher.

Meshorer, Y. 1981. *Sylloge Nummorum Graecorum, Palestine*. The Collection of the American Numismatic Society. New York: American Numismatic Society.

Meshorer, Y. 1982. *Ancient Jewish coinage I & II*. Dix Hills: Amphora Books

*TJC*: Meshorer, Y. *A treasury of Jewish coins*. 2001. Jerusalem and New York: Yad Ben Zvi Press and Amphora.

Mørkholm, O., Grierson, P., Westermark, U. 1991. Early Hellenistic coinage: from the accession of Alexander to the Peace of Apamea (336–188 B.C.). Cambridge: Cambridge University Press.

Price M. J. 1968 Early Greek bronze coinage. Kraay C. M. & Jenkins G. K., *Essays in Greek coinage presented to Stanley Robinson*: 90–104.

Price, M. J. 1979. The function of early Greek bronze coinage. *Instituto Italiano di Numismatica Annali, Supplemento al. v. 25*: 351–358.

Sperber, D. 1974. *Roman Palestine 200–400, money & prices*. Ramat Gan: Bar Ilan University Press.

*AJN* Second Series 21 (2009) pp. 123–150
© 2009 The American Numismatic Society

# Becoming Jupiter:
## Severus Alexander, The Temple of Jupiter Ultor, and Jovian Iconography on Roman Imperial Coinage

CLARE ROWAN***

This paper explores the evidence for Severus Alexander's conversion of the *Elagabalium* into a temple to Jupiter Ultor. Close analysis of the numismatic material calls into question modern ideas about the way in which legend and image interacted on Roman coinage, particularly on Jovian types. A new understanding of how Roman coinage communicated the increasing alignment between the emperor and Jupiter is employed to gain a better understanding of the numismatic evidence for the temple of Jupiter Ultor.

In AD 222, the emperor Elagabalus was overthrown and replaced by his cousin, Severus Alexander. Elagabalus' reign had been characterized by the worship of a cultic stone from Emesa, a move that proved unpopular with the elite of Rome. Severus Alexander came to power as the restorer of Roman *mores*, Roman culture and religion. The cult stone of Emesa was banished from Rome and the public space dedicated to the cult was intentionally transformed to signal the return to 'traditional' Roman cultic practices. Part of this process was the conversion of the *Elagabalium* on the Palatine, the temple constructed by Elagabalus to the Emesene god Elagabal.

* clare.rowan@students.mq.edu.au
** The research for this paper was conducted while a student at the American Numismatic Society Graduate Summer Seminar. I am indebted to all the staff of the ANS for their advice and assistance, and to those scholars who visited the ANS during the 2007 seminar and offered their expertise. Thanks are also due to the anonymous readers of this paper for their helpful suggestions and to the Australian Centre for Ancient Numismatic Studies for its continuing support of this project.

Figure 1. Coin of Elagabalus
(Sambon, 18 November 1907, lot 2546; *RIC* IV.2 Elagabalus 339).

This paper examines the archaeological and numismatic evidence for the construction of the *Elagabalium* on the Palatine, as well as the evidence for the temple's conversion. Given the complications presented by the numismatic evidence, this article will also suggest a new model for understanding the representations of Jupiter on imperial coinage. Rather than seeing Jovian imagery on a coin as a strict expression of the coin's legend, this paper suggests that image and legend could diverge, a phenomenon created by the alignment between the emperor and Jupiter in this period. The iconography and epithets of Jupiter developed significantly from the reign of Commodus in order to communicate the increasing association between the emperor and Jupiter in the second and third centuries AD. By understanding how Jupiter was presented on Roman coinage, we gain a better understanding of the temple of Jupiter Ultor, as well as the ideology of Severus Alexander's rule. It is clear that Jupiter acted as a patron deity under Alexander, in stark contrast to his predecessor.

## Monumentalizing the Foreign:
### The Temple to Elagabal on the Palatine

Literary evidence describes two structures to the god Elagabal in Rome. One temple was located on the Palatine, and the other in the outer suburbs of the city.[1] The site of the Palatine temple can be placed with some certainty on the site of the Vigna Barberini. Bigot was the first to propose this identification, observing that the remains of this site closely correlated to a temple shown on a coin of Elagabalus (Figure 1).[2] The piece shows a temple with a large area in front, surrounded by porticoes, and containing a monumental staircase with a *pentapylum* surmounted by statues. The legend reads P M TR P V COS IIII P P S C. It was once part of the Gnecchi collection and is in the Münzkabinett of the Staatliche Museum in Berlin, preserved only in a photograph in *I Medaglioni Romani* and in the Martinetti catalogue.[3] In the latter it is described as a *petit médaillon*, though it is listed in

---

1. Hdn. 5.5.8; SHA *Heliogab.* 1.6, 3.4–5.

2. Bigot (1911), 80–85.

3. Gnecchi III: 41 no. 6, pl. 152 no. 11. The coin was originally part of the Martinetti collection, and was sold in Sambon 11/18/1907. See Sambon, Canessa *et al.* (1907: pl. XXXII,

*RIC* as an *as*.[4] Without a recorded weight and without the piece to consult, it is difficult to assess whether it was a medallion or not. Nothing on the piece identifies the temple as the *Elagabalium*, though this is the likeliest interpretation considering the visual emphasis on the cult in Elagabalus' final years. Chausson believed that he saw the sacred stone of Emesa surmounted by an eagle behind the altar, and Brown suggested that the upright object in the *tympanum* of the temple may have been the sacred stone, but the poor quality of the surviving photographs prevent any conclusive identifications.[5] Four figures are shown sacrificing in front of the temple, probably Elagabalus (the largest figure) and Severus Alexander. The two other figures may represent the imperial women or sacrificial attendants. The piece dates from the final months of Elagabalus' reign, between December AD 221 and March AD 222.

French excavations of the Vigna Barberini have confirmed Bigot's hypothesis that the site probably housed Elagabalus' temple. It contains a Domitianic terrace measuring 180m by 120m, built over a Julio-Claudian *domus*.[6] This terrace supported a temple (60m by 40m) surrounded by porticoes, similar to the structure depicted on the piece of Elagabalus. The entrance to the complex comprised three large sections of stairs. Though the archaeological remains contain bricks stamped with the name of Faustina the Younger, the large amount of anepigraphic bricks (used from the reign of Caracalla) and other material found at the site strongly suggest a date in the second half of the Severan period.[7] The complex matches Herodian's description of Elagabal's temple as both large and beautiful.[8]

The location of the Vigna Barberini fits with the observation of the *Historia Augusta* that the *Elagabalium* was close to the imperial palace.[9] The church of Saint Sebastian, which once stood on the site, also provides incidental evidence to connect the area to Elagabalus. The church was erected on what was believed to be the place of the saint's martyrdom, 'the steps of Heliogabalus.'[10] Despite the rededication by Severus Alexander, it is evident that the area retained its earlier associations: problems surrounding the historical reliability of the *Acta* of Saint Sebastian do not detract from its topographical evidence. The site later housed a church dedicated to the Virgin Mary, Saint Sebastian, and Saint Zoticus. The inclu-

no. 2546). Münzkabinett, Staatliche Museen zu Berlin 1909/61, object number 18205364.

4. *RIC* IV.2 Elagabalus 339.

5. Chausson (1995), 737; Brown (1941), 161.

6. Broise and Thébert (1999), 730.

7. Broise and Thébert (1999), 740.

8. Hdn. 5.5.8.

9. Lugli's thesis that the phrase *iuxta aedes imperatorias* in the *Historia Augusta* referred to the temple of Augustus has since been convincingly refuted by Castagnoli (1979: 340).

10. *Acta S. Sebastiani Martyris* 23 (*PL* 17. Col 1056B).

Figure 2. Sestertius of Severus Alexander
(Hamburger, 19 October 1925, lot 1292; *RIC* IV.2 Severus Alexander 412.)

sion of the latter is significant when one recalls Elagabalus' lover was also named Zoticus.[11] It may be that this figure was chosen as a focal point for the conversion of the site from pagan to Christian.[12]

The confluence of evidence suggests that the Vigna Barberini was the site of Elagabalus' temple. The ability of an emperor to construct a large and magnificent temple in a four-year reign has been met with scepticism in the modern era. Jerome records that the temple was dedicated in AD 220, just two years into Elagabalus' rule.[13] Consequently, many believe that Elagabalus transformed an earlier structure into his *Elagabalium*.[14] The remaining literary and archaeological evidence belies this hypothesis. The verbs used to describe Elagabalus' actions (*constituere* and *facere* in the *Historia Augusta*, *aedificare* in Jerome) suggest that the structure was constructed from scratch.[15] The archaeological remains also indicate a single, coherent structure, built in the first half of the third century.[16] Situated on an older terrace, the *Elagabalium* was not a renovation of an existing structure; it was an entirely new building.

### Avenging Roman Religion: The Temple to Jupiter Ultor

As part of the restoration program of Severus Alexander, the *Elagabalium* was converted. The evidence for this is primarily numismatic, though the archaeo-

11. Dio 80.16.1ff; *SHA Heliogab.* 10.2–7.

12. Marchiori (2007), 273.

13. Jerome *Ad. Abraham* 296 g (Helm).

14. Castagnoli (1979: 332) provides a summary of the various suggestions of what may have stood on the hill before the reign of Elagabalus. These include a temple to Apollo, the temple of Augustus, the Adonea, the tomb of Antinoös (Grenier and Coarelli 1986: 230–253), a temple to Faustina the Younger (Cecamore 1999: 311–349) as well as the temple to Jupiter Victor.

15. Optendrenk (1969), 85.

16. Broise and Thébert (1999), 736–745.

logical remains also suggest two phases of building activity within a short time of each other, probably in the reign of Elagabalus followed by Severus Alexander.[17] Bigot was the first to suggest that Severus Alexander rededicated the *Elagabalium*, converting it into a temple to Jupiter Ultor.[18] The numismatic evidence here is compelling.

Coins of Severus Alexander display a structure remarkably similar to that seen under Elagabalus, accompanied by the legend IOVI VLTORI (Figure 2).[19] It is the similarity between the piece of Elagabalus and the structure shown on the coinage of Severus Alexander that forms the basis for the idea that the temple was converted.[20] Both the Elagabalian and Alexandrian pieces show a temple with a large area in front, surrounded by porticoes with a colonnade or gateway. Both also show evidence of *opus quadratum*. The similarities are so striking that one might suggest that the die engravers of the later coins were conscious of Elagabalus' earlier issue and set out to visually communicate the rededication of the building to a god more in keeping with traditional Roman religion. If this were the case, the temple was consciously portrayed in a similar manner to Elagabalus' piece to emphasise this conversion of sacred space. The epithet given to Jupiter in this instance is striking—VLTOR, or avenger. The legend reflected the wider rhetoric that accompanied the overthrow of Elagabalus and Alexander's rise to the throne. Normally an epithet of Mars, it had only ever appeared once before in relation to Jupiter, on an aureus of Commodus.[21]

The complete rededication of a Roman temple on the Palatine was extraordinary, although the conversion of buildings associated with an emperor who

17. Broise and Thébert (1999), 745.

18. Bigot (1911), 80–85.

19. Medallion: *BMC* VI Severus Alexander 209*, 210*. As: *RIC* IV.2 Severus Alexander 413. Sestertii: *BMC* VI Severus Alexander 208* Pl. 8; Hill 1960: pl. 8 no. 8; Münzhandlung Basel, Auction 3 (4 March 1935), lot 762 and 763 (described as a "petite medallion," diameter 27.2 mm); Gnecchi II no. 7; Glending (16–21 November 1950), lot 1802; Leu Münzen und Medallion (2–3 November 1967), lot 1422; J. Schulman (8–10 June 1966), lot 2045; Hamburger 96 (25 October 1932), lot 953.

20. The similarities between the structure portrayed on the piece of Elagabalus and that shown on the coinage of Severus Alexander had already been noted by Sambon. See Sambon, Canessa *et al.* (1907: 204, no. 2546).

21. *RIC* III Commodus 200, reliant on Cohen 261. I have not been able to find a specimen of the coin. Cohen may have been mistaken in his record (VLTORI and VICTORI look very similar on a worn legend) and thus Severus Alexander may have been the first to give the epithet VLTORI to Jupiter on imperial coinage. Cohen recorded that the specimen was in the British Museum, but the BM catalogue reports that it is not. Though there is no recorded *aurei* with the legend IOVI VICTORI for Commodus, there are *sestertii* bearing this legend (*RIC* III Commodus 291). Ultor as an epithet of Jupiter appears in inscriptions, but only rarely. See Angeli (1971: 151–152), also incidental evidence for the easy confusion between the epithets VICTOR and VLTOR.

Figure 3. Denarius of Severus Alexander (Dr. Busso Peus Nachfolger Auction 369, 31 October 2001, lot 688; *RIC* IV.2 Severus Alexander 144)

suffered *damnatio memoriae* had precedent.[22] The fact that the Romans took the unusual step of removing the Emesene god from Rome and converting the temple underlines just how closely the emperor Elagabalus and his deity were aligned. The *damnatio* of one necessarily entailed a *damnatio* of the other. The conversion of the temple was as necessary as the overthrow of the emperor; the vices of Elagabalus' regime were inherently connected with the structure.

The nature of the cult installed in the converted *Elagabalium* remains the subject of debate. Hill argued that Alexander merely re-installed the cult that had originally occupied the building. This viewpoint demands that Elagabalus had converted an existing structure. The foundations of Hill's argument were the coin types of Alexander that portrayed a seated Jupiter holding Victory and a scepter, with the legend IOVI VLTORI (Figure 3).[23] The image reproduces the iconic statue of Jupiter Victor. The representation of this particular statue type led Hill to suggest that Elagabalus converted the temple of Jupiter Victor, and that it was restored under Alexander. As noted above, however, archaeological remains show that the temple was a new construction.

A more sophisticated approach to the representation of Jupiter under Severus Alexander and his predecessors can reconcile the disparity between the numismatic and the archaeological evidence. Severus Alexander's coinage, and the iconographic divergences within it, is better understood from a larger contextual framework.

### Between Man and God: Jovian imagery on Roman imperial coinage

Traditionally in Roman Imperial numismatics the image on a coin has been seen as an expression of the accompanying legend. One expects IOVI VICTORI to be accompanied by a representation of the cult statue of this god holding a scepter and Victory. That is, the legend describes the image. The numismatic representation of the temple of Jupiter Ultor brings this strict framework of interpretation into question. Often the legend and image could possess subtly different nuances, and the

22. For example Nero's *domus aurea*, seen as an embodiment of the emperor's extravagance. Successive emperors went to considerable efforts to cover areas of the palace with pointedly utilitarian public buildings. See Griffin (1984), 137.

23. Hill (1960), 119–120.

legend came to be given greater weight in the expression of a coin's message. The focus of our discussion illustrates this point: Severus Alexander's *denarii* displayed the statue type of Jupiter Victor, but this image was accompanied by the legend IOVI VLTORI, an epithet that communicated the revenge of Elagabalus' offences. The legend could convey specific concepts and events with more detail than its pictorial counterpart. The Roman mint came to utilize this to great effect.

Hill employed a more traditional perspective and identified the statue in the temple of Jupiter Ultor from Alexander's *denarii* (Figure 3). He believed the statue in the temple was that of Jupiter Victor since this was what accompanied the IOVI VLTORI legend. This would make sense if Elagabalus had converted the temple to Jupiter Victor and Alexander had rededicated it. Hill believed this was the case, noting that regional catalogues list a temple to Jupiter Victor on the Palatine. He acknowledged the discrepancy between the statue type of Jupiter *Victor* and the legend naming Jupiter *Ultor*, and suggested that divine statue types could be given different names. For Hill, the same statue type of Jupiter could be given several different names according to the capacity in which the god acted. Jupiter Capitolinus could act as an avenger, a conserver, or in any other capacity. The statue type of Jupiter Capitolinus could thus be paired with the legend IOVI VLTORI, IOVI CONSERVATORI, or with any other epithet. Consequently (according to Hill) Severus Alexander could rededicate the temple of Jupiter Victor, but label it Jupiter Ultor, since here Jupiter Victor was acting in the capacity of revenge. Hill believed that the decision to place VLTOR on the coinage was to 'placate the god after the sacrilegious acts of Elagabalus.'[24]

The inherent messiness (to the modern mind) of Roman religious thought should not be underestimated, but Hill's interpretation remains unsatisfactory for a number of reasons. The epithet VLTOR on the coinage portraying the temple and the statue type of Jupiter Victor suggests that the temple was dedicated to Jupiter Ultor. If Alexander had restored the temple of Jupiter Victor, one would imagine he would restore the full cult, including the god's epithet. Tameanko also realized this problem and suggested that Elagabalus did convert the temple of Jupiter Victor, but that Alexander rededicated it to Jupiter Ultor.[25] If this were the case one would expect it to be named as such in the later regional catalogues, but only a temple to Jupiter Victor is mentioned.[26]

A better solution to the problem might be found through a closer examination of the coinage concerned. Such an investigation brings the identification of the cult statue of the temple into question. *Denarii* have been the main basis for the reconstruction of the cult statue, but an examination of the bronze issues is

---

24. Hill (1960), 119.
25. Tameanko (1999), 149.
26. Notitia Regio X Palatium 11: *aedem Iovis victoris.*

illuminating. The statue inside the temple does not hold Victory in his right hand, but another object, most likely a *patera* (cf. Figure 2).[27] Jupiter was commonly portrayed with this attribute in the provinces and is also portrayed seated with a *patera* on an issue of Caracalla.[28] The statue of the god in the temple was portrayed in a different fashion to those coins that only displayed Jupiter himself.

This may seem disconcerting, but a broader examination of Roman imperial coinage indicates that the epithets and iconography of Jupiter do not always correlate to modern ideas concerning the representation of cult statues. We would anticipate the legend IOVI VICTORI to be accompanied by the statue type of Jupiter seated, holding Victory and a scepter. In many instances this is the case.[29] Howeverer the same epithet is also accompanied by the image of Jupiter standing, holding Victory and a scepter (*RIC* IV.1 Clodius Albinus 25, 26), seated, holding a thunderbolt and Victory (*RIC* IV.1 Clodius Albinus 27), the head of Jupiter Ammon (*RIC* IV.1 Septimius Severus 272), and Jupiter in a *quadriga* hurling thunderbolts against the giants (*RIC* IV.1 Septimius Severus 204).

Conversely, the statue type of Jupiter Victor (seated, holding Victory and a scepter) appears on Roman coinage not only with the legends IOVI VLTORI and IOVI VICTORI, but with the legends IOVI CONSER(vatori), IOVI CAP(itolino) PR(aesidi) VRB(is), IOVI INVICTO, IOVI PRAE(sens) and IOVI PRAE(sens) OR(bis).[30] All of the latter epithets occur under Pescennius Niger and Septimius Severus, suggesting that a standard type of Jupiter was employed in a dialogue between the two competitors to the throne in the East. This particular usage occurred in (a) mint(s) outside Rome, as did Albinus' diverse iconography accompanying the legend IOVI VICTORI. One may be tempted to interpret this as the decision of a provincial die cutter to use a well-known type in the absence of a more sophisticated understanding of the intricacies of Jovian iconography, but the occurrence of the same phenomenon within the Roman mint negates this idea.

---

27. *BMC* VI Severus Alexander 207* lists the object as a thunderbolt. This is also a possible alternative, though the shape of the object, particularly on the medallion published in Gnecchi (no. 7) argues in favour of a *patera*. Whatever the object, it is clear that it is not Victory. Examples of this type can be found in n.19 above.

28. *RIC* IV.1 Caracalla 287. Jupiter is also shown standing with a *patera* on a coin of Vespasian with the legend IOVIS CVSTOS (*RIC* II Vespasian 124).

29. E.g. *RIC* I Vitellius 68, *RIC* II Domitian 253, *RIC* II Hadrian 251, *RIC* III Commodus 291, *RIC* III Marcus Aurelius 1612, *RIC* IV.1 Septimius Severus 441B, *RIC* IV.1 Caracalla 200.

30. CONSERVATORI: *RIC* IV.1 Pescennius Niger 42, *RIC* IV.1 Septimius Severus 111A, 130, 504A. IOVI CAP PR VRB: Bland, Burnett *et al.* (1987: 68), Group II no. 4. INVICTO: *RIC* IV.1 Septimius Severus 480. PRAE(sens): Classical Numismatic Group, Mail Bid Sale 61 (25 September 2002) lot 1850. IOVI PRAE OR: Fritz Rudolf Künker Münzenhandlung, Auction 83 (2003) lot 1018.

Here we have examined Jupiter Victor, but one may just as easily identify the same occurrence with other epithets and cult statues of Jupiter.[31] Hill's explanation that 'each aspect of the god could be, and often was, assumed by any one of the others' does not seem an adequate explanation for this divergence of legend and image on Roman coinage.[32] Jupiter could operate in any number of ways, but the giving of an epithet to a deity suggested that he had acted in that capacity.[33] IOVI VLTORI suggests that Jupiter had acted in revenge, not that Jupiter Victor had acted in this capacity. The epithet defined a particular aspect of a god.

A close examination of the legends referring to Jupiter on imperial coinage shows an increasing tendency towards new, very specific epithets for the god. The use of these specific epithets becomes particularly marked from the time of Commodus, under whom the following types were struck:[34]

1. IOVI EXSVPER. Jupiter seated l., holding branch and scepter (*RIC* III Commodus 138, 152–153, 483, 488). *Exsuperatoria* was an epithet taken by Commodus in AD 112, and was the new name for the month of November.[35]

2. IOVI IVVENI. Jupiter standing l., holding thunderbolt and scepter; at feet, eagle (*RIC* III Commodus 499, 525, 532). This type is perhaps best understood as an allusion to the return of the Golden Age (when Jupiter was young) under the youthful rule of Commodus.[36]

3. I.O.M. SPONSOR SEC AVG. Commodus standing l., holding globe and scepter; Jupiter standing l., placing r. arm on emperor's shoulder and holding thunderbolt (*RIC* III Commodus 255). This type was struck in AD 191, after the fall of Cleander.[37]

4. IOVI DEFENS SALVTIS AVG. Jupiter standing r., holding spear in l. hand and about to hurl thunderbolt in r.; in field, seven stars (*RIC* III Commodus 256, 597). Struck in AD 191, it can be connected with the type above.

5. IOVI CONSERVATORI. Jupiter standing l., holding thunderbolt and scepter; below thunderbolt, Commodus standing l., holding trophy (*RIC* Commo-

31. For example, Jupiter Conservator, who is normally portrayed standing, holding a thunderbolt and scepter. The legend CONSERVATOR is also on coins showing the statue type of Jupiter Victor (*RIC* IV.1 Pescennius Niger 41) and an eagle on a thunderbolt (*RIC* II Domitian 40). The type of Jupiter with a thunderbolt and scepter also appears with the legend IOV IVVEN (*RIC* III Commodus 173).

32. Hill (1960: 113).

33. Rives (2007: 15).

34. Only those coins with a specific legend are listed here; Commodus also struck several types of Jupiter without a specific epithet. This increase in the association of Jupiter with the image of the emperor is also noted by Fears (1981: 101).

35. Dio 73.15.3–4; Fears (1981: 111–112).

36. Hill (1960: 115).

37. Hill (1960: 115).

dus (as Caesar under Marcus Aurelius) 1524). Issued in AD 175/176, when Commodus was on military campaign.

(?) 6. IOVI VLTORI. Jupiter seated l., holding Victory and scepter. The existence of this coin is questionable (see n. 21 above).

What emerges from these examples is that the legend on the coin comes to have very specific reference to the emperor's situation. Epithets and attributes of Jupiter are employed to communicate personal imperial circumstances; even those epithets of Jupiter that are more traditional are used only when they allude to the emperor.[38] Such a development should not be surprising; the emperor and Jupiter were often closely aligned in Roman thought, both being the supreme rulers of their respective kingdoms. But in this period it appears the alignment between the human and divine ruler became more defined, and was expressed through specific epithets. The analysis of Commodus' rule by Hekster and Bergmann underlines this idea: Jupiter's image on coins of Commodus bears a striking resemblance to the emperor himself, particularly the god's eyes and beard.[39]

The 'Commodian' Jupiter highlights the fact that the close alignment between the emperor and the head of the Roman pantheon also developed within numismatic iconography. Jupiter as the *conservator* of the emperor had been a motif on coinage since the time of Trajan, with the god shown standing over a smaller figure of the emperor in a protective stance.[40] This type is developed under Commodus with his SPONSOR SEC AVG series (no. 3 above). The emperor is now the same height as his divine counterpart. The visual connection between Jupiter and the emperor gains even more specificity under Septimius Severus. Jupiter is shown towering over two children, presumably meant to represent Caracalla and Geta.[41] On an aureus of Septimius Jupiter is portrayed seated between the gods Liber Pater and Hercules.[42] The latter two gods were the tutelary deities of Lepcis Magna and acted as the emperor's patron deities during his reign. Their portrayal with Jupiter,

38. The phenomenon did not start with Commodus, merely became more prominent under his reign. An earlier, contextually specific use of the god is *RIC* I 62 (IVPPITER LIBERATOR, depicting Jupiter seated l., holding thunderbolt and scepter) struck during the civil wars of AD 68–69. Standard epithets of Jupiter (*Propagnator, Conservator*, and so on) also normally had topical reference. For example, *RIC* III Marcus Aurelius 1224, a coin with the legend PROPVGNATORI and portraying Jupiter hurling a thunderbolt at an enemy, was probably a reference to the triumph held for victories over the Germans and Sarmatians at the end of AD 176, or perhaps to plans for a military campaign in AD 178.

39. Bergmann (1998: 265); Hekster (2002: 102).

40. *RIC* II Trajan 249–250.

41. *RIC* IV.1 Septimius Severus 226, 233, 243. This type is also present on a medal of Marcus Aurelius (Gnecchi 52), though presumably here the two figures represent Aurelius and Lucius Verus.

42. Hill (1982: 159–60).

a unique numismatic type, was a result of their strong connection to Severus. Numismatic iconography thus also reflects the increasing articulation of the connection between the emperor and Jupiter.

We now return to the cult statue in the temple of Jupiter Ultor. It is likely that the statue in the temple of Jupiter Ultor was seated, holding a *patera* and scepter. This is what is portrayed on the coinage showing the temple itself. A different image (the statue type of Jupiter Victor) was employed on other issues, but this can be attributed to the methodology of the mint. In portraying the complex association between the emperor and Jupiter, the mint employed what might be described as a more creative approach to iconography and legends than was previously the case.

The first stage of this process was the depiction of the emperor in the direct company of Jupiter, who acted as the guarantor and protector of imperial power. This resulted in iconography that did not merely reproduce traditional cult statues (like Jupiter Victor), but employed imagery that captured the contemporary conceptualization of god and ruler. This is not to suggest that statues showing Jupiter protecting the emperor did not exist, merely that the artistic tradition that created both the statues and the numismatic types begins to express the connection between the emperor and the god in a way not seen before, at least on coinage.

This iconographic movement is followed by a growth in legends referring to specific and contemporary personal circumstances of the emperor and/or empire. The use of a new epithet to express a specific imperial situation did not necessarily result in the founding of a new temple or the creation of a new cult statue on which die engravers could base their designs. For instance, the connection between Jupiter and Commodus' new calendar (IOVI EXSVPER) may not have necessarily equated to a new cult statue or temple. Nor perhaps could the types marking Commodus' escape from the plot of Cleander (IOVI DEFENS SALVTIS AVG) necessarily draw upon a standard cult statue created for the occasion. Rather it seems that the Roman mint employed more standard images of Jupiter in conjunction with these new legends. In their desire to communicate the contemporary relationship between the emperor and Jupiter the mint began to express concepts more specific than could be encapsulated in a cult statue. Yet for the most part the mint was still reliant on an accepted repertoire of Jovian imagery. Jupiter had to remain recognizable. In consequence, the legend of the coin moved beyond the iconography. This explains how the image of Jupiter Victor came to be issued in conjunction with a series of diverse, yet contextually specific legends. The epithet referred to the imperial situation (for instance IOVI PRAE(sens) OR(bis) in the war between Severus and Niger), while the image remained a well known cult statue. This image still had significance and communicated the association of emperor and god, but it was not expected to be a strict representation of the legend. In this sense, there was a refinement of image and legend on Roman coinage.

Figure 4. Antoninianus of Gallienus (Münzen and Medaillen Deutschland Auction 8, 10 May 2001, lot 384; *RIC* V.1 Gallienus 53)

This point is further illustrated by the representation of Jupiter Ultor under Gallienus. Here the god is portrayed standing right, brandishing a thunderbolt (Figure 4).[43] Chausson suggested that the coin celebrated work performed on the temple of Jupiter Ultor (the only evidence for which is this coin type). He postulated that this work entailed the repair or replacement of the cult statue; hence the new iconography of the god.[44] A better understanding of Jovian iconography shows that this was not necessarily the case; the epithet of Jupiter was selected because it best captured the imperial situation (the coin is undated so a specific context cannot be postulated here) and a standard type of Jupiter was employed in conjunction with the legend.[45]

The separation of image and legend raises questions about the degree to which a coin type could have been understood by the differing segments of the population. Since the legend and image on a coin did not always equate, the literate segments of society would have gleaned more information from the coin than their non-literate counterparts.[46] But the continued use of iconic, standard images would have meant that an allusion to Jupiter was easily recognizable, even if the specific context of this reference was not immediately apparent. Indeed, the decision to use the same image of Jupiter Victor (though with differing legends) by Pescennius Niger and Septimius Severus in the East may have been because the cult statue was easily recognized.

There is thus no need to equate the temple of Jupiter Ultor with that of Jupiter Victor, as Hill did.[47] No temple to Jupiter Ultor is mentioned in later regional

43. *RIC* V.1 Gallienus 51, 220, 221.

44. Chausson (1995: 739).

45. The other Jupiter types of Gallienus bear out this hypothesis. The type of Jupiter standing or walking with a thunderbolt and scepter is accompanied by the legends IOVI CONSERVA (*RIC* V.1 Gallienus 47), IOVI PROPVGNATOR (*RIC* V.1 Gallienus 48), IOVIS STATOR(I) (*RIC* V.1 Gallienus 49, 50) and IOVI VLTORI (*RIC* V.1 Gallienus 51–53).

46. On the ability of various segments of Roman society to read a coin legend see Harris (1989: 213).

47. Hill (1965: 160).

catalogues, but Severus Alexander's temple may be one of the many monuments neglected by the authors.[48] The epithet Ultor communicated Jupiter's revenge of his neglect under Elagabalus, and Severus Alexander's role as the instigator of this revenge. The young emperor aligned himself with Jupiter from the very beginning of his reign: the *dies imperii* of Alexander is recorded in the *Feriale Duranum* as the 13th March, a day holy to Jupiter and in the later Chronography of 354 mentioned as a day sacred to Jupiter Cultor.[49]

The association between Jupiter and Alexander was not confined to the beginning of the emperor's principate. Jupiter continued to have a prominent place throughout Severus Alexander's reign, and the god's epithets and iconography changed to match contemporary circumstances. What follows is an exploration of the differing forms of Jupiter represented on Severus Alexander's coinage and their possible connection to the situation of the emperor. This overview illustrates in more detail the close association between emperor and god in this period.

## Severus Alexander and Jupiter AD (224–235)

In the following analysis the chronology of Carson in the *British Museum Catalogue* is followed. Since much of Alexander's coinage does not list his tribunician power (the easiest and most secure method for dating Roman imperial coinage), the date of many issues is not particularly clear. Carson's chronology, based on portraiture, hoard presence and type, remains the best means of dating Alexander's coinage.

This analysis will also add a quantitative dimension to illustrate the prominence of Jupiter in this period. Recent studies have illustrated the usefulness of coin hoards in estimating the relative size of a particular issue.[50] A similar methodology is employed here utilizing silver hoards, the details of which are listed at the end of the article. Gold hoards of this period do not provide sufficient quantity for an analysis of this kind, and *aes* production in the Severan period seems to have declined significantly.[51] In total, fifty-seven silver hoards were analyzed, containing 67,425 coins from the Severan period and 14,743 coins struck in Alexander's reign, which were entered into a database using the numbers assigned to types by *RIC*. It is not my purpose to attempt to recreate the total number of coins struck by Severus Alexander, or to recreate the precise composition of Roman currency in this period. The hoards are used to gauge the relative frequencies

---

48. Chausson (1995: 737–739).

49. Chausson (1995: 739) suggests that this may have been a corruption of *Ultor*. See also Coarelli (1987: 437).

50. Carradice (1983); Carradice (1998: 93–118); Carson (1983: 67); Christiansen (1988); Kemmers (2006: 197); Noreña (2001: 146–168).

51. Buttrey (1972: 33–58).

Figure 5. Denarius of Severus Alexander, AD 222 (Leu Numismatik AG Auction 91, 10 May 2004, lot 620; *RIC* IV.2 Severus Alexander 14)

of particular silver types and to allow Alexander's silver coinage to be viewed as a coherent whole. From this perspective we might glimpse what the silver coinage of this emperor looked like to his subjects. One might argue that every coin type was significant, regardless of quantity, since the very act of joining the emperor's personage to an image formed an official statement of the regime. And yet it is also useful to gauge what an emperor's coinage 'looked like' as a whole, since the totality of the imagery on an emperor's currency would have formed a wider public image presented to the populace.

## Jupiter Conservatori (AD 222–224)

Immediately upon Severus Alexander's succession the image of Jupiter was placed upon his coinage, initially without any specific epithets, then with the legend IOVI CONSERVATORI (Figure 5).[52] The epithet of Jupiter here has particular reference to the circumstances of Severus Alexander's succession. Both Dio and Herodian describe a plot of Elagabalus against his younger cousin, the failure of which led directly to Alexander's accession to the throne.[53] The *conservator* type can be seen as part of the rhetoric that surrounded Alexander's rise to power: his preservation from Elagabalus' murderous intent is attributed to the protection of Jupiter, who becomes the tutelary god of the young emperor's entire reign.

The epithet CONSERVATOR may also have had a secondary meaning. Elagabalus had bestowed this normally Jovian title on the Emesene god Elagabal.[54] The restoration of the epithet to Jupiter may thus also have signified the reinstatement of Jupiter as head of the Roman pantheon in the early years of Severus Alexander's reign.

Some tentative statements may be made from the hoard evidence. The percentage of these types as a total of all Severus Alexander's *denarii* (let alone all

---

52. Without an accompanying legend: *RIC* IV.2 Severus Alexander 4, 5, 387 (AD 222), 18-20 (AD 223), 34–35 (AD 224). The legend IOVI CONSERVATORI: *RIC* IV.2 Severus Alexander 140–141(AD 222).

53. Dio 80.19.1ff; Hdn. 5.8.3.

54. *RIC* IV.2 Elagabalus 61, 62, 64, 65; Numismatica Ars Classica, Auction 29 (11–12 May 2005) lot 596.

Table 1. Types of Jupiter on the Silver Coinage of Severus Alexander as represented in Selected Hoards*

| Date | RIC | Type | A | B | C | D | E | R-D | Total | Year % | Total % |
|---|---|---|---|---|---|---|---|---|---|---|---|
| 222 | 5 | Conservator | 35 | 64 | 4 | 34 | 3 | 148 | 288 | 19% | 2% |
|  | 141 | Conservator | 12 | 34 | 1 | 14 | 1 | 74 | 136 | 9% | 1% |
| 223 | 19 | Conservator | 21 | 63 | 1 | 35 | 1 | 151 | 272 | 16% | 2% |
| 224 | 35 | Conservator | 11 | 22 | 1 | 14 | 1 | 0 | 49 | 11% | <1% |
|  | 146 | Ultor (Temple) | 0 | 0 | 0 | 0 | 0 | 0 | 0 | 0% | 0% |
| 225 | 143 | Ultor | 0 | 7 | 7 | 7 | 0 | 4 | 25 | 2% | <1% |
|  | 144 | Ultor | 16 | 67 | 1 | 29 | 1 | 121 | 235 | 21% | <1% |
| 228–31 | 203 | Ultor | 0 | 0 | 0 | 0 | 1 | 0 | 1 | -** | <1% |
| 231 | 195 | Fides Militum | 0 | 2 | 0 | 0 | 0 | 0 | 2 | <1% | <1% |
|  | 198 | Conservator | 0 | 3 | 0 | 3 | 0 | 0 | 6 | <1% | <1% |
|  | 200 | Conservator | 4 | 18 | 0 | 6 | 0 | 54 | 82 | 3% | <1% |
|  | 202 | Stator | 5 | 11 | 0 | 7 | 0 | 27 | 50 | 2% | <1% |
|  | 235 | Propugnator | 3 | 38 | 0 | 20 | 5 | 71 | 137 | 6% | 1% |
|  | 236 | Propugnator | 0 | 0 | 0 | 5 | 3 | 0 | 8 | <1% | <1% |
|  | 240 | Propugnator | 0 | 0 | 0 | 0 | 0 | 9 | 9 | <1% | <1% |
|  | 241 | Propugnator | 0 | 2 | 0 | 1 | 0 | 1 | 4 | <1% | <1% |
| 232 | 238 | Propugnator | 4 | 27 | 0 | 13 | 0 | 161 | 205 | 12% | 2% |
|  | 239 | Propugnator | 0 | 57 | 0 | 8 | 0 | 0 | 65 | 4% | <1% |
| Hybrid | 201 | Propugnator | 0 | 0 | 0 | 0 | 0 | 0 | 0 | 0% | 0% |
| - | n/p*** |  | 0 | 3 | 0 | 0 | 0 | 0 | 3 | - | <1% |
| Total |  |  | 111 (16%) | 416 (14%) | 15 (16%) | 196 (12%) | 16 (14%) | 821 (12%) | 1577 (13%) |  | 13% |

A=Britain, B=West Continent, C=Italy, D=Danube, E=Eastern parts of the Empire, R-D=Reka Devnia. Due to the large size of this last hoard it was considered prudent to analyze it in a separate column.

* Year % is an expression of the Jupiter type in relation to all silver coins struck in the name of Alexander in that year, according to the dating system of Carson in the *BMC*. Total % is an expression of the Jupiter type in relation to all the silver coinage struck in the name of Severus Alexander throughout his reign.

** No equivalent for this coin is found in the *BMC*; consequently it has not been included in the yearly analysis, which is based on the chronology of the *BMC*.

*** n/p = not published in a standard catalogue.

the coinage in circulation at a particular time) is small (1–2%), as are the types discussed below (Table 1). However, when all the types referring to Jupiter are *combined* then it is apparent that Jupiter had a sizeable presence on the coinage of Severus Alexander (13%, Table 1). Although there are variations in the number of hoards and types between different regions, the imagery of Jupiter constitutes a similar proportion of Severus Alexander's coinage across the *entire empire*. The emperor's Jovian types in Britain (Zone A) constituted 16% of his coinage, in the West Continent (Zone B) 14%, in Italy (Zone C) 16%, along the Danube (Zone D) 12% and in the East (Zone E) 14%. The Reka Devnia hoard, found in modern day Romania, was analyzed separately due to its large size (more than 80,000 coins). It corresponds to the other hoard evidence, with Jupiter types constituting 13% of Alexander's *denarii*. Thus while the modern scholar may discuss the significance and meaning of one particular issue, and each type did have significance regardless of what quantities it was struck in, it is likely that only a general impression of the connection between the emperor and Jupiter was given by the coinage itself while in circulation. This distinction, between the iconography and message encapsulated in a particular issue and the impression conveyed by an entire body of coinage, must be kept in mind when considering the reception of ancient numismatic iconography.

## Jupiter Ultor (AD 224–225)

Given the discussion of the Jupiter Ultor type above, this section shall be brief. In AD 224, coin types were released showing the temple of Jupiter Ultor.[55] The following year (according to Carson) the IOVI VLTORI type with the statue of Jupiter Victor was struck.[56] The temple type (*RIC* IV.2 Severus Alexander 146) was completely absent from the hoard analysis, suggesting that it was a very small issue (Table 1). It may have been struck to mark the completion of the conversion of the *Elagabalium*. Perhaps the rededication of a temple in Rome had little visual significance outside the capital. Small as the issue was, the very act of striking the design was an important means of marking the transformation of urban space. By contrast, the more general issue with the image of Jupiter Victor and the legend IOVI VLTORI (*RIC* IV.2 Severus Alexander 143–144) has a stronger presence in hoards (Table 1). The type amounted to about 23% in the hoards of the emperor's *denarii* struck in AD 225. Considering the widespread circulation of *denarii* in this period (particularly their presence among frontier troops) a more general means of communicating the religious transformation of the empire may have been intentionally employed. The statue type of Jupiter Victor would have been widely

55. *RIC* IV.2 Severus Alexander 146, 412, 413.
56. *RIC* IV.2 Severus Alexander 142–145 (= *BMC* VI Severus Alexander 232–238, Issue 5).

Figure 6. Denarius of Severus Alexander (Gorny & Mosch Giessener Münzhandlung Auction 156, 5 March 2007, lot 2245; *RIC* IV.2 Severus Alexander 200.)

recognized throughout the empire and for the literate the legend was a powerful statement of Severus Alexander's religious intent.

## Jupiter Conservator (AD 230/1?)

In AD 230, news reached Rome of a Persian invasion. The decision to issue coinage with the image of Jupiter at this juncture (AD 230-231), after a gap of six years, is telling. Jupiter evidently formed part of the ideology of Severus Alexander before he left for the Persian War. The god once again appears as *Conservator*, in the style discussed above and with a new variant, depicting the emperor in the company of the god (Figure 6).[57] The epithet of Jupiter here probably has reference to the preservation of the emperor in the upcoming war, though it could also be connected with the *Fides Militum* series discussed below.

## Jupiter Conservator and the Fides of the Roman Army (AD 231)

In AD 231 a series of coins and medallions were struck with the legend FIDES MILITVM, showing the emperor in the company of Jupiter.[58] A bronze medallion was also struck with the legend IOVI CONSERVATORI, showing Severus Alexander, Jupiter and a soldier holding two standards.[59] Jupiter Conservator thus seems to have had a particular association with the military. This series and the one immediately above may have been thematically connected. Jupiter Conservator had been associated with military activity under Septimius Severus, Caracalla, and Elagabalus.[60] The *conservator* types released at the beginning of Severus Alexander's reign may also have had this implication: according to literary evidence the young

57. *RIC* IV.2 Severus Alexander 197–200 (*aureii* and *denarii*), 558–559 (*sestertii*).

58. *RIC* IV.2 Severus Alexander *195* (denarius*), 555–556* (sestertius and *as* respectively), *662 (dupondius* and *as); BMC* VI Severus Alexander 734–736 *(Aes* Medallion*).*

59. *BMC* VI Severus Alexander 736* (*Aes* Medallion); *Gnecchi* II no. 5 (*Aes* Medallion).

60. *RIC* IV.1 Septimius Severus 130 has the legend IOVI CONSERVATORI with the image of Jupiter Victor and was struck in the aftermath of Severus' Parthian Victory in AD 198. *RIC* IV.1 Caracalla 301, *RIC* IV.2 Elagabalus 90 and 91 connect this particular aspect of Jupiter with the military in a more direct manner. On these types the legend IOVI CONSERVATORI is accompanied by an image showing Jupiter with two standards.

emperor was saved from Elagabalus by the Roman army.[61] The emphasis on the loyalty of the army was particularly poignant in AD 231: Dio mentions that many of the troops in the east had revolted and were joining the invading Persians.[62]

The denarius of this type (*RIC* 195) had only two occurrences in the hoard analysis, both in the Niederaschau hoard. Again the mere act of designing and striking the image of Jupiter protecting the emperor and the *fides* of the Roman may have been where the significance of the issue lay.

## Jupiter Stator (AD 231)

In AD 231, a type was struck for Severus Alexander showing Jupiter Stator on the reverse.[63] The epithet Stator had previously appeared on the coinage of Antoninus Pius but the god had a connection with Rome stretching back to its foundations.[64] According to tradition, a temple was vowed to Jupiter Stator by Romulus at a critical moment in the battle against the Sabines.[65] The Roman army was losing the encounter and had begun to flee, but returned under the auspices of Jupiter Stator ("stayer"). This particular temple was never constructed, but M. Atilius Regulus later made a similar vow that he fulfilled in the war against the Samnites.[66] For this reason Jupiter Stator has been interpreted as the god who stays panic in battle, who "remains" on the battlefield.

The appearance of Jupiter Stator on the coinage of Antoninus Pius has been connected with his military activities in Britain in AD 142, but the coin is better seen as part of the emperor's celebration of the significant events in the history of Rome. Many of Pius' types between AD 140–144 refer to myths and legends from Rome's early history: Aeneas, Anchises, Rhea Silvia, and the she-wolf and twins, for example.[67] The Jupiter Stator type should be viewed within this context, particularly since Romulus' intended temple and Regulus' actual building had become conflated in the Roman mind.[68]

Considering the origins of Jupiter Stator and his appearance under the religiously conservative Antoninus Pius, the god's presence on the coinage of Severus Alexander at this juncture is significant. The type alludes to the religious restoration and traditionalism of the emperor through a connection with Romulus, while

---

61. Dio 80.19.2ff; Hdn 5.8.1ff.
62. Dio 80.4.1–2.
63. *RIC* IV.2 Severus Alexander 773, 927.
64. *RIC* III Antoninus Pius 72, 607, 773, 927.
65. Livy 1.12.3–6; Ov. *Fast.* 6.794.
66. Livy 10.36.11, 10.37.15.
67. Toynbee (1925: 170–173).
68. Mattingly and Sydenham (1930: 6). For the conflation between the two temples see Cic. *Cat.* 1.13.33.

at the same time making reference to the upcoming military campaign. Romulus featured on several of Alexander's coin types, and on one particular issue the association between Rome's founder and Alexander is made explicit. The image of Romulus carrying the *spoila* is combined with the legend VIRTVS AVG.[69] The viewer is uncertain whether the image is that of Romulus or of the emperor; the ambiguity casts Alexander as a founder of Rome and directly compares his *Virtus* to that of Romulus.[70] The Jupiter Stator type only appears on a single denarius (Figure 7), and had a small presence in the hoard analysis.[71]

Also struck in this period (AD 228–231) was another IOVI VLTORI issue.[72] This may have been a "commemorative" like that postulated by Hill for the earlier Severans.[73] It is more likely, however, that Jupiter "the Avenger" was employed within the context of the upcoming war. Like Jupiter Stator, Jupiter Ultor was used to connect the religious conservatism of the emperor with the military campaign: Stator and Ultor conveniently encapsulated Alexander's religious traditionalism while simultaneously referring to military ideology. This Ultor issue was found in a single hoard in southeast Turkey.

### Jupiter Propugnator (AD 231–232)

The image of Jupiter hurling a thunderbolt with the epithet IOVI PROPVGNATOR(I) appeared on Alexander's coinage from AD 231–232 (Figure 8).[74] This epithet has clear military overtones and is probably connected to Severus' Persian campaign. A variant of this type (*RIC* 238 ) shows Jupiter holding an eagle and thunderbolt, again indicating that the images on coins at this period did not always strictly reflect cult statues (Figure 9). The type shows a wide distribution, though there are certain regional variations (Table 1).

---

69. Romulus: *RIC* IV.2 Severus Alexander 85–86, 96–97, 103–104. Romulus with the legend VIRTVS AVG: *RIC* IV.2 Severus Alexander 223–225, 625–626.

70. Indeed, the ambiguity between the two images meant that Cohen, and consequently *RIC*, lists two different coin types: Romulus, bareheaded, walking r., carrying spear and trophy (*RIC* IV.2 Severus Alexander 223–224, 625–626) and the emperor in military dress, walking r., carrying spear and trophy (*RIC* IV.2 Severus Alexander 225). Inspection of the coins concerned suggests that this is the same image, a conclusion also reached by Carson, who described the type (and indeed all the 'Romulus' types) as 'Severus Alexander as Romulus' (*BMC* VI Severus Alexander 481, 482).

71. *RIC* IV.2 Severus Alexander 202.

72. *RIC* IV.2 Severus Alexander 203.

73. Hill (1964: 173).

74. AD 231: *RIC* IV.2 Severus Alexander 234–236, 240, 241, 628–630. AD 232: *RIC* IV.2 Severus Alexander 237–239, 631–634. The division is based on the chronology of Carson, who places the type in Issue 14 (AD 231) and Issue 15 (AD 232) in the *BMC* catalogue.

Figure 7. Denarius of Severus Alexander (Auktionhaus H.D. Rauch GmbH Mail Bid Sale 10, 2 March 2006, 603; *RIC* IV.2 Severus Alexander 202)

Figure 8. Denarius of Severus Alexander (Auktionhaus H.D. Rauch GmbH Mail Bid Sale 11, 12 September 2006, lot 995; *RIC* IV.2 Severus Alexander 235)

Figure 9. Denarius of Severus Alexander (Numismatica Ars Classica Auction 39, 16 May 2007, lot 145; *RIC* IV.2 Severus Alexander 238)

## CONCLUSIONS

It is clear that Severus Alexander used Jupiter as a patron deity throughout his reign, clearly distancing himself from his predecessor. It is also evident that the Roman mint utilized the different epithets of the god to express divine assistance in different contexts. In this the mint was following an earlier tradition that had developed under Commodus, where the close association between the emperor and Jupiter came to be expressed in a distinct and creative way. The rededication of the *Elagabalium* into a temple to Jupiter Ultor would have only underlined the connection between emperor and god.

Table 2. Jupiter on the Coinage of the Severan Emperors (to nearest whole per cent)

| Emperor | Zone A | | | Zone B | | | Zone C | | | Zone D | | | Zone E | | | Total | | |
|---|---|---|---|---|---|---|---|---|---|---|---|---|---|---|---|---|---|---|
| | J | T | % | J | T | % | J | T | % | J | T | % | J | T | % | J | T | % |
| Septimius Severus | 152 | 4408 | 3% | 98 | 1791 | 5% | 14 | 223 | 6% | 395 | 8752 | 5% | 23 | 576 | 4% | 682 | 15750 | 4% |
| Caracalla (sole reign) | 83 | 815 | 10% | 129 | 1380 | 9% | 10 | 66 | 15% | 386 | 2942 | 13% | 28 | 265 | 11% | 636 | 5468 | 12% |
| Elagabalus | 14 | 1072 | 1% | 49 | 2178 | 2% | 2 | 81 | 2% | 88 | 5184 | 2% | 3 | 67 | 4% | 156 | 8582 | 2% |
| Severus Alexander | 111 | 665 | 17% | 416 | 2895 | 14% | 15 | 95 | 16% | 1017 | 8422 | 12% | 16 | 116 | 14% | 1575 | 12193 | 13% |

J = Total coins displaying the image of Jupiter.
T = Total number of coins struck in the emperor's name.

The focus of Severus Alexander on the cult of Jupiter can be quantified through a comparison with the earlier Severan dynasty (Table 2). Using the same hoard evidence to examine the Jupiter types of Alexander's predecessors reveals startling results that quantifies the large role Jupiter played in the emperor's rule. Under Septimius types of Jupiter constituted approximately 4% of silver types struck in the emperor's name. During the sole rule of Caracalla, Jupiter rose to occupy 13% of the emperor's types, in keeping with the largely divine emphasis of Caracalla's coinage. A real decline is seen under Elagabalus, with Jupiter types falling to a mere 2%. It is apparent that the types released by the Roman mint, and their respective quantities, reflected the religious emphases of a particular emperor. During the reign of Severus Alexander Jupiter types rise to approximately 13% of the emperor's total coinage. We can thus identify the religious polarity between Elagabalus and Severus Alexander through numismatics. For the population of the Roman Empire, the differing religious policy of these emperors was reflected in their coinage; the overall impression gained from each emperor's coinage would have resulted in contrasting public images. The comparison between the two rulers (exaggeratedly) presented by the *Historia Augusta* is also reflected in the numismatic record.

## HOARDS

**Britain:**

Bristol, (AD 208, 1,480 coins)
  Mattingly, H., and B. W. Pearce. 1938. The Bristol hoard of denarii, 1937. *Numismatic Chronicle* 18: 85–98.

Muswell Hill, London (AD 210, 654 coins)
  Mattingly, H. 1929. Muswell Hill. *Numismatic Chronicle* 9: 315–319.

Darfield II, South Yorkshire (AD 215, 500 coins)
  Corder, P. 1948. A second hoard of Roman denarii from Darfield. *Numismatic Chronicle* 8: 78–80.

Edston, Peebles-Shire, Scotland (AD 222, 290 coins)
  Holmes, N., and F. Hunter. 1997. Edston, Peebles-Shire. *Coin Hoards from Roman Britain* 10: 149–168.

Shapwick Villa, Somerset (AD 224, 9,238 coins)
  Abdy, R., and S. Minnitt. 2002. Shapwick Villa. *Coin Hoards from Roman Britain* 11: 169–233.

Denbighshire, Wales (AD 226, 507 coins)
  Mattingly, H. 1923. Find of Roman denarii in Denbighshire. *Numismatic Chronicle* 3: 152–155.

St. Mary Cray, Bromley (AD 228, 376 coins)
  Robertson, A. S. 1935. The St. Mary Cray hoard. *Numismatic Chronicle* 15: 62–66.

East England (AD 230, 3,169 coins)
  Evans, J. 1898. A hoard of Roman coins. *Numismatic Chronicle* 18: 126–184.

Falkirk, Scotland (AD 230, 1,925 coins)
  MacDonald, G. 1934. A hoard of Roman denarii from Scotland. *Numismatic Chronicle* 14: 1–30.

Cambridge (AD 248, 193 coins)
  Boyd, W. C. 1897. A find of Roman denarii near Cambridge. *Numismatic Chronicle* 17: 119–126.

Darfield, South Yorkshire (AD 250, 481 coins)
  Walker, J. 1946. The Darfield hoard of Roman denarii. *Numismatic Chronicle* 6: 147–150.

Brickendonbury, Hertfordshire (AD 250, 430 coins)
  Evans, J. 1896. Roman coins found at Brickendonbury, Hertford. *Numismatic Chronicle* 16: 191–208.

Stevenage, Hertfordshire (AD 263, 387 coins)
  Bland, R. 1988. Stevenage, Hertfordshire. In *The Normanby hoard and other Roman coin hoards*, CHRB 8, R. Bland and A. Burnett, eds., 43–71. London.

Caistor by Yarmouth, Norfolk (c.AD 270, 847 coins)
  Jenkins, G. K. 1947. The Caister by Yarmouth Hoard. *Numismatic Chronicle* 7: 175–179.

**France:**

Aïn, Rhône-Alpes (AD 215, 446 coins)
  Salama, P. 2001/2002. Le trésor de deniers d'Aïn Témouchent et ses "satellites" dans l'Afrique romaine. *TM* 20: 185–222.

Viuz-Faverges (AD 252, 2,306 coins)
  Pflaum, H. G. 1981. Le Trésor de Viuz-Faverges. *Trésors Monétaires* 3: 33–76.

Nanterre, Paris (AD 254, 1,968 coins)
  Gentilhomme, P. L. 1947. La Trouvaille de Nanterre. *Revue Numismatique* 9: 15–114.

Eauze, Gers (AD 261, 28,003 coins)
  Schaad, D., P. Agrinier, *et al.* 1992. *Le Trésor d'Eauze.* Toulouse.

**Belgium:**

Elligines-Sainte-Anne (AD 240, 276 coins)
Lallemand, J. 1968. Le trésor d'Elliginies-Sainte-Anne: deniers de Marc-Auréle à Gordien III. *Revue Belge de Numismatique* 114: 138–168.

Clavier, Liège (AD 255, 1,680 coins)
Lallemand, J. 1969. Le trésor de Clavier III: deniers et antoniniens de Commode à Valérien-Gallien. *Revue Belge de Numismatique* 115: 263–331.

**Italy:**

Vicenza, Veneto (AD 235, 110 coins)
No. 45/3(1) in *Ritrovamenti Monetali de età Romana nel Veneto* IV.1.

Via Tritone, Rome (AD 244, 828 coins)
Cesano, L. 1925. Nuovi Ripostigli di Denari di Argento dell'Impero Romano. *Atti e Memorie dell'Istituto Italiano di Numismatica* 5: 57–72.

**Germany:**

Welzheim, Baden-Württemburg, (AD 225, 652 coins)
No. 4,596 in *Die Fundmünzen der römischen Zeit in Deutschland* II.4.

Baden-Baden, Baden-Württemburg (AD 228, 611 coins)
No. 2,196 in *Die Fundmünzen der römischen Zeit in Deutschland* II.2.

Mainz, Rhineland (AD 228, 186 coins)
No. 1,153 in *Die Fundmünzen der römischen Zeit in Deutschland* IV.1.

Eining, Bayern (AD 235, 73 coins)
No. 2,034 in *Die Fundmünzen der römischen Zeit in Deutschland* I.2.

Kirchmatting, Bayern (AD 235, 1318 coins)
No. 2,116 in *Die Fundmünzen der römischen Zeit in Deutschland* I.2.

Kempten Lindenberg III (AD 235, 640 coins)
No. 7,186 in *Die Fundmünzen der römischen Zeit in Deutschland* I.7.

Pfünz (AD 235, 94 coins)
No. 5,042 in *Die Fundmünzen der römischen Zeit in Deutschland* I.5.

Wiggensbach, Bavaria (AD 235, 401 coins)
No. 7,199 in *Die Fundmünzen der römischen Zeit in Deutschland* I.7.

Köln (AD 238, 4,169 coins)
No. 1,004 3a-b in *Die Fundmünzen der römischen Zeit in Deutschland* VI.1.1.

Niederaschau, Bayern (AD238, 766 coins)
No. 1,229 in *Die Fundmünzen der römischen Zeit in Deutschland* I.1.

Wiesbach, Rhineland-Palatinate (AD 254, 402 coins)
No. 1,082 in *Die Fundmünzen der römischen Zeit in Deutschland* III.

Linsberg (AD 238, 286 coins)
Dembski, G. 2007. Ein römischer Münzschatzfund aus Linsberg, Gem. Erlach, BH wieder Neustadt. *Numismatische Zeitschrift* 115: 33–55.

Gunzenhausen, Bavaria (AD 244, 510 coins)
No. 5,057 in *Die Fundmünzen der römischen Zeit in Deutschland* I.5.

**Romania:**

Ghirişa, Beltiug (AD 198, 151 coins)
No. 141 in Depeyrot, G., and D. Moisil. 2008. *Les Trésors de Deniers de Trajan à Balbin en Roumanie.* Wetteren.

Frânceşti, Vâlcea (AD 219, 1,365 coins)
Depeyrot, G., and D. Moisil. 2004. *The Trésor Frânceşti (Roumanie).* Wetteren.

Munteneşti, Valsui (AD 228, 742 coins)
No. 183 in Depeyrot, G., and D. Moisil. 2008. *Les Trésors de Deniers de Trajan à Balbin en Roumanie.* Wetteren.

Barza, (AD 235, 1,337 coins)
No. 174 in Depeyrot, G., and D. Moisil. 2008. *Les Trésors de Deniers de Trajan à Balbin en Roumanie.* Wetteren.

Taga (AD 239, 962 coins)
Protase, D., and I. H. Crişan. 1968. Tezaurul de Monede Imperiale Romane de la Ţaga. *Studii şi Cercetări de Numismatică* 4: 139–173.

**Hungary:**

Kecel, Bács-Kiskun (AD 215, 255 coins)
Katalin, B. S. 1986. A keceli éremlelet. *Cumania* 9: 27–74.

Ercsi, Fejér (AD 228, 386 coins)
Soprini, S. 1964. Az ercsi éremlelet. *Numizmatikai közlöny* 62/63: 9–17.

Börgöndi, Székesfehérvár (AD 235, 587 coins)
Aladár, R. 1936. A börgöndi éremlelet. *Numizmatikai közlöny* 34/35: 24–27.

**Slovenia:**

Leskovec (AD 236, 122 coins)
No. 408 in *Die Fundmünzen der römischen Zeit in Slowenien* II.

Postojna, Carniola (AD 238, 339 coins)
No. 91.2 in *Die Fundmünzen der römischen Zeit in Slowenien* I.

Gračič, Zreče (AD 253, 431 coins)
No. 176 in *Die Fundmünzen der römischen Zeit in Slowenien* III.

**Bulgaria:**

Nicolaévo (AD 249, 936 coins)
Seure, G. 1923. Trésors de Monnaies Antiques en Bulgarie III: Le Trésor de Nicolaévo. *Revue Numismatique* 26: 111–153.

Rustschuk (AD 249, 1,602 coins)
Muschmow, N. A. 1918. Münzfunde aus Bulgarien. *Numismatische Zeitschrift* 11: 43–51.

Reka-Devnia, Devnya (AD 251, 81,096 coins)
Mouchmov, N. A. 1934. *Le Trésor Numismatique de Réka-Devnia (Marcianopolis)*. Sofia.

Plevna (AD 259, 3,296 coins)
Mattingly, H., and F. S. Salisbury. 1924. A find of Roman coins from Plevna in Bulgaria. *Numismatic Chronicle* 4: 210–238.

**Macedonia:**

Usküb (Skopje) (AD 249, 1,022 coins)
Kubitschek, W. 1908. Ein Denarfund aus der Gegend von Usküb. *Numismatische Zeitschrift* 41: 37–47.

**Serbia:**

Singidunum, Belgrade (AD 254, 2,445 coins)
Kondic, V. 1969. *The Singinudum hoard of denarii and antoniniani (Septimius Severus-Valerian)*. Belgrade.

**Turkey:**

South East Turkey (AD 251, 1,911 coins)
Bendall, S. 1966. An eastern hoard of Roman imperial silver. *Numismatic Chronicle* 6: 165–170.

Haydere, Aydin (AD 264, 2,330 coins)
    Ashton, R. 1991. The Haydere hoard and other hoards of the mid-third cen-
    tury from Turkey. In *Recent Turkish coin hoards and numismatic studies*, C.
    S. Lightfoot, ed., 91–180. Oxford.

## Syria:

Syria (AD 212, 261 coins)
    Cesano, L. 1925. Nuovi Ripostigli di Denari di Argento dell'Impero Roma-
    no. *Atti e Memorie dell'Istituto Italiano di Numismatica* 5: 57–72.

Dura Europos III and IV (AD 218, 402 coins)
    Bellinger, A. R. 1949. *The excavations at Dura Europos Volume 6: The coins.*
    New Haven.

## REFERENCES

Angeli, M. G. B. 1971. A proposito di un'epigrafe da Ciunia di recente riedita. *Epi-
    grafica* 33: 150–152.
Bergmann, M. 1998. *Die Strahlen der Herrscher. Theomorphes Herrscherbild und
    politische Symbolik im Hellenismus und in der römischen Kaiserzeit.* Mainz: P.
    von Zabern.
Bigot, P. 1911. Le Temple de Jupiter Ultor et la Vigne Barberini. *Bullettino della
    Commissione Archeologica Comunale di Roma* 39: 80–85.
Bland, R. F., Burnett, A. M., et al. 1987. The mints of Pescennius Niger in the light
    of some new aurei. *Numismatic Chronicle* 147: 65–83.
Broise, H., and Thébert, Y. 1999. Élagabal et le Complexe Religieux de la Vigna
    Barberini. *Mélanges de l'École Française de Rome* 3: 729–747.
Buttrey, T. V. 1972. A hoard of Sestertii from Bordeaux and the problem of bronze
    circulation in the third century A.D. *American Numismatic Society Museum
    Notes* 18: 33–58.
Carradice, I. 1983. *Coinage and finances in the reign of Domitian.* Oxford: B.A.R.
———. 1998. Towards a new introduction to the Flavian coinage. In *Modus Ope-
    randi. Essays in honour of Geoffrey Rickman*, M. Austin, J. Harries, and C.
    Smith, eds., 93–118. London: University of London.
Carson, R. A. G. 1983. Coin hoards and Roman coinage of the third century AD. In
    *Studies in numismatic method presented to Philip Grierson*, C. N. L. Booke, B.
    H. I. Stewart, J. G. Pollard, and T. R. Volk, eds., 65–74. Cambridge: Cambridge
    University Press.
Castagnoli, F. 1979. Su alcuni problemi topografici del Palatino. *Atti della Acca-
    demia Nazionale dei Lincei* 34: 331–347.
Cecamore, C. 1999. *Faustinae Aedemque Decernerent (SHA, Marcus, 26).* Les frag-
    ments 69–70 de la *Forma Urbis* et la Première dédicace du temple de la Vigna
    Barberini. *Mélanges de l'École Française de Rome* 111.1: 311–349.

Chausson, F. 1995. *Vel Iovi Vel Soli:* Quatre études autour de la Vigna Barberini (191–354). *Mélanges de l'École Française de Rome* 107: 661–765.

Christiansen, E. 1988. *The Roman coins of Alexandria: quantitative studies: Nero, Trajan, Septimius Severus.* Aarhus: Aarhus University of Press.

Coarelli, F. 1987. La situazione edilizia di Roma sotto Severo Alessandro. In *L'Urbs. Espace urbain et Histoire (1er siècle av. J.-C.- IIIe siècle ap. J.-C.)* eds., 429–456. Rome: École Française Rome.

Fears, J. R. 1981. The cult of Jupiter and Roman imperial ideology. *Aufstieg und Niedergang der römischen Welt VI.1 (?):* 3–141.

Grenier, J. C., and Coarelli, F. 1986. *(Porticus) Adonaea, Aedes Heliogabli, Aedes Iovis Ultoris.* La Tomba di Antinoo? *Mélanges de l'École Française de Rome* 98.1: 230–253.

Griffin, M. T. 1984. *Nero. The end of a dynasty.* London: Batsford.

Harris, W. V. 1989. *Ancient literacy.* Cambridge, Massachusetts: Harvard University Press.

Hekster, O. 2002. *Commodus. An emperor at the crossroads.* Amsterdam: J. C. Gieben.

Hill, P. V. 1960. Aspects of Jupiter on coins of the Rome mint, AD 65–318. *Numismatic Chronicle* 20: 113–128.

———. 1964. Notes on coinage of Septimius Severus and his family AD 193–217. *Numismatic Chronicle* 4: 169–188.

———. 1965. Some architectural types of Trajan. *Numismatic Chronicle* 5: 155–160.

———. 1982. A new gold type of Septimius Severus. *Numismatic Circular:* 159–60.

Kemmers, F. 2006. *Coins for a legion. An analysis of the coin finds from the Augustan legionary fortress and Flavian canabae legionis at Nijmegen.* Mainz: Von Zabern.

Marchiori, M. L. 2007. Art and reform in tenth-century Rome—The paintings of S. Maria in Pallara. Ph.D. diss., Queen's University.

Mattingly, H., and E. A. Sydenham. 1930. *The Roman imperial coinage III: Antoninus Pius to Commodus.* London: Spink.

Noreña, C. F. 2001. The communication of the Emperor's virtues. *Journal of Roman Studies* 91: 146–168.

Optendrenk, T. 1969. *Die Religionspolitik des Kaisers Elagabal im Spiegel der Historia Augusta.* Bonn: R. Habelt.

Rives, J. B. 2007. *Religion in the Roman empire.* Oxford: Blackwell.

Sambon, A., Canessa, C., et al. 1907. *Collections Martinetti & Nervegna, médailles grecques et romaines aes grave. (Sambon 18/11/1907).* Bologna.

Tameanko, M. 1999. *Monumental coins: buildings and structures on ancient coinage.* Iowa: Krause Publications.

Toynbee, J. 1925. Some 'programme' coin-types of Antoninus Pius. *Classical Review* 39: 170–173.

*AJN* Second Series 21 (2009) pp. 151–226
© 2009 The American Numismatic Society

# Early Byzantine Coin Circulation in the Eastern Provinces: A Comparative Statistical Approach

ANDREI GÂNDILĂ*

*Number is the ruler of forms and ideas and the cause of gods and demons*
Pythagoras (Taylor 1818: 78)

This paper addresses two major issues in the study of early Byzantine coinage. First, the statistical validity of large public collections of Byzantine copper coins is established as a reliable indicator of coin production. Second, based on the rhythm of coin output inferred from the evidence of the public collections, a comparison is attempted between coin finds in the three major geographical areas of the Eastern Empire: the Balkans, Anatolia, and Syria-Palestine. This comparative analysis reveals a great deal of regional variation, but also common patterns in coin circulation.

As early as the first half of the nineteenth century antiquarians and collectors became interested in developing means of organizing and systematizing Byzantine coin series. The chief concern was to create "suites monétaires," an attempt to gather all the known coin types issued by the Byzantine state. The pioneering works of de Saulcy and Sabatier in the nineteenth century had been an important starting ground for the subsequent catalogue of the collection published by Count Tolstoi between 1908 and 1911.[1] However, the standard work for more than fifty years

---

* andrei.gandila@ufl.edu. University of Florida, History Department.

1. de Saulcy (1836); Soleirol (1853); Sabatier (1862); Tolstoi (1912–1914). Equally important are Mionnet's second volume of *De la rareté et prix des médailles romaines* (1827), the second part of Christian Thomsen's collection, Erslev (1873), as well as the contribution to the classification of coins of Justinian I by Friedländer and Pinder (1843).

would become the catalogue of Byzantine coins in the British Museum. What made it atypical for this early period was the decision to publish an entire collection, whose purpose would be twofold: to fill the gaps in the Byzantine coin series and to provide scientific access to an entire collection, including duplicates.[2]

The breakthrough made after the publication of the major collection at Dumbarton Oaks, assembled through mass purchases, opened a new era in terms of the methodology behind the study of Byzantine coinage.[3] Alfred Bellinger and especially Philip Grierson embarked on the task of reassessing many of the old datings and attributions in what became a seminal work for our understanding of early Byzantine coinage (hereafter EBC). Cécile Morrisson went a step further by cataloguing the old and important collection of the Bibliothèque Nationale in Paris, enriched with the donations of leading scholar-collectors such as Gustave Schlumberger. Equally significant have been the major private collections of Byzantine copper coins made available to the scientific world, such as those of Rodolfo Ratto and George Bates.[4] Creating a corpus of all known Byzantine coin finds, as the latter has pleaded for in the introduction to his catalogue, might prove to be an illusory endeavor if we take into account the large number of coins currently on the market. Nonetheless, the number of coins in national or local museums from the Balkans, Turkey or the Middle East has greatly increased in the past fifty years due to extensive archaeological research, often performed by international teams of scholars at Apamea, Sardis, Berytus and Caesarea Maritima to name a few of the most important. In addition, the collections assembled by museums and universities in Western Europe contribute to the wealth of EBC available for study.[5] The stupendous task of assembling all known Byzantine coin types was attempted by Wolfgang Hahn in his series *Moneta Imperii Byzantini*.[6] However, few initiatives have been taken towards a statistical understanding of the monetary circulation at the scale of the entire empire,[7] although the use of quantitative tools was promoted and employed for assessing local provincial patterns in coin circulation.[8]

The use of statistical tools in Byzantine numismatics is largely a post-war development. The growing interest in elaborate means of quantification lies both

2. Wroth (1908).

3. Bellinger and Grierson (1966–1968).

4. Ratto (1930); Bates (1981).

5. Most important are the collection of the Hunter Coin Cabinet in Glasgow (Bateson and Campbell 1998), the collection Köhler-Osbahr from the Duisburg Museum (Althoff 1998–1999), the collection of the University of Göttingen (Sommer 2003), and the collection of the Bottacin Museum in Padova (Callegher 2000).

6. Hahn (1973–1981).

7. Morrisson (2002).

8. Metcalf (1964); Pradwic-Golemberski and Metcalf (1963); Pottier (1983); Morrisson and Ivanišević (2006); Noeske (2000).

in the need for a more complex method of analyzing the increasing number of coins and in the introduction of computer-based programs which facilitated such an approach. Mathematical tools have always been employed in numismatics; by necessity, coins needed to be counted and classified based on chronological and typological criteria, but no attempt was made to analyze them statistically.[9] D. M. Metcalf has been a pioneer in this respect.[10] His study of Byzantine coins in Sirmia and Slavonia represents the first elaborate attempt to use statistics in order to understand the EBC circulation in that region. It also represented an opportunity to make use of comparative statistics, which permitted a number of generalizations at the scale of the Eastern Empire, based on the evidence available from the excavations at Corinth, Athens, Antioch, and Sardis.[11] Starting from the early 1980s one can observe an explosion of studies employing more or less sophisticated statistical tools. The main impetus had been provided by the organization of a Round Table dedicated to the use of statistics in numismatics, in which reputed numismatists and professional statisticians collaborated for a better implementation of statistics in numismatic research.[12]

Overtime, the work diversified and the aims turned more ambitious, to analyses of metrology and calculations of mint output. Again, D. M. Metcalf should be mentioned for his role as a pioneer. His work on particular early Byzantine issues, the Anastasian small module coins and the Justinianic coinage from Thessalonica, represent early attempts to determine Byzantine mint output.[13] However, calculations of mint output based on die studies have not moved too far for the Byzantine series. Aside from the work of D. M. Metcalf, calculations have been attempted by W. E. Metcalf and C. Morrisson for small issues such as the joint reign *solidi* of Justin I and Justinian I and gold issues of Carthage, respectively.[14] The sheer size of the Byzantine base coinage has prohibited scholars from attempting any such calculations and the situation will probably remain the same in the foreseeable future. Consequently, students in the field of Byzantine numismatics have been less engaged in the lively debate of the last two decades centered on the question of

9. Bell (1916); Edwards (1933); Mosser (1935); Bellinger (1938); Waage (1952); Thompson (1954).

10. For an early methodological essay see Metcalf (1958).

11. Metcalf (1960).

12. Carcassone and Hackens, eds., (1981). For the statistical method see also Carcassone and Guey (1978); Carcassone (1987).

13. Metcalf (1969); Metcalf (1976).

14. Metcalf (1988); Morrisson (1981); Morrisson (1988). Although removed from the chronological focus of this article, the comprehensive die-study done by Füeg (1991) on the eighth century gold issues remains seminal for a general understanding of Byzantine gold coinage even if extrapolations can be problematic.

mint output.[15] Steps have been taken, however, to understand the metrology of the multi-denominational system of Byzantine coinage. The publication of the large collections of Dumbarton Oaks and Paris provided the opportunity for metrological calculations based on large samples. In addition, Henri Pottier contributed a seminal book for the metrological study of Byzantine coinage but also for the monetary circulation in Syria, based on comparative statistics.[16]

In the past two decades, a number of statistic methods in Byzantine numismatics have been used in studies dealing with a substantial sample of coins, either hoards or stray finds. Coin hoards from the Balkans, Anatolia, and the Middle East were processed mainly using a statistical apparatus. One should mention here a substantial article by Florin Curta on hoards from Eastern Europe with a thick appendix of statistical results, the monumental trilogy of Hans-Christoph Noeske on Byzantine coin circulation in Egypt and the Near Eastern provinces, of which the last volume comprises a few dozen graphs derived from statistical calculations, and the collaborative work coordinated by C. Morrisson, V. Popović, and V. Ivanišević on the coin hoards found in the Balkans and in Anatolia.[17] At the same time, studies of stray and single finds from major archaeological sites have included statistical analyses of recent finds and also previously published material.[18]

## I. The Statistical Relevance of Museum Collections

The purpose of this study is twofold: first, it attempts to identify general fluctuations in the production of base-metal coinage, based on the evidence of the major public collections, and secondly, it draws a series of comparisons between coin finds in the major geographical units of the Eastern Empire. This study deals exclusively with copper coins issued in the major Eastern mints: Constantinople, Thessalonica, Nicomedia, Cyzicus, and Antioch. The reasons behind this decision are both technical and practical; most of the EBC finds originate in the eastern part of the empire, from the Danube to the Eastern Mediterranean provinces, while the monetary system itself was not standardized throughout the Empire. Egypt was largely self-sufficient, Italy and the African mint at Carthage had different rhythms of coin production than the Eastern mints, and the ratio between gold and copper seems to have had regional particularities.[19] Therefore, in order to insure the accuracy of statistical parameters and ultimately of the historical conclusions drawn

---

15. Esty (1986); Buttrey (1993, 1994, and 1997); Duncan-Jones (1994) with an extensive review by W. E. Metcalf (1995); Callataÿ (1995).

16. Pottier (1983). See more recently Pottier (2004).

17. Curta (1996); Noeske (2000); Morrisson et al. (2006).

18. Marot (1998); Sheedy (2001); Butcher (2003); Evans (2006); Gândilă (2008).

19. Hahn (1973–1981).

from this material, Western provinces, including North Africa were left out. In quantitative terms, this means working with more than 10,000 bronze coins located in five major collections (hereafter 'museum collections')[20] and another c. 8,000 from the major urban centers of the Eastern Empire .

The single finds resulting from systematic archaeological research are unevenly distributed over the geographical area under consideration. The material from the Balkans is by far the most abundant, followed by the Near East, where numerous Syro-Palestinian sites have been excavated. Christopher Lightfoot has sketched the current state of the Byzantine research in Anatolia and drew attention to the lack of interest for Byzantine archaeological layers in favor of the presumably more sophisticated classical period.[21] Recent research by Zeliha Demirel Gökalp has shown that the Turkish archaeological museums preserve a wealth of EBC found in Anatolia, which awaits publication.[22] Although a few tentative steps have been taken towards a broad understanding of the coin circulation in the Balkans and the Middle East,[23] little has been done with respect to gathering the numismatic material for an in-depth comparative analysis, partly because of the still insufficient evidence. The case of the border province of Scythia is a unique situation, given that Romanian numismatists have constantly published comprehensive catalogues of recent finds and museum collections,[24] bringing the total number of EBC finds to a dazzling figure of more than 3,000 specimens.

20. The collections under consideration are Dumbarton Oaks and the Whittemore collection (DOC); Bibliothèque Nationale in Paris (BNP); the collection of the British Museum (BMC); the collection Köhler-Osbahr in Duisburg (KOD); and the vast collection of the American Numismatic Society (ANS), still unpublished. They were chosen based on size and on the preponderance of copper issues, including numerous duplicates. The collections of Tolstoi and Ratto are not included in the statistical analysis, as the former published a type catalogue and the latter a sale catalogue and therefore neither was interested in including duplicates. Even if they remain outside the scope of this study, such collections retain a statistical significance for the understanding of mint output by looking at the coin types they were unable to find in their desire to assemble the entire Byzantine coin series.

21. Lightfoot (2002).

22. I wish to express my gratitude to Zeliha Demirel Gökalp for allowing me to consult her unpublished PhD dissertation and two other unpublished catalogues of the Byzantine coins from the Malatya and Bolu museums.

23. Morrisson (1989a); Morrisson (1998); Walmsley (1999); Gândilă, (2008).

24. See the chronicles of the recent finds compiled by B. Mitrea and Gh.Poenaru Bordea from *Dacia*, "Découvertes de monnaies antiques et byzantines en Roumanie" along with the ones regularly published in *Pontica* by Gh. Papuc, R. Ocheşeanu, G. Custurea, A. Vertan and G. Talmaţchi under the title "Cronica descoperirilor monetare din Dobrogea." While the coins published in the Romanian journals were mainly single finds resulting from archaeological research, in Bulgaria such articles are devoted exclusively to hoards, see T. Gerasimov's series "Kolektivni nahodki na moneti" from *Izvestiia na Arkheologicheskiia Institut*.

The relevance of site finds has been a debated issue. Philip Grierson has argued that the structure of site finds tends to favor the smaller coins because they were easily lost and not retrieved and thus they cannot offer a completely reliable image of their circulation.[25] What seemed acceptable at the time when Grierson was suggesting such an interpretation of site finds is no longer tenable in light of the material coming from the Balkans, Anatolia and the Near East. His conclusions were chiefly based on the major centers of the early Byzantine Empire, Corinth, Athens, Sardis, Antioch, and Constantinople where excavations had yielded a large number of small denominations. The idea that small coins were more easily lost due to their size seemed perfectly reasonable both because of the structure of finds and a sort of natural logic suggesting that the smaller the coin (and the lesser the value) the higher the probability of it being lost.[26] This, however, does not help to explain why more than 80 percent of the coins coming from archaeological excavations in the Balkans and some Anatolian and Near Eastern sites are *folles* and *½-folles*.[27] The argument that excavators missed the smaller coins cannot be a valid explanation given the wealth of fourth–fifth century material recovered from the same archaeological sites, many coins being half the size of a Byzantine *pentanummium*. We must therefore accept the possibility that people were primarily losing coins based on availability, not size.

Setting a pattern of the coins in circulation might be regarded as an endeavor both daunting and risky. While assessing the mint output based on die studies may be a fruitful approach for rare specimens or gold/silver issues, it is hardly a viable course of action for the circulating base metal coinage. Even if the method was profitable it could only point to the *potential* number of issues. The real number is effectively connected to minute mechanisms of the Byzantine monetary economy, whose purpose clearly was not to use dies until worn-out, but to control the market through a regulated inflow of fresh currency, to pay the army and the administrative apparatus, and to insure the collection of taxes. The lively debate initiated during the last decades has pointed to variables in determining mint output, which ultimately compromised the value of this method as a definitive tool in assessing absolute coin production volumes.[28] The devastating criticism of T. V. Buttrey in a period when such applications were flourishing has precisely the merit of pointing to problems with this model. Although the discussion was centered on Greek and

25. Grierson (1986, 42). But see Metcalf (1969, 94), who argued that *"folles* [...] stand the same chance of being lost."

26. This interpretation held as a general applicable rule is still advocated, especially for sites in the Middle East. See, for example, Sheedy (2001, 5).

27. Gândilă (2008, 318); Sheedy (2001, 44); Bellinger (1938, 95–119); Marot (1998, 322); Demirel Gökalp (2007).

28. See n. 15.

Roman coinage, his arguments were generally applicable to any ancient coin series. The skepticism regarding figures drawn for gold and silver series turns into total despair in the case of copper issues characterized by large die-populations and high wear factors due to intensive circulation.[29] Even if we could take advantage of the fact that most of the copper coins were dated with the regnal year starting with 538, and could hypothetically determine the mint output for a certain type based on the number of surviving dies, we would still be nowhere near having a great understanding of the phenomenon of coin production. What is needed, and is unfortunately illusory, is the absolute numbers for the varieties of denominations, mints, *officinae* and dates in a given period.

The only approach capable of producing relevant statistical figures, insofar as they can be determined with our current body of knowledge, is one based on the coin sample at our disposal. The statistical representativity of museum collections first came into discussion in the 1950s when scholars were trying to make sense of the transformations that brought the once prosperous Byzantine Empire into a "Dark Age." Using numismatic material from the British Museum, Alexander Kazhdan argued that the number of bronze coins decreased dramatically towards the end of the seventh century and remained at a low level for the next two centuries.[30] George Ostrogorsky, on the other hand, using the same material from the British Museum, showed that the gold coinage, which he took to be more important than the base currency, in fact witnessed an important numerical increase during the same period. Furthermore, he introduced new data in the equation by analyzing two other major collections, those in Leningrad and Washington.[31] What is important here is not the debate *per se*, but the fact that the evidence provided by the largest collections of Byzantine coins was brought into question as a valid argument. Shortly after that, Grierson, perhaps the highest authority in Byzantine numismatics at the time, completely refuted the concept that such collections could ever project a realistic picture of the money in circulation at any given time.[32] His position, reiterated in the following decades, was based on the assumption that collectors contributing to what were to became the major public collections were driven by a general desire to gather full series of issues.[33] The numerous types of *solidi* introduced by the emperors of the house of Heraclius thus explained the abundance of seventh century gold coins in the major collections. Although he was mainly discussing gold in his attempt to respond to the claims made by Ostrogorsky, Grierson in fact drew a general conclusion regarding the

29. See also Hendy (1985, 7–8).
30. Kazhdan (1954).
31. Ostrogorsky (1959)
32. Grierson (1961, 445–446); Grierson (1967a, 323–324).
33. Grierson (1986, 38–39).

statistical representativity of public collections: "Les grandes collections, malgré le nombre considérable des pièces qu'elles possèdent, ne constituent donc pas un échantillon représentatif de la masse monétaire à un moment donné."[34] What was never taken into account, however, is the large body of sixth century material, namely copper issues, available in such collections, many of the common types being represented by dozens of duplicates. Such coins elude the parameters set by the reputed Byzantinist for the gold series. Constantina Katsari has recently made a similar argument regarding the representativity of museum collections for statistical studies. Her focus was on Roman provincial bronze coins and her conclusion was that "museum curators did not discriminate greatly against particular types of bronze provincial coins, although in the past they may have shown a preference for certain types of silver and gold coinages."[35]

The major collections included in the present analysis have the advantage of being heterogeneous with respect to geographical sources of origin. Each of them in fact reunites smaller collections gathered at different times and in different places, and it is reasonable to suppose that they cover the entire Eastern Empire, albeit perhaps unequally so. The museums have usually kept records of their purchases, visible in the catalogues' footnotes or more extensively in introductions revealing the historical background of the collection. Nevertheless, it is hard to trace back the mechanisms of gathering a particular collection.[36] It is rather a "detective's quest" and one is often faced with having to sleuth back in time as far as the age of Enlightenment. Famous collectors have been recently discussed by scholars and more information on their life and collections has been brought to light.[37] However, first hand accounts of find spots are hard to obtain even for current acquisitions given the discretion of many collectors and their providers, let alone for those almost a century old.[38]

Another methodological issue involves so-called "collector behavior" and is related to a more significant issue, namely that of establishing whether the sample of coins in various collections is representative of the total mass of coins produced in ancient times. To what extent can we safely trust the statistical results based on specimens from private collections? How much is the collectors' preference for certain specimens going to color the big picture? A few arguments presented below point to the fact that a collector's/ curator's choice, although inherently present, does not have a dramatic effect on the type of material selected for this analysis.

34. Grierson (1986, 39).
35. Katsari (2003, 52).
36. Grierson in *DOC* I, xiii–xviii.
37. Bendall (2002); Grierson (1998); Morrisson (2001).
38. Grierson (1965, vi).

This study is devoted exclusively to copper issues, which softens the effect of selectivity. By eliminating gold coins which are always more carefully selected and more rigorously arranged in a collection, we are left with a base metal series subject to a more random selection.[39] One wonders, for example, how much selectivity there could have been in the creation of the Swiss collection purchased for Dumbarton Oaks which amounted to over 10,000 coins, mostly copper. The collector did not keep a personal record of the coins, and therefore any suggestion that such a collection had a clear direction in terms of its structure is problematic.[40] The often huge number of copper coins in such collections suggests quantity and randomness as a major characteristic besides the basic desire to gather as many different types as possible.[41]

Furthermore, some collectors did not even specialized in Byzantine coinage.[42] Perhaps the best example in this regard is the Köhler-Osbahr collection from the Duisburg Museum, in which the entire Byzantine series represents less than 5 percent of the 70.000 coins collected by Dr. Köhler, which included ancient, medieval, and modern coins. The collection is particularly strong in Greek, German, and Asian coinage. Numismatics itself was just one focus of his collecting interests, as Dr. Köhler assembled a very diverse collection of jewelry and minor arts covering a huge time period, from 3000 B.C. to the modern age. Ralf Athoff, who published the catalogue of Byzantine coins, confirmed the fact that Dr. Köhler had no special interest in the Byzantine coins, whose purchase was less a process of systematic selection than a need to cover this important historical period in his huge collection.[43]

Each large collection contains an important number of duplicates. Doubtless some selection occurs on the part of museum curators. The large collection at Dumbarton Oaks, for example, was subjected to the removal of the poorly pre-

39. With few exceptions the major private collections focused on gold issues mixed with rare silver and bronze coins. Some of the outstanding collections falling under this category are the ones gathered by William Herbert Hunt (Sotheby's 1990 and 1991); Nadia Kapamadji (Boutin 1983); P. J. Donald (Baldwin's 1995); Hugh Goodacre (Christie's 1986); Anton C. R. Dreesmann (Spink 2000); and the collection sold by Bonham's in December 1980.

40. Cf. Grierson (*DOC* I, xvi).

41. O'Hara in Bonham's sale catalogue of Dec. 1980, 5, discussing an important collection of Byzantine gold and silver coins: "The collection of four hundred coins has been formed over many years on the basis of academic interest, rarity, style and chronology, rather than as so frequently happens in these days of 'investment portofolios' amassing rows of identical coins of somewhat dubious quality"

42. Many of the collectors who donated their Byzantine coins, such as E. T. Newell, de Salis, Köhler, and H. C. Lindgren had only a marginal interest in Byzantine coins.

43. I am grateful to Ralf Althoff from the Kultur- und Stadthistorischen Museum Duisburg for the valuable information provided on this important collector.

served duplicated when the collection was published, but the state of preservation itself is often governed by statistical principles. How curators define a duplicate is also important. For the purpose of this study a duplicate signifies a coin of the same denomination, date, mint, *officina* regardless of other variations pertaining to the use of different dies. Especially when large collections are involved curators may choose to define a duplicate as a coin struck with the same die(s), but this rarely occurs in the case of common coppers.

The unpublished collection of the American Numismatic Society (hereafter ANS) meets the criteria for a statistically acceptable sample. The collection numbers more than 5000 early Byzantine coppers from the Eastern mints dated between 498 and 616 and is primarily the result of donations *en masse* in the last decades.[44] In this area duplicates were never cleaned, removed, sold, or exchanged regardless of their condition, as long as they were legible. The major donations of bronze coins of this period are Lindgren (1984),[45] Milrod (1984, ex George Bates),[46] Clark (1972), Wales (1983) and Newell (1944), of which only the group belonging to E. T. Newell can be characterized as a sample selected with quality and workmanship as the main criteria, but not necessarily rarity.[47] Therefore, most coins are in mediocre condition at best and include numerous duplicates, which suggests a high degree of randomness. Most of the few purchases made by the ANS date to the early 1970s and the acquisition records point to a price range of $1–2.50 per coin.

Only Eastern mints are included in the study, leaving out the more desirable and sought-after Western mints. Sixth-to-seventh century Byzantine coppers from mints such as Constantinople, Nicomedia, Thessalonica, Cyzicus, and Antioch have been the most common and cheapest coins on the market since the nineteenth century.[48] Mass purchases of such cheap types are typical for major collectors.

44. The ANS collection is by far the largest; by comparison, the collection at Dumbarton Oaks, which is the second largest, has only c. 2800 pieces.

45. H. C. Lindgren is best known for his collection of Roman provincial coins from Asia Minor, sold at public auctions. A few hundreds of the EBC donated to the ANS have an identical green patina and similar dirt incrustations which suggest that they were part of a large hoard. The age structure of the group is typical for the large hoards found in Syria, containing numerous pre-538 issues, very few dated coins of Justinian and a closing date in the first decades of the seventh century. This group of coins was excluded from the statistical analysis of the ANS collection.

46. Bates (1981).

47. As a collector E. T. Newell is, of course, best known for his splendid collection of Greek coins, now at the ANS.

48. As early as the mid-nineteenth century Sabatier was pricing the Justinianic *follis* from the East at 2–10 francs while a *follis* from the Western mints ranged from 20 to 50 francs. The criterion is not so much style but degree of rarity and this considerable difference in

Quality is not always an issue; all collections under scrutiny have poorly preserved specimens even from the most common types. They include specimens on which details such as the regnal year, the officina, or the mint mark are no longer legible. A large number of smaller denominations, often less appealing to the collector's eye, represent an important percentage of the group, which suggests quantity not quality as a criterion. The hundreds of duplicates themselves point to the largely random nature of these collections. Admittedly, as Philip Grierson has argued on several occasions,[49] some collectors intended to gather all the known (and hopefully unknown) types that they could find. However, the mere fact that none of them was able to achieve this ultimate goal, coupled with the fact that all of them seem to have been very successful at gathering the same particular issues (certain regnal years, mints, officinae, etc.) points to the fact that some types were more readily available than others. The fact that different collectors had the same success with some types and shared a similar failure in finding others indicates a fluctuation in coin production which inevitably translates into the varying numbers of coins available today.

Furthermore, there is a striking resemblance between the five major collections in terms of structure and consequently, of statistical results (Figure 1). What counts in the end is the observable similarity of these collections, even when they are tested at the detailed level of annual fluctuations. We do not have sufficient information on each of the major individual collectors in order to make meaningful comparisons, but even so it is very unlikely that they all shared the same collecting behavior.

Finally, and most importantly, in many respects the archaeological evidence confirms the general pattern of annual fluctuation. Unfortunately, the only archaeological samples comparable in size with the large museum collections are the single finds from the province of Scythia and a number of large circulation hoards from the Near East.[50] By necessity, the analysis has to follow the nature of the evidence. The dating structure of the Near Eastern hoards makes them suitable for an analysis of the second half of the sixth century, for which the material is abundant (Figures B–D). On the other hand, the coins from Scythia are less useful

valuation proves that collectors of Byzantine coins were already having a rough quantitative image of the Byzantine coin series and were therefore able to determine the degree of rarity for each type. Tolstoi's estimations, Ratto's sale catalogue with prices realized, and David Sear's *Byzantine Coins and their Values* (1987) confirm this difference of appeal up to this day.

49. Grierson 1967, 323–324; 1986, 39.

50. The most important hoards for this purpose are Chyrrus, Tell Bissé, Amman, Baalbek, Khirbet Fandaqumya, Quazrin, and a number of hoards with uncertain provenance in the Near East. See Todd (1987); Mansfield (1995a, 1995b); Ariel (1996); Bates and Kovacs (1996); Pottier (1983); Noeske (2000, II); Naismith (2004).

for a close analysis of the last quarter of the century when the region was menaced by the attacks of the Slavs and Avars, but offers a good sample for the preceding decades (Figure A). The comparison between the collections and the finds from Scythia and the Near East offer a high degree of correlation and is perhaps key to demonstrating the randomness of museum collections.[51] Even more, Figure D clearly shows that those who assembled the major collections did not limit their collecting behavior to "one coin of each type." The first years of the reign of Heraclius shown here by way of example suggest that the museum collections follow the pattern of the single finds and hoards and not the variety of types. Obviously, both the single finds from Scythia and the hoards from the Near East represent types of evidence that were never subjected to selection at the hands of collectors and museum curators. Such statistical similarities indirectly undescore acceptable degree of randomness in the large collections under consideration.

## II. A Comparative Approach to Early Byzantine Coin Circulation. Museum collections, Site Finds, and Hoards.

The present study is not an attempt to determine the absolute number of coins produced by a certain mint or in a certain year.[52] The graphs highlight the fluctuations in the quantity of fresh currency produced each year and therefore it has nothing to do with calculating the entire coin population in circulation at a given moment. The evidence of hoards shows that coins issued by Anastasius were still circulating during the reign of Heraclius. Due to factors such as loss, hoarding, wear, and state policy of withdrawing certain issues, no precise calculations can be made in this respect.[53]

Private and public collections, single finds and hoards need to be employed as complementary types of numismatic evidence, moving away from the sterile debate over which is the more capable of producing an accurate reflection of the coin production and circulation in ancient times. Large collections, provided that they were amassed with an acceptable degree of randomness, can provide important indications about the rhythm of production. It has been shown often that site

51. The spikes observable in Figure B on coins from Scythia dated from 568 to 571 are explained by the significant number of coins issued at Thessalonica, a phenomenon best illustrated by Figure 4.

52. Unpublished catalogues of the Byzantine coins from the Isparta and Bolu museums and lists of coin finds from Pisidian Antioch and Melitene, referred to in the following section, were kindly provided by Zeliha Demirel Gökalp from Anadolu University.

53. With these caveats in mind, Figure 3 is most useful for observing annual fluctuations in coin production within shorter chronological units (e.g., reigns, monetary reforms, decades) and less for comparing, say, the coin output in 538/9 and 612/3.

finds, if they amount to a statistically relevant sample, are useful for observing the evolution of coin circulation in time in a circumscribed geographical area. Comparative analyses of site finds in a broader region provide a better understanding of the monetary economy in a larger unit of analysis, such as an administrative province, as has been shown for Scythia, Pisidia, and Arabia.[54] Finally, the evidence of circulation hoards, which has been privileged by prominent Byzantinists and numismatists, usually informs us about the circulating medium at a certain time and in a certain place. Again, comparison is needed, in the sense of the exemplary analysis done by Henri Pottier and Hans-Christoph Noeske for the Near East[55] and the team of scholars coordinated by Cécile Morrisson for the Balkans,[56] in which ideally a number of contemporary hoards concealed in the same geographical area are available for study.

In the next sections the discussion will be based on several chronological and thematic parameters ranging from the general to detailed: *nummia* / year of reign (Figure 1), quantity of *nummia* / year of reform (Figure 2a; 5a–c),[57] quantity of *nummia* year-by-year (for the period 538–616) (Figure 3), mints (Figures 6–19), and denominations (Figures 20–32). Obviously, the collections differ in size. In order to make the comparison possible, a common denominator had to be provided and therefore all the numbers are percents from a given total, e.g., within each collection, the percentage represented by the number of *nummia* from the reform period 538–542 out of the total number of reforms from 498 to 616 (taking into account the time span of each reform), or the percentage of the volume of *nummia* from 565/6 out of the total quantity of *nummia* from Justin II's reign, in each collection. The chosen time span, 498–616, opens with the reform of Anastasius and ends with the abrupt decline in coin circulation after 616 in several major centers of the Eastern Empire.[58] The province of Scythia provides us with a

---

54. Marot (1998); Gândilă (2008); Demirel Gökalp (2007).

55. Pottier (1983); Noeske (2000).

56. Morrisson et al. (2006).

57. A conversion into *solidi* based on the ratios proposed by Hahn (see n. 75) is provided in Figure 2b, which gives a more accurate picture of the purchasing power of the base coinage in the early Byzantine period.

58. Wastage rates are sometimes included in analyses when long periods of circulation are involved. For the methodology and applications to Roman coinage see especially Duncan-Jones (1994, chapter 14). However, the extrapolation of modern wastage rates to ancient coinages remains of somewhat dubious value. Moreover, Figure A does not reveal any clear signs of wastage for the dated series of Justinian from Constantinople (27 years). Stray finds from Scythia, which are the direct result of wastage (i.e., casual losses) should theoretically contain a higher number of coins from the early regnal years (as a result of longer circulation) than circulation hoards, which should reflect the effects of wastage at the time when the hoards were concealed (i.e., fewer coins from the early regnal years).

Map 1. Early Byzantine Coin Finds: Major Sites and Local Museums

number of coins that parallels the size of the large public collections and represents the only substantial sample of coins with a secure geographical provenance and usually with a clear archaeological context. For comparison purposes, hoards and various site finds or local museum collections from the Balkans, Anatolia, and the Near East will be used throughout the following discussion, the main criterion for inclusion being the total number of EBC available for study (Map 1).

## II.1. The reform of Anastasius and the pre-538 coinage

In 498 Anastasius introduced a new system for the base-metal currency, one that would put an end to the crisis of the fifth century, which rendered the low value currency almost worthless.[59] However, as shown by Figure 2a, the number of small-module coins struck after the reform does not seem to be very high, if compared with the quantity issued after a second reform in 512. In geographical terms, a larger number of small-module issues can be found in the Danube area[60] and, to an even larger extent, in a number of urban centers in Syria-Palestine—Jerusalem, Pella, Gerasa, Beth She'an (Scythopolis)—and especially Berytus where a unique situation can be noted.[61] In Anatolia, urban centers such as Sardis, Sagalassos, Side, Pisidian Antioch, and Melitene point to a rather reduced impact of the reform in the first period.[62] To return to the special case of Berytus, almost 70 percent of the total number of EBC is represented by small-module issues. Berytus might well have represented an idiosyncratic circulating micro-medium, a semi-closed monetary environment which might have encompassed a larger area of Phoenicia,[63] but it does, nevertheless, raise an important question regarding the withdrawal of these coins from circulation, once a new reform in 512 doubled the weight of the copper coin. As Kevin Butcher has shown in his discussion of the Anastasian coins from Berytus, many of the small module specimens were found in layers dating from the reign of Justinian, which means that the small coins were still in

59. For the reform of Anastasius and its impact see in particular Blake (1942); Grierson (1967b); Metcalf (1969).

60. Especially at Tomis (9 out of 26 coins of Anastasius) and Dinogetia (3/8): Gândilă (2003–2005, 129–144); Shumen (4/16): Zhekova (2006, 65–66). The highest concentration has been recorded in Constantinople, at Saraçhane and Kalenderhane (19/26), Hendy (1986, 285–287); Hendy (2007, 196–198). These types are scarcer among finds from the Western Balkans, in Serbia (5/39): Radić and Ivanišević (2006, 92–96), and Albania (3/21): Spahiu (1979–1980, 366–368), while in Greece the reform had little immediate impact: Hohlfelder (1978, 63); Bellinger (1930, 45); Edwards (1933, 121); Edwards (1937, 249); Mac Isaac (1987, 135); Thompson (1954, 66–67).

61. Metcalf and Payne (1965, 130–131); Sheedy (2001, 128–130); Marot (1998, 461–464); Bellinger (1938, 95–97); Bijovsky (2002, 511–512); Butcher (2003, 257–264). One can add a few more sites or regions with a smaller quantity of EBC, of which a good proportion is made up of small-module coins of Anastasius. Such cases are Capernaum: Spijkerman (1975, 29, 31), Fayran: Noeske (2001, 708), and Mesopotamia: Prawdzic-Golemberski and Metcalf (1963, 90–92). A special case is the synagogue at 'En Nashut where half the small batch of EBC are small module issues, Ariel (1987, 151, table 1).

62. Bell (1916); Bates (1971); Buttrey (1981, 212); Scheers (1993, 254; 1995, 314; 1997, 332; 2000, 525); Atlan (1976, 77). No such coins can be found in the local museums in Amasra (ancient Amastris): Ireland and Atesogullari (1996, 132); Bolvadin (vicinity of ancient Polybotos): Ashton, Lightfoot, and Özme (2000, 183). However, see a few specimens at Amasya (ancient Amaseia): Ireland (2000, 101), and Pessinus: de Wilde (1997, 107); Devreker (1984, 211). A few specimens found in Anatolia are now kept in the archaeological museum in Zagreb: Mirnik and Šemrov (1997–1998, 143–145, n. 11, 36).

63. See the hoard of small module *folles* found at Sarafand south of Beirut, Taylor (1977, 87).

circulation at that time.[64] It is hard to determine with any certainty their precise relation to the Anastasian and later, Justinianic, heavy standard. An analogy with a seventh century measure might reinforce a hypothesis established in the past decades. Special marks were placed on the reformed heavy coins introduced by Constantine IV (M on ½-*folles*, K on ¼-*folles*) indicating that the new coins were worth twice as much as the old, smaller ones.[65] Although no such clear marks are present on the heavy coins of Anastasius, the small-module issues might have remained in circulation based on the same rationale of using them for a different face-value.[66] To be sure, these small and ephemeral issues remained in circulation throughout the sixth century as testified by hoards found in the Eastern Empire.[67] Despite their small size, such coins remain outside the danger of "Gresham's Law," as the state did not have to fear that the circulation of the newly introduced heavier specimens might be disrupted by the existence of those lighter issues, as long as their face-value was halved. The reuse of late Roman, early Roman and even Greek coins, based on a similar size and weight is not uncommon in the large centers of the empire and is also testified by hoards containing such specimens.

The museum collections confirm the high proportion of coins issued in Constantinople, over 75 percent in all cases, the rest being struck at the sub-metropolitan mint of Nicomedia (Figures 7a–b). There is a fairly balanced proportion of *folles* and ½-*folles* both in the collections and in the samples found during archaeological excavations, while the ¼-*folles* are themselves well represented (Figures 21a–b). This phenomenon shows that the divisionary system was functional and

64. The evidence of hoards seems to point in the same direction. Several hoards containing a large number of small module *folles* were found in collapsed buildings associated with the earthquake of 551. Butcher (2003, 283–286); Beliën (2005); Abou Diwan (2008).

65. Schindler (1955, 33–35).

66. See Mecalf (1969, 41–43), followed by Pottier (1983: 227–230) who suggested that the countermarks often found on small module coins from the Middle East are a sign that the state was attempting to regulate the use of the pre-reform coins. The reduction of the face value was also accepted as a plausible hypothesis by Grierson (1982, 60) and Hahn and Metlich (2000, 30). Recently, Abu Diwan challenged this common wisdom by pointing to the abnormal circulating pattern of Berytus, which raises important questions regarding the uniform implementation of the monetary reforms throughout the Empire, Abu Diwan (2008, 316–317).

67. In the Balkans and Anatolia out of 36 hoards containing coins of Anastasius, seven include small module types. The latest of these hoards, Caricin Grad 1952, ends in 595/6, testifying to the longevity of the small-module coins of Anastasius (Morrisson et al. 2006, 299). In the Near East small-module coins occur occasionally in large hoards ending in the seventh century such as Tel Bissé, Baalbek, Khirbet Fandaqumya and "Northern Syria," Noeske (2000, II); "Lebanon" Kruszynski (1999). This evidence clearly contradicts Noeske's supposition that the small-module series was immediately withdrawn in 512 (Noeske 2000, I, 150–151).

smaller denominations were used frequently in minor transactions. The museum collections, however, hardly contain any specimens of the smallest denomination, the *nummus*, found especially in Greece (Athens, Corinth, Kenchreai),[68] Anatolia (Sardis, Sagalassos),[69] and Palestine (Caesarea Maritima, Beth She'an, Ramat Hanadiv, Hammat Gader)[70] and to a much lesser extent in the Balkans and at the Danube border.[71] The retrieval of large numbers of *minimi* accumulated in special circumstances, like the water basins at Ramat Hanadiv and Hammat Gader, or the hoards found in Palestine, Greece, Dobroudja, and in Istanbul,[72] might signal the fact that we are largely underestimating the sheer quantity of low value coins still in circulation deep into the sixth century.[73] The contrasting image offered by Sardis awaits more information from other centers in Western Anatolia in order to determine whether this is a particular case or a more general phenomenon. Philip Grierson attributed the paucity of *minimi* at Sardis to the negligence of the excavators,[74] but recent research in Anatolia, at Melitene and Pisidian Antioch shows that *minimi* are generally scarce.

The period 512–538 is homogeneous in many respects, largely due to a stable ratio between the gold *solidus* and the copper *follis*, most probably 1:360.[75] Figure

68. Thompson (1954, 66); Edwards (1937, 249); Fisher (1984, 245); Hohlfelder (1978, 64). See also the case of Nemea where John Mac Isaac argued that *minimi* continued to circulate during the sixth century, Mac Isaac (2005, 185).

69. Bates (1971); Scheers (1993, 254; 1997, 332; 2000, 525).

70. Hamburger (1956, 115–138); Evans (2006, 180–203); Bijovsky (2002, 507–512); Barkay (2000, 413, table 4); Barkay (1997, 300). See also the hoard of *minimi* from Gush Halav, Bijovsky (1998, 77–106), and a hoard of *minimi* and ⅛-*folles* probably found in Lebanon, Phillips and Tyler Smith (1998); A significant number of one-*nummus* pieces have been found during the excavations on the *Limes Arabicus*, primarily at Lejjūn, Betlyon (1988, 171–172).

71. Gândilă (2008,318, table 5).

72. Gush Halav, Bijovsky (1998, 77–106), with a comparative discussion of the circulation of *minimi* in the first half of the sixth century (Morrisson et al. 2006) Greece: several hoards in Thebes, Athens, Corinth, and Kenchreai; Thasos 1977, Argos 1892–1895, Hagios Nikolaos 1935, Kenchreai 1963, Kleitoria 1933, Megara before 1884, Patras 1938, Pellene 1937, Priolithos 1979, Spata 1982, Trype 1935, Zacha, Chersonissos. Dobrudja: Constantza 1929; Histria 1974. Several small hoards in Istanbul (Hendy 2007, 271–276).

73. See also the case of Gerasa where Marot has shown that late Roman coins are still present in sixth century archaeological contexts, Marot (1998, 304).

74. Grierson (1965, xi).

75. The ratio between *solidus* and *follis* has been taken from Hahn's *MIB* I (1973, 27); *MIB* II (1975, 14–17), and *MIB* III (1981, 16). A consensus is yet to be reached regarding the calculation of this ratio and different propositions have been made in the past decades: Callu (1982), Pottier (1983, 252), Morrisson (1989b, 248); Morrisson and Ivanišević (2006, 51); Hendy (1985, 478).

2 points to an important increase in coin production during this period, although not a continuous one, the reign of Justin I usually providing a larger number of finds than the first decade of Justinian's reign. In the larger framework of the "long sixth century," however, the coins minted between 512 and 538 stand at a lower point than the post reform coinage of Justinian and the inflationary peak reached during the reign of Justin II.

The larger quantity of coins from Justin I has already been noticed in the Near Eastern provinces,[76] although it is hardly a general phenomenon and the evidence is still too scant to permit a conclusion in this respect.[77] The phenomenon is conspicuous in the province of Scythia, where all the major sites without exception display a peak reached during the reign of Justin I.[78] This is by no means characteristic for the Balkan area as a whole. The neighboring province of Moesia II offers a contrasting image with a high occurrence of coins of Anastasius.[79] A similar contrast is found in Greece in the cases of Corinth and Athens, while in the western Balkans, there is a fairly balanced proportion of the two periods, with somewhat higher numbers for Justin I (Figure 5a).[80] In Anatolia the evidence available from Sagalassos, Sardis, Side, Amaseia, Amastris, Pisidian Antioch, and Melitene offers a mixed picture (Figure 5b)[81] and so does the evidence from Cyprus, at Paphos, Salamis and Curium.[82] The major Syro-Palestinian sites seem to be more correlated, with the notable exception of Berytus (Figure 5c). Overall, the apparent contrast between neighboring areas in the Balkans and Anatolia in particular suggests local patterns of circulation rather than a controlled macro-economic policy.

The museum collections suggest a slight decrease in coin production during the reign of Justinian I, prior to his major reform in 538 (Figure 2). The archaeological evidence indicates that such a phenomenon is very clear in the Balkans[83] and to a large degree in Anatolia,[84] but seems to be somewhat irregular in the Near Eastern sites, where, without a clear distribution according to provinces, we

76. Grierson (1967b, 296); Walmsley (1999, 344).

77. Butcher (2003, 103, fig. 75). Almost half of the sites tabulated by Butcher provide a larger quantity of coins from Anastasius without the possibility of discerning between different provincial patterns of supply.

78. Gândilă (2008, 322, table 3 and 4), where 10 major sites are compared.

79. Mihailov (2008, 281, table 4).

80. Thompson (1954, 67); Edwards (1933, 121); Mac Isaac (1987, 135); Radić and Ivaniševic (2006, 92–104), Ivaniševic (1988, 90–94); Janković (1981, 72, table 6).

81. Scheers (2000, 525); Bates (1971, 19–26); Atlan (1976, 78); Ireland (2000, 102); Ireland and Atesogullari (1996, 132–123).

82. Nicolaou (1990, 192–204); Callot (2004, 41–43); Cox (1959, 77–78).

83. Gândilă (2008, 306, table 1); Radić and Ivaniševic (2006, 110–125); Edwards (1933, 121–122). The situation is somewhat balanced in Albania: Spahiu (1979–1980, 368–377).

84. Bates (1971, 28–44); Ireland (2000, 102–105); Ireland and Atesogullari (1996, 133).

find all three possible situations —the prevalence of coins from 518–527 (Pella),[85] a balanced proportion (Gerasa, Nessana),[86] and a larger number of coins from 527–538 (Caesarea Maritima, Hama, Antioch) (Figures 5a–c).[87] Aside from these fluctuations, the Near Eastern provinces yield the highest volume of finds dated to the pre-538 period. This characteristic is confirmed by the structure of the hoards found in the area, which contain a good number of pre-reform coins, even if most of these hoards were concealed after 600.[88] As a general observation the quantity of Justinianic pre-reform issues depends on the influence of the mint of Antioch, which is rather insignificant in the Balkans and most Anatolian sites (Pisidian Antioch and Amaseia being two major exceptions) (Figure 10b).

According to the evidence from the collections, Constantinople is the most important mint during the period 512–538. Its influence, however, gradually diminishes in favor of the Antioch mint, which greatly increases its output during the first decade of Justinian's reign, even surpassing Constantinople. The mint of Nicomedia retains a secondary role, while Cyzicus and Thessalonica, re-opened by Justin I have only a modest output at this time (Figures 8a–10a). The mints issued especially *folles* and, somewhat surprisingly, a large number of ⅛-*folles*, particularly during the reigns of Anastasius and Justin I and to a lesser degree at the beginning of Justinian's reign. Except for this latter period, the ½-*follis* is struck in smaller quantities. The role of the ¼-*follis* appears to be less significant during this period and it seems that, in most cases, it was the large number of ⅛-*folles* which fulfilled the role of small change in the market (Figures 22a–24a).

This phenomenon is less visible in the Balkans, where, with the exception of Ahtopol (Agathopolis),[89] on the Black Sea coast, and of Constantinople,[90] the urban centers and border fortresses yielded a very small number of eight-*folles*. Especially in Scythia, the balanced proportion between *folles* and ½-*folles* indicates that the latter was the only fraction required in a market whose intensity of small transactions was relatively low.[91] In the western Balkans the proportion of *folles* is overwhelming, which could indicate that the severe disruption of urban life in the fifth century had long-term consequences.[92] In Anatolia the most substantial

85. Sheedy (2001, 130–131).

86. Bellinger (1938, 98–102); Marot (1998, 465–471); Bellinger (1962, 71–72).

87. Evans (2006, 183–188); Thomsen (1986, 62); Waage (1952, 149–155).

88. Noeske (2000 II) (Baalbek, Khirbet Fandaqumya, Syria 1974, Khirbet Dubel, Khirbet Deir Dassawi, Rafah, Amman), Pottier (1983); Metcalf (1975, 110–112); Mansfield (1995a, 348–350); Naismith (2004, 296–297).

89. Iordanov, Koicev, and Mutafov (1998, 71, table I).

90. Hendy (1986, 287–295); Hendy (2007, 197–206).

91. Gândilă (2008, 318, table 5).

92. Spahiu (1979–1980, 366–377); Radić and Ivanišević (2006, 92–125); see also at the Iron Gates of the Danube (Janković 1981, 66, table 3).

evidence comes from Sardis, as usual, where the ⅛-*follis* represents the main de-nomination in the period following the reform of 512, but its volume gradually decreases in the following decades prior to 538 in favor of the *follis*. At Amasya, Amastris, Side, Melitene and Pisidian Antioch the pattern of denominations re-sembles the situation in the Balkans where the main role is played by the *follis*, followed by the ½-*follis*. In the Near East we find once again a mixed picture. It can be argued that the smaller denominations are more present in the Near East-ern provinces, especially in Antioch where the ⅛-*follis* is prevalent in this period, but also in other major sites like Caesarea Maritima, Nessana, and Berytus.[93] As already mentioned, another characteristic is the high presence of *minimi* in Beth She'an, Rammat Hanadiv, and Hamat Gader. In the last two cases most of the coins were found in the tunnel of a spring and a large bath complex, respectively, which might be less reflecting the real structure of denominations in circulation and more the habit of throwing small coins into the water as a symbolic offering.[94] In Syria II - at Hama (Epiphania), in Palaestina II - at Pella, and in Arabia - at Gerasa the structure resembles the one seen in the Balkans and in Anatolia, with very few small denominations (Figures 22b–24b). A constant feature of the Near Eastern provinces is the larger role played by the Antioch mint than in Anatolia or the Bal-kans (Figures 8b–10b). However, in centers like Pella, and especially Nessana, very far from Antioch, in Palaestina III, the mint of Antioch is less influent.[95]

## II.2. The post-reform coinage of Justinian I

The four-year period following the reform of 538 is one of the most intriguing. It is also the only point in which the five major collections under scrutiny present higher quantitative variation. Although there certainly was a dramatic increase in output immediately after the reform, we can also accept that a certain bias existed in favor of collecting the eye-catching, impressively large *folles* of Justinian. This is highly visible in the cases of *DOC* and *BNP* (Figure 3). Interestingly, the coin finds from Scythia, where no collector's choice is involved, share this high peak reached in the period 538–542. In all cases, including Scythia, the numbers point to a continuous decrease in mint output during the next two reform periods in the reign of Justinian, 542–550 and 550–565 (Figure 2a).[96] The economy was not able to sustain a constant high output of heavy *folles*, whose introduction in the first place must have relied on both economic and propagandistic agendas. It is signifi-cant in this respect that the majority of coins both in the collections and in Scythia

93. Evans (2006, 180–188); Bellinger (1962, 72); Butcher (2003, 263).
94. See the discussion by Barkay (2000, 415–417).
95. Walmsley (1999, 337, table 4); Bellinger (1962, 71–72); at Nessana the influence of Alexandria, geographically much closer than Antioch, is more visible among the EBC.
96. For a possible explanation of this phenomenon see Pottier (1983, 241–242).

are comprised of *folles*, in a proportion usually higher than 70 percent (Figures 25a–b). The situation changed dramatically in the second half of the 550s when a huge number of ¼-*folles* flooded the market (Figures 27a–b). They were issued by the mint of Constantinople, but in even higher numbers by Nicomedia and Cyzicus. It is hard to determine what caused this sudden shift. It seems to correspond to a wider set of measures taken by Justinian in the last years of his reign. According to the current information, Nicomedia and Cyzicus stopped minting *folles* and ½-*folles* after 561 and concentrated almost exclusively on striking ¼-*folles*, while Thessalonica abandoned its idiosyncratic denominational system and began issuing ½-*folles* in 562.[97] These measures might have been caused by a need for small denominations after the market had been overwhelmed by a high number of *folles* for two decades. Furthermore, the increased production of ¼-*folles* can be seen in all the regions of the Eastern Empire. At Noviodunum, on the Danube, 57 percent of the coins from 550 to 565 are ¼-*folles*; at Tomis, on the Black Sea, they represent 75 percent; at Corinth, 73 percent; at Sardis in Lydia, almost 70 percent of the finds, and at Antioch, 55 percent (Figure 27b). Even when very few coins are reported for this time interval we find ¼-*folles* among them. Such is the case at Capidava on the Danube, Sagalassos and Side in Anatolia, Curium and Salamis in Cyprus, Berytus, Gerasa, Caesarea Maritima, Hammat Gader, Rammat Hanadiv, Dibon in the Near East.[98]

The mint of Constantinople gradually reduced its output in favor of Nicomedia, Cyzicus, and especially Antioch during the last reform period, 550–565 (Figure 13a). Thessalonica still had a secondary role largely restricted to supplying the area of the western Balkans (Figure 13b).[99] A geographic anomaly can be noted in the case of the Antioch mint: for reasons that are not clear, Antioch is very well represented in the collections of the museums in Amasra and Amasya, while closer to Antioch, at Side it is less well represented. In the Near Eastern provinces, as was to be expected, Antioch plays a more important role, although still up to half the total number of coins come from the central mint in Constantinople.[100] The mint of Antioch appears to serve primarily the needs of the city but its influence can be far-reaching as shown by the cases of Amasra and Amaseia. The higher presence

97. Hahn and Metlich (2000, 56–62).

98. Gândilă (2006–2007, 114–116); Scheers (2000, 525); Atlan (1976, 79–81); Callot (2004, 44); Cox (1959, 78); Butcher (2003, 268–269); Ariel (1986, 142); Lampinen (1992, 172); Evans (2006, 186–187); Barkay (2000, 413, table 4); Tushingham (1972, 199).

99. Radić and Ivanišević (2006, 122); Ivanišević (1988, 92); Spahiu (1979–1980, 376–377). The mint is rather under-represented in Greece proper and D. M. Metcalf (1976, 8) has explained its geographical distribution by restricting its role to military expenditure at the Balkan border.

100. Ariel (1982, 326); Morrisson (1995, 79); Walmsley (1999, 337, table 4–5); Evans (2006, 48, fig. 17); Butcher (2003, 257–269).

of coins from Antioch in urban centers located close to the sea, such as Caesarea in Palestine and Amastris on the Black Sea could point to the distribution of coins through commercial activities.

The monetary reform of 538 raises a number of interesting issues regarding the use and function of the large copper coins in a monetary system in which the mass of coins in circulation was up to 25 percent lighter. Even more problematic in the circulating scheme of the "long sixth century" is the role of such heavy specimens after the weight-standard of the copper coin began to slide until it was finally established at half the weight of the Justinianic large *follis*.[101] "Bad money drives out good" was an economic principle well understood in early Byzantium. The reform of Constantine IV, briefly mentioned above, is a case in point. If the small-module *follis* of Anastasius posed no serious circulating problems, the state would certainly have been interested in recalling the large coins of 538–542, either by coercion or by discouraging potential hoarding by temporarily raising their market value until they could be withdrawn from circulation. Certainly this represents only a logical, yet speculative, scenario and the actual process of withdrawing certain issues remains obscure. The complexity of the early Byzantine monetary economy should be neither under- nor over-estimated by viewing it from the perspective of modern economic policies. Both single finds and hoards suggest that the state had a good control over its major urban centers and was less able to impose its economic policies at the periphery. The intensive excavations at Saraçhane and Kalenderhane in Istanbul have yielded close to 500 coins dated 491–616 and not a single one of them was a heavy *follis* or a ½-*follis* of Justinian. In Antioch, out of more than 2300 EBC, only two *folles* and four ½-*folles* are dated to 538–542. Large cities where imperial mints were located, as was the case at Constantinople and Antioch, certainly had tighter control over the circulating mass of coins in their urban areas.

In the Balkans, both hoards and single finds point to an abundance of such heavy coins and, more significantly, their persistence until the last decade of the sixth century. In Scythia, coins from 538–542 represent more than 10 percent of the entire group of EBC, while the proportion is much higher in Moesia II and in the north-western Balkans, in Serbia.[102] It is interesting that the major urban centers of Scythia, namely Tomis, Histria, and Noviodunum, yielded a smaller number of large *folles*, while none of the four hoards found at Histria contains such coins.[103] In the fortresses defending the Danube frontier the situation is different. At Durostorum, 40 percent of the coins of Justinian are heavy issues from

101. *BNP* I, 61.

102. Gândilă (2008, 306, table 2); Belgrade museum (18.42 percent), Radić and Ivanišević (2006); Shumen museum (22.18 percent), Zhekova (2006).

103. Gândilă (2008, 322, table 4). Morrisson et. al. (2006, 170–174).

538–42.[104] A small hoard of 51 coppers recently found at Capidava contains coins up to Tiberius II, and yet one third are heavy *folles* of Justinian. The coins were kept in a small textile container and were found overlapped in a row on the floor of a room destroyed by fire. The lack of intentionality allows a glimpse of an ordinary purse of coins probably handled by a soldier on the Danube frontier in the early 580s.[105] Such examples suggest that the process of withdrawing the heavy series was more readily applicable in the major centers where control was tighter.

Nevertheless, the coin hoards from the Balkans, as a general characteristic, contain heavy specimens as late as the 580s, as testified by such finds across the peninsula, in Greece, Serbia, Bulgaria, and Romania.[106] It is significant that, with one exception (Veliki Gradac), no such coins seem to appear in any of the hoards concealed in the 590s, a possible sign that the big coins of Justinian had been almost completely removed from circulation by the end of the century.[107] Another phenomenon might suggest that the 590s represented a time of intensive withdrawal of heavier issues, namely the overstriking of Maurice *folles* on previous Justinianic *folles*, after the flan was trimmed to meet the demand of the new weight standard. Several public collections[108] and catalogues of site finds and hoards[109] contain such overstruck specimens. Most of them date from the early 590s and correspond to the period when the Justinianic large *folles* disappear from hoards in the Balkans. Such a late date of withdrawal might be related to the difficulty encountered by Justin II and Tiberius II in collecting the taxes from the border provinces of the Balkans, which received particular mention in the legislation of 566 and 575.[110] The collection of taxes was also an opportunity to regulate the circulating mass, and a disruption of this system could have delayed the process of calling in the heavy Justinianic coinage. We may also use a later account from Theophanes

104. Author's file cards.

105. Author's file cards.

106. Morrisson et. al (2006). Most significant hoards are Koprivec, Zhalad, Adamclisi 1908, Athens 1908, and Eleusis 1893.

107. Morrisson et al. (2006). Hoards ending in the 590s: Reselec, Rakita, Sofia, Histria (5 hoards), Caričin Grad 1952, Bosman, and Horgeşti, Movileni, Unirea, north of the Danube, in "barbaricum."

108. Sommer (2003, 59, n. 288); *DOC* (307, n. 33e2); *BNP* (185, n. 16); *BMC* (160–161, n. 138, 139). Ratto (51, n. 1105); *KOD* (111, n. 123). The ANS collection contains fourteen overstruck coins from this period, of which ten clearly show Justinianic undertypes. An even larger number of coins, of every denomination have trimmed planchets indicating a revaluation exercise.

109. Viminacium: Ivanišević (1988, 94, n. 56); Sardis: Bates (1971, 68, n. 562); Caesarea Maritima: Ariel (1986, 143, n. 67); Evans (2006, 193, n. 2472) (half-*follis*); Tell Bissé hoard, Leuthold (1952–1953, 39); Quazrin hoard, Ariel (1996, 75, n. 6).

110. Popescu (2005, 379).

Confessor who argued that the imperial treasury could no longer sustain the regular payment of the troops, so the state was forced to cut a quarter of the salaries in 587.[111] The decision to resize and overstrike larger issues, thus gaining additional metal and insuring the payment of troops in "new" coin, can be ascribed to the difficult financial situation mentioned in the written sources.

In Anatolia the big coins are less well represented than in the Balkans but still represent an important proportion of the total number of EBC. Excavations at Side, Pergamum, and Sagalassos have yielded a number of specimens while the local museums in Bolvadin, Amasra, and Amasya also contain heavy *folles* dated 538–542. There is also variation: at Pisidian Antioch 25 percent of the coins are heavy issues while at Melitene they represent only 3 percent, to provide only the two extremes. Much like the Balkans, the hoards concealed in the 590s lack any large coins of Justinian.[112]

There is an apparent scarcity of such coins in the Near East. D.M. Metcalf has long suggested that the post-reform coinage of Justinian was not introduced in Palaestina and Arabia. Philip Grierson ascribed their scarcity to their withdrawal from circulation, while Henri Pottier and Cécile Morrisson have pointed to the fall in circulation between 538 and 565 and suggested that wars and natural disasters are important factors explaining this situation.[113] More recently P. J. Casey attempted a closer analysis of the post-reform coinage by looking at the evidence from site finds and hoards across the Eastern Empire. His point of departure was a written source, Procopius' *Secret History*, especially a passage where the Byzantine historian claims that Justinian stopped paying the *limitanei* on the Eastern frontier. Seeking to assess the veracity of this statement by analyzing the numismatic and archaeological evidence from Syria-Palestine, Casey concluded that such circumstances may indeed explain the virtual absence of post-reform coins from Palestine, but admitted that such an argument is less compelling in the case of Syria.[114] Finally, disregarding the evidence from the Balkans and Anatolia, Noeske has recently suggested that the post-reform coinage was struck in limited quantities and was unsuited for the circulating medium of the Near Eastern provinces due to its heavy weight standard.[115]

111. See the discussion by Yannopoulos (1987, 129).

112. Unfortunately, the information comes from a single major source, Sardis, where at least 4 hoards (found 1913, 1958, 1961, and 1968) ending after 590 are relevant for this discussion. Another hoard, from Anemurium in Isauria, ends in 602 and has no coins prior to 578. Morrisson *et al.* (2006).

113. Grierson (1967b, 296); Pottier (1983, 55); Morrisson (1989, 192); Morrisson and Ivanišević (2006, 52).

114. Casey (1996, 220).

115. Noeske (2000, I, 152–153).

Although coins dated 538–542 are indeed conspicuously hard to find, some are still reported at Jerusalem, Caesarea Maritima, Antioch, Berytus, Pella, and Nessana in six different provinces of the Near East.[116] Coins issued during the remainder of Justinian's reign, 542–565 are more common and they are found in almost all excavations conducted in the region, and in a number of hoards.[117] It is thus fair to conclude that the post reform coinage did penetrate into the Near Eastern provinces, perhaps in smaller quantities than in the Balkans. This contrast should not be exaggerated, however, if we take into consideration the level of urbanization in the two regions. As noted, the major towns in Scythia yielded fewer heavy coins and a tighter control of the coins in circulation can certainly be envisaged in a highly urbanized region like Palestine, for instance.

Antioch, the mint whose chief purpose was to serve the major Syrian city and its vicinity, issued coins in this period in especially high numbers starting from the late 540s (Figure 13a), of which only a small percentage reached more distant parts of the Empire such as the Balkan provinces. Coins minted in Constantinople and Nicomedia are extremely common among finds in the Near East and, judging by their increased output immediately after the reform in 538, it is hard to imagine that the coins were artificially kept out of the Eastern provinces. Doubtless catastrophic events such as the plague, the Persian invasions starting from 540, the Samaritan revolt in 555, and major earthquakes such as the one of 551 affected the circulation, but a long term disruption of the influx of new coinage seems rather improbable.[118] The argument advanced by Casey might be acceptable for the frontier region only, but is unsuited for explaining the coin circulation in urban centers unrelated to any frontier business. As a matter of fact, although Casey's central argument concerns Palestine, his comparative table includes only one, remote, Palestinian center, Nessana, notwithstanding his discussion of the hoards, concealed late in the sixth or early in the seventh century and consequently less relevant for the discussion.[119] The urban record is still decidedly thin, but in the light of the

116. Fitzgerald (1929, 117); Ariel (1986, 142); Waage (1952, 152–154); Butcher (2003, 266–268); Sheedy (2001, 132); Bellinger (1962, 72).

117. From the major site finds discussed throughout this article only Nessana and Hama failed to produce any finds from 542–565. The relevant hoards are "Northern Syria" (Pottier), Syria 1974, Khirbet Dubel, Tell Bissé, Baalbek, Khirbet Deir Dassawi, cf. Noeske (2000, II); Qazrin (Ariel 1996, 70, table 1); "Northern Syria" (Todd 1987,178–179); "Near East 1993" (Mansfield 1995b, 355); "Near East 2003" (Naismith 2004, 297), and a Near Eastern hoard which includes Arab-Byzantine issues as well (Bates and Kovacs 1996, 166).

118. The mint of Antioch ceased minting coins in years 14–15 of Justinian's reign when the city was sacked by the Persians and in Justinian's regnal years 17, 18, and 19 because of the Great Plague. See DOC, 143. For a list of the major earthquakes in Palestine see Russell (1985). However, once the crises were overcome, the mint was reopened.

119. Casey (1996, 217).

new evidence, mostly but not completely inaccessible to Casey, it is more plausible to suggest that the heavy specimens did circulate in the area, but were more efficiently withdrawn from circulation at a later period.

The large coins disappear from hoards in the Balkans in the last decade of the sixth century, although the process might have started even earlier. It is hard to say if the Near Eastern provinces followed the same pattern, largely because the major coin hoards from this region, with the exception of Rafah and a "North Syrian hoard,"[120] have a closing date after 595. The hoard of Rafah has a "closing coin" dated 573/4, but despite the early date of closing it contains no post-reform coins of Justinian. The "North Syria Hoard," however, ends in 584/5 and has 16 post reform coins out of a total of 60 pieces, which means more than 25 percent of the entire hoard. Almost half the coins from this hoard were issued in Antioch so it might be safe to conclude that it was formed in the region and not brought from a more distant province of the Empire. The hoard found in the synagogue of Meroth in Palestine is particularly interesting for this discussion. It was found in a secret chamber where the treasury of the synagogue was kept and represents a slow and gradual accumulation throughout the sixth century and into the seventh.[121] The hoard contains 55 base-metal coins of Justinian of which 16 are post-reform issues, meaning almost 30 percent of the total. Six of the post-reform coins belong to the heavier standard.[122] Because of its special nature, as an "open" savings hoard, fresh coins were constantly fed into this treasury and many were never taken out. This is probably the reason why these heavy *folles* escaped the process of withdrawal. It also confirms once again the presence of the post reform coinage of Justinian in Palestine, possibly in much greater numbers than we are inclined to believe, based on the surviving specimens from site finds and later hoards. It seems so far that a policy of withdrawing the heavier issues was implemented in the Near East even earlier and more efficiently compared to the Balkans and even Anatolia. This would explain the pronounced scarcity of the big coins among finds in Syro-Palestinian sites, given the fact that they circulated for a shorter period.

The fact that the large coins were withdrawn from circulation can also be indirectly reinforced by the unusual number of pierced coins.[123] Without attempting

120. Noeske (2000, 634–639); Todd (1987, 176–182).

121. Kindler (1986).

122. I owe this information to Gabriela Bijovsky from the Israel Antiquities Authority whom I thank once again for allowing me to study the still unpublished catalogue of the coins from the Meroth hoard.

123. Pierced coins from the following decades, 542–616, are seldom found in public collections or among site finds. An interesting case was signaled at the early Byzantine church from Khirbat al-Karak, where several tombs contained holed sixth century coins possibly pointing to a habit of wearing coins as pieces of jewelry (Delougaz 1960, 51 and plate 46).

to be comprehensive, I assembled the most significant instances where pierced *folles* of Justinian have been noted, both in public collections[124] and among site finds from the major geographical areas of the Eastern Empire, the Balkans,[125] Anatolia,[126] and the Near East.[127] Significantly, most of the coins are pierced at 12 o'clock, above the emperor's head, which suggests that the coins were worn as pendants. One specimen from Pella is holed six times and was probably sewn to a textile garment. Many were found in a clear archaeological context and therefore the hypothesis that such coins might have been found and pierced at a much later date is not plausible. The sheer number of cases itself points to a period closer to the time of their striking. No less than 7 percent of the total number of *folles* dated 538–542 in the Dumbarton Oaks and the ANS collections are pierced, so this is hardly an isolated phenomenon from a later period. It is unlikely that such coins, once demonetized, would be taken out of the necklace and reintroduced in circulation. It is more probable that such large coins began to be transformed into pieces of jewelry only after the entire series was officially withdrawn from circulation. Although it is not entirely impossible for the two phenomena to coexist, the symbolic value of the coin turned into a pendant is much more powerful when the hundreds or thousands of similar pieces were no longer showing up in local market transactions. Furthermore, the owner of such a coin would have acknowledged its special nature only after Justin II had introduced a *follis* half its weight. The big coins of Justinian were therefore highly regarded by the common people and perhaps reminded them of an ambitious age of military achievements and building programs, both lacking in the decades when such coins were probably being pierced.

## II.3. Inflationary tendencies and decline (565–616)

The reign of Justin II witnessed a dramatic increase in coin output with a peak reached in the interval 570–575, after a general tendency of accretion during the first five years. The prominent peak from 574/5 might be artificially produced by the inclusion of numerous types described by Hahn as *Moneta Militaris Imitativa*,

124. *MIB* I (112, plate 22); Sommer (2003, 38, n. 106, plate 2); several specimens in *BNP*, *DOC* and in the ANS collection, the latter including a gold plated piece; Ratto (26 , n. 495 and 30, n. 583); *KOD* (56, n. 333, plate XV); Bateson and Campbell (1998, 13, n. 13, plate 2); Arslan (2000, 38, n. 14, plate III).

125. Radić and Ivanišević (2006, 117, n. 318, plate 20); Mirnic and Šemrov (1997–1998, 150, n. 102, plate 8); Poenaru, Ocheşeanu, and Popeea (2004, 35, n. 206); Hohlfelder (1978, 65, n. 1017, plate IV).

126. Bell (1916, 77, n. 639); Morrisson (1993, 55, n. 765, plate 8); Callot (2004, 191, fig. 18, n. 274).

127. Sheedy (2001, 132, n. 021 and 023, plate 10); Ariel (1986, 142, n. 54, plate I); Metcalf and Payne (1965, 185, n. 48).

which bear the regnal year 10 (type *MIB* 89–93). The last years of the reign mark a sharp downfall in coin production, which coincide with the adoption of Tiberius as co-regent (Figure 3). These fluctuations in coin output derived from the study of the museum collections are paralleled by the numerous finds for Scythia, where the massive contribution of the mint of Thessalonica forces a more dramatic increase until 570 (see also Figure 4).

Numismatists have long drawn attention to the inflationist tendencies of the reign of Justin II, in direct relation with the devaluation of the *follis*, which went down from 216 *folles / solidus* to 525 and then 720. The huge volume of coins issued during this period is sometimes interpreted as a sign of crisis not of economic prosperity or increasing commercial activities.[128] This is undoubtedly the reflection of Justinian's prodigal policy of expenditure on warfare and buildings, as well as of demographic decline caused by natural disasters such as large epidemics and intensified seismic activity. However, this is by no means a crisis of catastrophic proportions. The monetary economy remained fairly stable until 616, at least if we judge by the *follis / solidus* ratio, and Tiberius II Constantine was ambitious enough to attempt a return to the Justinianic standard. Moreover, the difference in mint output between the previous reform period (550–565) and the reign of Justin II as a whole is higher than the difference in purchasing power (Figure 2b). This means that the volume of coins produced supersedes the theoretical level of inflation triggered by the devaluation of the *follis*. This can be interpreted either in economic terms suggesting that a certain level of prosperity still existed, or in relation to the military situation of the Empire and the need to pay the army. The high level of coin output might also be related to the policy of withdrawing the heavy coins of Justinian, which was a more or less successful process, as we have seen. At any rate, such a procedure would have provided both the means (raw material) and the need to issue a large quantity of fresh coins.

The mint of Constantinople is the most active in the first reform period, 565–570, covering approximately 40 percent of the total coin output. An important development is the importance gained by Thessalonica and its ½-*folles* issued in great numbers during these years (Figure 14a). A few major changes occur in the second reform period, 570–578, when Constantinople, while still the major supplier, is closely followed by Antioch, which increased its output probably due to the conflict with Persia. Cyzicus became more important after a period of low activity, while Thessalonica drastically reduced its output for reasons discussed in the following section (Figure 15a). More than half the coins issued during the reign of Justin II are *folles*. The ¼-*follis* is less present, a sign that the monetary policy sustained by Justinian in his last years of reign was discontinued. The mint of

128. Poenaru (1981, 374–375).

Antioch alone continued to issue ¼-*folles* in significant quantities.[129] The decline in the production of smaller denomination is considered a general characteristic of the second half of the sixth century,[130] but this is not entirely accurate. Although ¼-*folles* are indeed rather scarce, the production of ⅛-*folles* maintains and even surpasses the levels of the preceding decades (Figure 28a). Their presence in urban settings, as it will be shown below, is an indication of a still vibrant monetary economy (Figure 28b).

There is a sudden influx of coins in the Danubian provinces after Justin II's decision to abandon the policy of regular payments sent to the northern barbarians in order to secure the border provinces. It is very probable that such a shift implied the arrival of additional troops to be stationed in the border fortresses along the Danube. The enlarged garrisons brought about an increased number of coins and this phenomenon is clearly visible in fortresses such as Noviodunum, Dinogetia, Capidava, Durostorum, Aquis, Viminacium, and Sirmium.[131] This is not only a frontier-related phenomenon. Numerous finds from this period are also reported in major urban centers, such as Corinth (and Kenchreai), Athens, and Tomis, and to a lesser degree in rural areas,[132] which gradually become isolated from the urban monetary economy. The extensive mint output at Thessalonica explains the large number of coins in the provinces of the Balkans. Thessalonica is especially influential in the western half of the peninsula, in Greece, Albania, and Serbia[133] and to a lesser degree in the east, at Odartsi, Agathopolis and in the region of Shumen.[134]

Although the evidence for Anatolia is still insufficient for broad generalizations, there is strong indication of a general increase in the volume of coins during the reign of Justin II. Apparently surprising, Thessalonica is a major supplier of coins at Sardis, where, at least in the first stage, 565–570, the coins struck by the Macedonian mint cover almost 35 percent of the finds (Figure 14b).[135] This seems to be a general characteristic of towns from western Anatolia, close to the coast,

129. See also the observations of Pottier (1983, 186).

130. Pottier (1983, 150).

131. Gândilă (2008, 322, table 4); Janković (1981, 66, annex 3); Ivanišević (1988, 93–94); Popović (1978a, 181–185).

132. Bellinger (1930, 46–47); Edwards (1933, 125–127); Mac Isaac (1987, 135–136); Hohlfelder (1978, 68–71); Thompson (1954, 68–69); Gândilă (2008, 322–323, table 4); Oberländer-Târnoveanu (2005, 383–384).

133. Edwards (1933, 125–127); Hohlfelder (1978, 68–71); Thompson (1954, 68–69); Spahiu (1979–1980, 378–381); Radić and Ivanišević (2006, 132–135). See also the composition of hoards found in these areas: Morrisson et al. (2006).

134. Gândilă (2008, 323, table 5); Iordanov, Koicev, and Mutafov (1998, 72, table 4); Zhekova (2006, 79).

135. Bates (1971, 54–55).

judging by the similar finds from Pergamum, Ephesus, and Side,[136] whereas further to the west the proportion dwindles, 15 percent at Pisidian Antioch, while no coins of Thessalonica are so far recorded at Amaseia, Pessinus, and Melitene.[137] Surprisingly, no such coins were found in the region of Bolu and Amasra close to the Black Sea, so we are still far from establishing a clear pattern. Coins from the second half of the reign are abundant at Melitene, which was a strategic position in the Armenian campaigns organized by Tiberius, now co-emperor with Justin II.

In the Near Eastern provinces the heavy influx of coins of Justin II has been often noted, especially because of the contrast with the post reform period of Justinian I, which is less prominent among finds. The number of finds is conspicuously high at Gerasa in Arabia and in Palaestine at Pella, Hammat Gader, Caesarea Maritima and to a lesser extent at Jerusalem and Nessana.[138] Although they are fairly well represented at Antioch, Hama, and Apamea,[139] no coins of Justin II have been reported among the admittedly small group of finds from Bālis,[140] and they have a generally weaker presence in the rural settlements from Syria, such as Çatal Hüyük and Déhès,[141] which parallels the situation observed by Ernest Oberländer-Târnoveanu in the case of the eastern Balkans.[142] It also accords with the observations made by Clive Foss for rural settlements in Syria where the archeological evidence suggests a period of decline after 550.[143]

The large number of coins of Justin II at Gerasa has been described by Alfred Bellinger as the most salient feature of EBC finds in this important city of the Decapolis.[144] The situation was rightly ascribed to the high presence of coins from Nicomedia, partially confirmed by the subsequent finds from the "Macellum." No clear explanation is given for this peculiar development.[145] Dealing with a similar situation at Pella, Kenneth Sheedy has suggested that it might reflect a new deployment of troops in the East for another episode of the war with Persia in the early 570s (Figure 5c).[146] There is no such parallel at Antioch, but indeed at Apamea,

136. Morrisson (1993, 55); Milne (1925, 390); Atlan (1976, 81–82).

137. Ireland 2000, (105–106); de Wilde (1997, 107); Devreker (1984, 195–196).

138. Bellinger (1938, 103–113); Marot (1998, 472–480); Sheedy (2001, 134–136); Barkay (2000, 299, table II); Evans (2006, 188–190); Ariel (1982, 326); Bellinger (1962, 72–73).

139. Waage (1952, 155–157); Balty (1984, 240–244); Thomsen (1986, 62).

140. Hennequin and Abū-l-Faraj (1978, 7–8).

141. Vorderstrasse (2005, 498); Morrisson (1980, 279).

142. Oberländer-Târnoveanu (2004, 348).

143. Foss (1997).

144. Bellinger (1938, 13).

145. This characteristic can be also noticed in most Syro-Palestinian hoards: Baramki (1939, 83–84); Leuthold (1971, 15); Mansfield (1995a, 350–351); Ariel (1996, 70); Bates and Kovacs (1996, 166); Naismith (2004, 298).

146. Sheedy (2002, 49).

the number of coins from Nicomedia is overwhelming.[147] Such an explanation is, however, weakened by a similar situation noticed in two distant sites, Amaseia and Pisidian Antioch, where although no invasions are recorded, the mint of Nicomedia has an unusually significant presence (Figure 14b).[148]

The collections point to a high output of *pentanummia* during the reign of Justin II (Figure 28a). This is indeed confirmed by finds in Constantinople and Pessinus where more than 75 percent of the finds are *pentanummia* pieces;[149] at Tomis, Sardis, and Antioch they represent approximately one third of the total, while in Greece they cover less than 20 percent (Figure 28b).[150] The cluster of small change in large urban centers points to a necessity of the market, which seems to be less felt in small towns and fortresses and even less in rural contexts. Less than 15 percent of the coins found in Scythia are *pentanummia*, while in Moesia Secunda they amount to a mere 4 percent.[151] No such coins are recorded among the published finds from Albania, Amaseia, Melitene, Caesarea Maritima, Pella, and Gerasa to name only the most important.[152]

In 579 Tiberius II, now sole ruler, attempted an ambitious reform designed to celebrate his consulship. The weight of the *follis* was lifted to a Justinianic standard and the collections as well as the numerous finds from Scythia indicate a high mint output for this special series (Figure 3). His measure, no doubt popular with the masses, was short-lived and most likely was never intended as a true reform meant to re-establish the heavy standard of Justinian. Albeit less spectacular, the heavier *folles* introduced by Maurice in 602 with the occasion of his consulship testify to the irregular nature of these special issues.

As usual, the mint of Constantinople issued more than half the coins put in circulation, followed by Antioch and Nicomedia. The mint of Thessalonica is ranked higher than Cyzicus, probably because of the increasing military activity at the Danube border (Figure 16a). The production of the peculiar 30-*nummia* introduced by Tiberius II was perhaps less impressive than the collections would let us believe. This scarcer denomination was likely to attract the collectors' attention which explains their heavy presence in the collections, on average amounting to 10 percent of the entire number of coins attributed to Tiberius II (Figure 29a). Scythia offers a more

147. Balty (1984, 240–244).
148. Ireland (2000, 105–106).
149. Hendy (1986, 297–300); Hendy (2007, 208–211); de Wilde (1997, 107); Devreker (1984, 211).
150. Isvoranu and Poenaru Bordea (2003, 153, table 3); Bates (1971, 49–61); Waage (1952, 156).
151. Gândilă (2008, 318, table 5); Mihailov (2008, 281, table 4).
152. Spahiu (1979–1980, 378–381); Ireland (2000, 105–106); Ariel (1986, 142); Lampinen (1992, 172); Evans (2006, 188–190); Sheedy (2001, 134–136); Bellinger (1938, 98–102); Marot (1998, 465–471).

realistic proportion, with the 30-*nummia* accounting for less than 4 percent.[153]

In the three major regions of the Eastern Empire the influx of coins issued by Tiberius II is characterized by a high degree of variation. At the Danube border it appears that the coins of Tiberius II made little impact as can be seen in the catalogue of finds from Dinogetia, Capidava, Aquis, Viminacium, and the Belgrade museum.[154] On the western sector of the *limes* the coins from Thessalonica played an important role, and indeed in Greece, at Corinth and Athens, where close to 40 percent of the coin finds are issued by the Macedonian mint.[155] The mint of Antioch becomes more important in the Balkans, and it is possibly a sign that some troops were brought from the eastern front, despite Tiberius' tendency to concentrate on the war with Persia.[156] There is a generally higher number of coins of Tiberius found on the Black Sea coast, Histria, Callatis, and Accres Castellum being a few major examples.[157] Another characteristic of the Balkan settlements is the fact that in most cases when the coin circulation dropped during the reign of Tiberius II it never recovered in the following decades, a sign of the gradual disintegration of urban life in the area.

Very few coins have been found in Constantinople, at Saraçhane and Kalenderhane,[158] and a similar situation can be seen in the northern part of Anatolia judging by the coins from the museums in Amasya and Bolu, as well as in Pisidia at Antioch, Sagalassos and in the area of modern Isparta.[159] Sardis and Melitene, far apart on the map of Anatolia, share the same tendency and it seems so far that only Side provides a larger number of coins from Tiberius II (Figure 5b).[160] Jumping to the island of Cyprus one notices a contrasting image: at Salamis and Curium the number of coins of Tiberius II is conspicuously high given his short reign.[161] Considering that Caesarea Maritima in Palestine has yielded a similarly high number of coins from this period,[162] we can advance a provisional hypothesis that the coins of Tiberius II circulated more intensively on sea routes.

The observation regarding the circulation of smaller denominations made for the reign of Justin II remains valid for the short reign of Tiberius II (Figure 29a).

153. Gândilă (2008, 318, table 5).

154. Gândilă (2008, 322–323, table 4); Janković (1981, 66, annex 3); Ivanišević (1988, 94); Radić and Ivanišević (2006, 136).

155. Edwards (1933, 128–129); Mac Isaac (1987, 136); Thómpson (1954, 69).

156. Whitby (1988, 87).

157. Gândilă (2008, 322–323, table 3).

158. Hendy (1986, 300–301); Hendy (2007, 212).

159. No coins of Tiberius can be found among the four excavation reports from Sagalassos mentioned in n. 62.

160. Bates (1971, 63–66); Atlan (1976, 84).

161. Callot (2004, 46–47); Cox (1959, 79).

162. Evans (2006, 190–191).

Aside from a few urban centers such as Constantinople, Antioch, Tomis, Corinth, Pisidian Antioch, and Sardis the 10- and 5-*nummia* pieces become scarcely used across the Eastern Empire (Figure 29b). Antioch and Constantinople remain the main mints issuing small denominations, no doubt partly because of the local needs of the two metropoleis.

During the reign of Maurice the value of the copper *follis* remained stabilized at 600 *folles* per *solidus*. The collections point to a general decrease in mint output during the last two decades of the sixth century, when only two peaks reached in 589/90 and 602 resemble the quantity of coins issued by Justin II (Figure 3). The first peak is partly due to the high output of Antioch. During regnal year 8 the old type inherited from Tiberius II continued to be struck along with the new type introduced by Maurice, which increases the total number of coins from this year. The other peak, in 602, coincides with the consulship assumed by the emperor. A special type was struck for this special occasion having the emperor represented in consular robes instead of the usual military cuirass. A large number of coins were issued in a very short time interval, which explains why many specimens are over-struck on previous issues. It also points to a crisis of raw material for striking fresh coins, a typical phenomenon in the first two decades of the seventh century.

The outstanding feature in mint activity is the high output of Antioch through-out the period, sometimes surpassing the production of Constantinople (Figure 17a). The intense military activity which characterizes the reign of Maurice is an important factor in explaining this phenomenon. The high number of troops in-volved in the war against Persia in the 580s and in the Balkans in the 590s increased the demand for fresh coins. The major role of Antioch even after the eastern front was closed, coupled with the unusually low output of Constantinople in the last years of the sixth century when the Empire was waging war against the Slavs and Avars are somewhat perplexing. Between 7 and 22 percent of the coins of Maurice in the northern Balkans, including the Danube fortresses were issued in Antioch. Especially in the western sector of the Lower Danube the coins from Antioch are found in larger numbers. Conversely, in towns located on the Black Sea coast, such as Tomis, Callatis, Accres Castellum and Agathopolis, very few such coins have been found.[163] This is also true for the coins found in Constantinople, at Kalender-hane and Saraçhane (Figure 17b).[164]

It is unlikely that the mint of Antioch was commissioned to insure the pay-ment of troops stationed in the Balkans. It is more probable that the coins were brought by the large number of troops transferred by Maurice after the war with Persia was brought to an end. This does not help to explain the low activity of the mint of Constantinople especially between 597 and 602 (excepting the consular

163. Gândilă (2008, 322–323, table 4); Iordanov, Koicev, and Mutafov (1998, 73, table 6).
164. Hendy (1986, 301–305); Hendy (2007, 213–215).

type in 602) when the war against the Avars was in full motion. Michael Whitby considers that the emperor's decision to leave the troops stationed north of the Danube for the winter of 602 had specific military purposes, *contra* Theophylact, who suggested that financial considerations were behind this decision.[165] Although multiple factors might have been at play, the low mint output of Constantinople and also Nicomedia, Cyzicus, and Thessalonica point to a serious financial crisis which must not be underestimated, despite the emperor's expenditure with the occasion of his consulate.

The coin finds from the Balkans concentrate on the eastern part, in the provinces adjacent to the Black Sea. The payment of the troops stationed in the Danubian fortresses seems to have been a serious problem. The numerous finds from the province of Scythia show a high level of coin loss for the regnal years 5 and 10, which seem to coincide with the distribution of the quinquennial *donativa* to the troops. One would have expected a similar peak in 597 as well, which is hardly the case.[166] Its absence is due to the low activity of the mints of Constantinople, Nicomedia, Cyzicus and Thessalonica, already mentioned, and coincides with some serious military setbacks at the Danube frontier, menaced by the Avars who reached as far as Tomis, the capital of Scythia, besieged in 597–598.[167] The low ebb in coin production during the last five years of the century indicates that military payments in the Balkans were delayed; discontent was certainly building up in the frontier garrisons and would eventually turn into rebellion in 602. Theophanes Confessor, though a later source, informs us about the deep financial crisis of the state, forced to pay the soldiers' salaries only one third in coin and the rest in commodities.[168]

Thessalonica, whose coinage was a major source of payment for the troops stationed on the Danube, reduced its output dramatically during the last years of the sixth century. The activity of this mint has been a debated issue in the last decades and it is primarily connected with the dating of the siege of Thessalonica.[169] Figure 4 represents a comparison between the coins from the collections (336 coins) and the finds from Scythia (248 coins). The trend is clearly similar, while the peculiarities of Scythia are marked by the high peaks of 568/9/70 and 574/5, which are consistent with the situation in Serbia: the collection of the National Museum in Belgrade provides forty-six specimens from Justin II of which eighteen are dated 569/70 and thirteen, 574/5.[170]

165. Whitby (1988, 165–169).
166. Gândilă (2008, 311).
167. Madgearu (1996, 50)
168. See the discussion by Yannopoulos (1987, 129).
169. Popović (1975, 459–464) ; Popović (1978b, 622); Metcalf (1991, 142).
170. Radić and Ivanišević (2006, 132–135).

The year-by-year fluctuations bring forth even more interesting facts about the Thessalonican mint output after 578. D. M. Metcalf maintained that 580 was a critical moment when the mint activity was virtually paralyzed.[171] Figure 4 partly confirms Metcalf's assertion with respect to the mint's influence in the Balkans around year 580, although a few specimens are available in the Belgrade collection as well as in Scythia. While this might be true for the Balkans (579–582 provides a striking difference in the comparison chart), the major collections provide six specimens from 580/1 and less for the next three years. Therefore, one can conclude that Metcalf's statement is true as a local feature and not necessarily a problem of mint output. The same goes with the theory introduced by Vladislav Popović who supposed that the mint activity at Thessalonica virtually ceased in 585/6, and yet we find four specimens in the collections and no less than five (only single finds included) in Scythia.[172] The most critical period in the mint's activity occurred toward the turn of the century, 597–600, and is a more general phenomenon of the monetary economy.

The statistical value of coin finds of Maurice in Anatolia is usually double the value established for the Balkans (Figures 5a–b). The frequent invasions and the general devastation of the Danube provinces are certainly among the major reasons for this striking difference. Much as in the Balkans, however, the numerous coin finds from urban sites like Sardis, Amaseia, Pisidian Antioch, Side, and Malatya usually form a continuous sequence until 595.[173] The scarcity of coins from the later years and the similarity with the Balkans force us to conclude that economic reasons affecting the mint output should be held responsible for this situation and not military activity, pervasive in the Balkans, but almost nonexistent in most of Anatolia. Another distinctive characteristic is the large influence of the Antioch mint in Anatolia. At Amaseia and Melitene around 50 percent of the coins were struck in Antioch, while the average for most of the towns for which we have sufficient information is more than 20 percent.

Two prominent exceptions are Sardis and Amasra where the mint of Antioch is less significant or not present at all. In both towns, however, the coins from Thessalonica represent an important proportion of the group, suggesting different channels of coin distribution in Anatolia, not necessarily based on geographic location (Figure 17b).[174] The collection of the archaeology museum in Bolu (ancient Claudiopolis), in the ancient province of Bithynia, far from Antioch, has no coins of Maurice from Thessalonica, but many from Antioch, amounting to 30 percent of the total. This is a general characteristic of the collection for the entire sixth

171. Metcalf (1991, 142).
172. Popović (1978b, 622); Gândilă (2008, 320).
173. Bates (1971, 67–78); Ireland (2000, 106–107); Atlan (1976, 84–86).
174. Bates (1971, 72–73); Ireland and Atesogullari (1996, 124).

century. Jumping to the island of Cyprus we notice a combined influence of Antioch and Thessalonica at Salamis and Curium, no doubt because of the maritime dimension of both the towns and the mints.[175]

In Syria-Palestine the proportion of coins issued by Maurice is slightly higher than in Anatolia. Antioch itself provides a high number, due to the presence of the mint in the city and its influence is also felt in the vicinity, if less overwhelming, at Hama, Déhès, Apamea, and Çatal Hüyük.[176] Southward, on the coast, at Berytus and Caesarea, a large number of coins from Antioch are recorded among finds, perhaps a sign of commercial activities and also in towns from the Palestinian inland, such as Jerusalem and Nessana.[177] The large coin hoards found in the Near Eastern provinces testify to the fact that Antioch played a more important role in this region, compared to the Balkans and Anatolia.[178] The decline in coin circulation is now felt in some previously prosperous towns, most importantly at Pella and Gerasa. Kenneth Sheedy has explained this situation by the impoverishment of the two centers,[179] while Alan Walmsley has suggested that state consignments ended in this period.[180] It is hard to make any generalizations at the scale of the entire province of Arabia or Palaestina II since the coin samples for most settlements are too small to observe any clear tendencies in coin circulation. It should be noted, however, that in most cases finds from Maurice Tiberius are present.

The lower denominations continued to be struck in limited numbers and their use was generally restricted to the urban economy (Figure 30b). Both the collections and site finds point to a sharp decline in the production of ⅛-*folles*, which remain abundant only among the finds from Constantinople and to a lesser degree at Sardis and Ephesus.[181] The ¼-*follis* is found in a wider variety of settlements, in major urban centers such as Tomis, Pisidian Antioch, Salamis, and Antioch, and occasionally in rural settlements like Déhès, in Syria.[182]

A new increase in coin output can be noticed during the reign of Phocas, which is another reason to reconsider the merits of his reign (Figure 2a). Historians in the past have relied perhaps too heavily on written sources biased against Phocas to describe his reign in overly negative terms. The collections prove that his coin-

175. Callot (2004, 48–51); Cox (1959, 80).

176. Waage (1952, 159–160); Thomsen (1986, 62); Morrisson (1980, 279); Balty (1984, 240–244); Vorderstrasse (2005, 498–499).

177. Butcher (2003, 271–273); Ariel (1986, 142–143); Evans (2006, 193–194); Ariel (1982, 326); Bellinger (1962, 73).

178. Noeske (2000, II); Morrisson et al. (2006).

179. Sheedy (2001, 52).

180. Walmsley (1999, 345).

181. Hendy (1986, 301–305; 2007, 213–215); Bates (1971, 67–78); Milne (1925, 390).

182. Isvoranu and Poenaru Bordea (2003, 153, table 3); Callot (2004, 51); Waage (1952, 159–160); Morrisson (1980, 279).

age was abundant, although it must be noted that a good proportion of his copper coinage is made of overstrikes, usually on coins of Maurice. This is not so much a case of *damnatio memoriae* as a direct result of a shortage of copper building up in the course of the sixth century as a consequence of inflation, hoarding, and casual loss. Chiefly *folles* were overstruck and mainly in Constantinople, Nicomedia, and Cyzicus. Based on the evidence of the collections, the overstruck group represents on average c. 25 percent of the total, while the carefully published finds from Sardis reveal that c. 22 percent of the *folles* of Phocas are overstruck.[183] The mint of Antioch is excluded from these calculations because it rarely overstruck its issues.

Except for the collection in Paris,[184] there is a strong indication of decline in mint output in the last regnal years, probably because of the turmoil created by the Heraclian revolt. The mint of Antioch continues to be the second most important after Constantinople and its output can be related to the new offensive initiated by the Persian king after the deposition of Maurice. Surprisingly, the two major mints are closely followed by Cyzicus, which became extremely active after having a minor role throughout the sixth century (Figure 18a).

The military conditions in the Balkans become aggravated after the rebellion of 602. Although the thesis of the collapse of the Danube *limes* in 602 is no longer tenable,[185] numerous fortifications, particularly on the western sector, were severely affected. There is a marked difference in coin circulation between the settlements on the border, such as Capidava, Novae, Aquis, and Viminacium,[186] where few or no coins of Phocas were found, and towns further away from the military operations, such as Tomis, Accres Castellum, Corinth, Athens, and Constantinople itself, where the volume of finds marks a visible increase compared to the reign of Maurice (Figure 5a).[187] A very similar tendency can be observed in Anatolia, where most of the urban settlements have yielded a large number of finds from Phocas (Figure 5b). One major exception is Melitene situated close to the front line after the Persians had occupied the main strategic towns in Upper Mesopotamia. The mint of Antioch, less visible in the Balkans, covers more than 30 percent of the

183. Bates (1971, 67–78).

184. The collection of the Bibliothèque Nationale shows a prominent peak in 609/10, apparently inexplicable (Figure 3). A closer examination of the coins' provenance reveals the fact that all coins belonged to the Schlumberger collection; most of them were minted in Antioch and were purchased in Aleppo by the French scholar and might be part of a hoard.

185. Barnea (1990).

186. Gândilă (2008, 322–323, table 4); Dimitrov (1998, 111); Janković (1981, 66, annex 3); Ivanišević (1988, 94).

187. Gândilă (2008, 322–323, table 4); Bellinger (1925, 46–47); Edwards (1933, 130–131); Fisher (1984, 245); Mac Isaac (1987, 136); Thompson (1954, 69–70); Hendy (1986, 305–308); Hendy (2007, 216–218).

coins found in Anatolia, an important increase compared to the reign of Maurice. As expected, the finds from the Near Eastern provinces show an even more pronounced influence of Antioch, especially at Gerasa and Caesarea, probably itself a sign of the threat posed by the Persian armies (Figure 18b).[188] However, the influence of Antioch stops being so pervasive in the Near East. At Hama, Jerusalem, and Nessana, where Antioch had always been an important supplier of fresh coins, no such finds have been reported.[189] This is not only a matter of distribution but also a problem of coin supply, since in many towns from Syria-Palestine, unlike what we have seen in the Balkans and Anatolia, the volume of fresh coins stagnates or decreases during the reign of Phocas (Figure 5c). The extreme scarcity of coins from Thessalonica, which had been a minor but steady supplier of coins since the reign of Justin II, is possibly another sign of decline. The low number of smaller denominations adds to this picture of fall in coin circulation (Figure 31b). Besides Antioch, no other urban center in Syria-Palestine provides such issues.[190] The rare hoard of small change found in Aleppo could originate from the circulating medium of the great Syrian metropolis.[191] By comparison, Tomis and Odartsi in the Balkans,[192] Sagalassos, Pisidian Antioch, and Sardis in Anatolia,[193] and Salamis in Cyprus[194] continued to receive lower denominations, ¼-folles and even ⅛-folles.

It is often considered that the long reign of Heraclius marks the end of Antiquity. The empire lost its eastern provinces to the hands of the Arabs and its influence in the Balkans to the repeated attacks of Slavs and Avars. By necessity, this comparative analysis has to end with the first decade of Heraclius' reign, when the coin circulation drops in Scythia, our main element of comparison with the museum collections. The first years of reign are characterized by an abundant coinage with a high peak reached in 612–614 (Figure 3). It coincides with an important change in iconography, the frontal bust of the emperor being replaced with the standing figures of Heraclius and his son Heraclius Constantine. One could argue that the successive changes in iconography are the reason why the collections possess so many coins from this time interval. This is not the case, since the abundant material from Anatolia and Syria shows a very similar peak in the same years and is, of course, un-

188. Bellinger (1938, 114–116); Marot (1998, 481–483); Ariel (1986, 143); Evans (2006, 195–196).

189. Thomsen (1986, 62); Ariel (1982, 326); Bellinger (1962, 73–74). See, however, the group of coins purchased in Jerusalem in 1963 in which 30 percent of the coins of Phocas come from Antioch (Metcalf and Payne 1965, 209).

190. Waage (1952, 161–162).

191. Mansfield (2003, 354–355).

192. Isvoranu and Poenaru Bordea (2003, 153, table 3).

193. Scheers (1995, 314); Bates (1971, 88–89).

194. Callot (2004, 52–53).

affected by selection in the hands of collectors or museum curators (Figure D).[195]

Even from these early years of reign, the complexity of the early Byzantine monetary system began to slowly break down. The mint of Antioch was closed, never to be reopened for regular issues, while the mints in Cyzicus (615/6) and Nicomedia (618/9) were temporarily shut-down. The multi-denominational system ceased to be functional, after the mints stopped issuing ⅛-*folles* and concentrated c. 90 percent of their activity on the production of *folles* (Figure 32a). Over 90 percent of the coins from the first six years of reign are overstruck, especially the ones belonging to the second type of Grierson's classification.[196] The "conversion" of large quantities of coins issued by Maurice and Phocas affects the quantitative estimation for these two reigns. To give one example, the number of undertypes of Phocas in *DOC* would increase by 30 percent the total number of *folles* issued during his reign.

The Balkans witness a severe downfall in coin circulation in the second decade of the seventh century. Isolated spots of Byzantine control usually located around urban centers from the Black Sea coast or Danubian fortresses still held by the Empire continued to receive fresh coins. With the exception of Durostorum, the number of coins found at Capidava, Sacidava, Novae, and Viminacium are too meager to represent anything but the last payments sent to the small garrisons still holding the Empire's position at the Danube.[197] Urban life continued its course to some extent at Tomis and Mesembria and especially at Corinth and Athens, to name the most important centers (Figure 5a),[198] but later in the century the eastern Balkans would be menaced by a new and long lasting enemy of the Byzantine state, the Bulgars. Most of the coins found in the Balkans were issued either in Constantinople and Nicomedia, while Cyzicus and Thessalonica have a negligible presence (Figure 19b). As expected, most of them are *folles*, over 80 percent on average, and ½-*folles*; ¼-*folles* are lacking, even among finds from Constantinople (Figure 32b).

In Anatolia we encounter a totally different situation. The coins of Heraclius are among the most common EBC found during excavations or in local archaeology museums. In statistical terms they usually represent between 20 and 40 percent of the total number of finds, which is in sharp contrast to the picture offered by the Balkans. Excavations at Sardis and Side yielded a particularly high number of finds (Figure 5b), while the coins preserved in the Bolu and Isparta museums

195. Bell (1916, 82–95); Bates (1971, 95–109).

196. *DOC* II/1, 226.

197. Oberländer-Tărnoveanu (1996, 97–127); Gândilă (2006–2007, 118); Gândilă (2003–2005, 140); Dimitrov (1998, 111); Ivanišević (1988, 94).

198. Gândilă (2008, 322–323, table 4); Edwards (1933, 131–132); Mac Isaac (1987, 136); Thompson (1954, 70).

point to a massive influx of coins in the respective areas.[199] It should be noted however that the abundance of coins in these early years predates the Persian invasion, which initially affected the south-eastern part of Anatolia but soon got deeper into the Byzantine heartland where the Persians sacked Caesarea, Ancyra, and Sardis and took the island of Rhodes.[200] The abundance of early Heraclian issues is most striking in the islands, in Cyprus,[201] at Salamis, Curium, and Paphos and on Samos[202] in the Aegean, where an impressive number of coins have been recovered from the Tunnel of Eupalinos, among which are some rare ¼-*folles*. The developments in Cyprus have been ascribed to an increased strategic importance of the island after Antioch was occupied by the Persians, which might also explain the ephemeral presence of an official mint on the island.[203]

The first decades of the seventh century brought an unprecedented series of invasions led by the Persians and later Arabs which sealed the fate of the Byzantine provinces in Syria-Palestine. The increased number of hoards testifies to the growing insecurity in the area after 602.[204] Site finds, however, provide us with a mixed picture. Relatively few early coins of Heraclius found their way into Antioch and Apamea,[205] the two major cities of the region, the finds being two or even three times fewer than in Anatolia, somewhat resembling the situation encountered in the northern Balkans. Surprisingly, at Hama[206] the finds are much more numerous and correspond with an unexpected period of reconstruction late in the sixth century.[207] In Palestine we notice a sensible increase in coin finds, at Caesarea, Jerusalem, and Pella,[208] but they are by no means characteristic of the region as a whole (Figure 5c).[209]

199. Bates (1971, 95–109); Bell (1916, 82–95); Atlan (1976, 88–92).

200. Foss (1975, 721–747).

201. Callot (2004, 54–75); Cox (1959, 80–81); Nicolaou (1990, 194–199).

202. Jantzen (2004, 156, 160).

203. Metcalf (2001, 135).

204. The relevant hoards are Khirbet Dubel, Tell Bissé, Baalbek, Khirbet Fandaqumya, Khirbet Deir Dassawi, Cyrrhus, "Syria," and Deir Dassawi Noeske (2000, II); Quazrin Ariel (1996); "Northern Syria" Mansfield (2003); "Lebanon" Kruszynski (1999), and probably also three hoards with uncertain Near Eastern provenance buried after 602, Mansfield (1995); Naismith (2004); For a recent catalogue of hoards from Palestine see Waner and Safray (2001).

205. Waage (1952, 162–164); Balty (1984, 240–245).

206. Thomsen (1986, 62–63).

207. Foss (1997, 259).

208. Evans (2006, 197–198); Ariel (1982, 326); Sheedy (2001, 139–141).

209. Few or no early Heraclian coppers have been reported among the fairly large number of finds from Hammat Gader, Chorazin, Tel Jezreel, and Samaria, see Barkay (1997, 279–300); Kloetzli (1970, 367–369); Moorhead (1997, 162–163); Fulco and Zayadine (1981, 221–223).

## Conclusion

The statistical validity of large collections of EBC can no longer be overlooked. The comparison of five major collections with the numerous finds from the province of Scythia and the hoards from the Near East has revealed a number of quantitative similarities, which need to be addressed. The purpose of analyzing the collections from a statistical perspective is not to provide us with absolute figures. Unfortunately the statistical tools often used in numismatics are far more sophisticated and precise than the sampled evidence, which is most of the time fragmentary. There are too many lacunae in our knowledge of the monetary policies conducted by Early Byzantium to attempt any definitive propositions. The nature of the evidence and the inherent methodological limitations are an invitation to caution.[210] Any statistical results will need to be confirmed and re-confirmed by future evidence before attempting any conclusive remarks. Relative fluctuations can, however, be discerned at this point and the large number of copper coins in the major museum collections offer a solid base on which to re-construct the rhythm of mint output and from which to draw a number of general remarks. Accounting for variation in the volume of output is of course more difficult and much more needs to be done in the realm of interpretation to explain such fluctuations. Such an understanding cannot be accomplished only by studying the de-contextualized coins from the public collections. Archaeological excavations in the Balkans, Anatolia, and the Near East offer the most promising perspectives for understanding regional patterns in a comparative fashion. Nonetheless, the high correlation of the major collections of EBC remains instrumental for a better understanding of annual coin production. Where significant site finds are available they should be analyzed against this pattern and if anomalies (i.e., local particularities) are spotted they need to be explained within a geographical and historical framework. Many interpretations based on political/military events, including some of my own conclusions regarding the coin circulation in Dobrudja,[211] need to be reassessed, because "abnormal" levels in coin circulation can not be properly detected and understood without basic knowledge of the "normal" pattern. It will soon become apparent that low points in the statistical curve of a region are very often reflections of coin production and distribution at the center and less the result of provincial developments alone.[212]

210. See Robertson (1989) for a methodological discussion and an invitation to caution in the case of Roman coins, which could be easily extrapolated to the Byzantine period as well.

211. Gândilă (2003–2005).

212. The activity of provincial mints should be part of the general explanation regarding local particularities. Indeed the mint of Thessalonica will heavily influence the coin distribution in the western Balkans, while the mint of Antioch will have a similar effect in Syria

I have shown in the previous sections that, in spite of the still insufficient evidence, an analysis can be undertaken at the inter-regional level, which is undoubtedly the most appropriate course of action, enabling us, at least provisionally, to examine, understand, and explain regional peculiarities and different levels of monetization and economic integration. Studying coin circulation in a single province without reference to the circulating medium in other corners of the Empire can lead to false generalizations and unreliable interpretations of the numismatic material. The coin finds from a major urban site will not inform us sufficiently about coin circulation in the whole province, while the finds from a province will not be necessarily relevant for an entire region. Therefore, I have tried to paint, perhaps in overly broad strokes, a comparative tryptich of circulation, with one panel devoted to the Balkans and two others for Anatolia and Syria-Palestine in the hope that future studies will soon correct and improve this provisional effort. The broad outlines drawn for Anatolia, and to a certain extent for the Near East, are subject to change as new evidence surfaces. At least in the northern Balkans the current body of evidence is large enough to insure the stability of present analyses although, of course, at more detailed level the overall scheme will certainly require minor adjustments. The common features observed in many urban centers of the Near Eastern provinces are likely to endure, although new data is expected to color the grey areas in the big picture and perhaps to bring more homogeneity in what seems like a very diverse landscape. Anatolia is by far the most sensitive region to future developments and constitutes the most promising avenue to test both the uniting and the distinctive features of coin circulation in the major geographical units of the Eastern Empire.

## ACKNOWLEDGEMENTS:

I wish to express my gratitude to Dr. Florin Curta for reading and critiquing several drafts; Ralf Althoff, Gabriela Bijovsky, Dr. Zeliha Demirel Gökalp, Dr. Ernest Oberländer-Târnoveanu, and Dr. Alan Stahl for commenting on the final draft and for providing valuable information and access to unpublished material from the Balkans, Anatolia, and Palestine, and to the curatorial staff of the American Numismatic Society for allowing me to study their rich collection of Byzantine coins. Sections of this paper were presented in 2009 at the International Congress on Medieval Studies, Kalamazoo, at the Summer Seminar of the American Numismatic Society, New York, and at the International Numismatic Congress, Glasgow. I thank all these audiences for their questions and comments.

(Figures 6–19). Given the different channels of distribution, towns from Syria and Macedonia will certainly differ to some extent in their circulation patterns.

## ABBREVIATIONS

ANS = American Numismatic Society

BMC = Wroth, W. *Catalogue of the imperial Byzantine coins in the British Museum*, vol. 1. London, 1908.

BNP = Morrisson, C. *Catalogue des monnaies byzantines de la Bibliothèque Nationale (491–1204). Tome prémier: D'Anastase à Justinien II (491–711)*. Paris: Bibliothèque Nationale, 1970.

DOC = Bellinger, A. R., and P. Grierson, eds. *Catalogue of the Byzantine coins in the Dumbarton Oaks collection and in the Whittemore collection*. vol. I–II. Washington, DC: Dumbarton Oaks Center for Byzantine Studies, 1966–1968.

KOD = Althoff, R. Sammlung Köhler-Osbahr. *Band V/1–2. Byzantinische Münzen und ihr Umfeld*. Duisburg, Kultur und Stadthistorisches Museum, 1998–1999.

MIB = Hahn, W. *Moneta Imperii Byzantini*, 3 vol. Vienna: Verlag der Österreichischen Akademie der Wissenschaften, 1973–1981.

Ratto = Ratto, R. *Monnaies byzantines et d'autres pays contemporains à l'époque Byzantine*. Lugano, 1930; reprint by J. Schulman. Amsterdam, 1959.

## REFERENCES

Ariel, D. T. 1982. A survey of coin finds in Jerusalem. *Liber Annuus* 32: 273–326.

———. 1986. The coins. In *Excavations at Caesarea Maritima, 1975, 1976, 1979: Final Report*, L. I. Levine and E. Netzer, eds., pp. 137–148. Jerusalem: Hebrew University of Jerusalem.

———. 1987. Coins from the synagogue at 'En Nashut. *Israel Exploration Journal* 37: 147–156.

———. 1996. A hoard of Byzantine *folles* from Qazrin. *'Atiqot* 29: 69–76.

Arslan, E. A. 2000. *Catalogo delle monete bizantine del Museo Provinciale di Catanzaro*. Catanzaro: Amministrazione Provinciale di Catanzaro.

Ashton, R., C. Lightfoot, and A. Özme. 2000. Ancient and Medieval coins in Bolvadin (Turkey). *Anatolia Antiqua* 8: 171–195.

Atlan, S. 1976. *1947–1967 Yılları Side kazıları sırasında elde edilen sikkeler*. Ankara: Türk Tarih Kurumu Basımevi.

Baldwin's. 1995. *Byzantine gold coins from the P. J. Donald collection, October 11*. London.

Balty, J. 1984. Monnaies Byzantines des maisons d'Apamée: étude comparative. In *Apamée de Syrie: bilan des recherches archéologiques 1973–1979: aspects de l'architecture domestique d'Apamée: actes du colloque tenu à Bruxelles les 29, 30 et 31 mai 1980*, J. Balty, ed., pp. 239–248. Bruxelles: Centre belge de recherches archéologiques à Apamée de Syrie.

Baramki, J. 1939. A hoard of Byzantine coins. *Quarterly of the Department of Antiquities in Palestine* 8: 81–85.

Barkay, R. 1997. Roman and Byzantine coins. In *The Roman baths of Hammat Gader. Final Report*, Y. Hirschfeld et al., pp. 279–300. Jerusalem: The Israel Exploration Society.

———. 2000. The coins of Horvat 'Eleq. In *Ramat Hanadiv excavations. Final report of the 1984–1998 seasons*, Y. Hirschfeld et al., pp. 377–419. Jerusalem: The Israel Exploration Society.

Barnea, Al. 1990. Einige Bemerkungen zur Chronologie des Limes an der unteren Donau in spätrömischer Zeit. *Dacia* 34: 283–290.

Bates, G. E. 1971. *Byzantine coins*. Cambridge MA: Harvard University Press.

———. *A Byzantine Coin Collection*, Boston: Privately Printed, 1981.

Bates, M. L., and F. L. Kovacs. A hoard of large Byzantine and Arab-Byzantine coppers. *Numismatic Chronicle* 156: 165–173.

Bateson, J. D, and I.G. Campbell. *Byzantine and Early Medieval Western European Coins in the Hunter Coin Cabinet*. London: Spink, 1998.

Beliën, P. 2005. A hoard of Byzantine *folles* from Beirut. *Numismatic Chronicle* 165: 314–322.

Bell, H. W. 1916. *Sardis*, vol. XI, part I, 1910–1914: *Coins*, 76–95. Leiden: Brill.

Bellinger, Alfred R. 1930. *Catalogue of the coins found at Corinth, 1925*. New Haven: Yale University Press.

Bellinger, A. R. 1962. Coins. In *Excavations at Nessana*, H. D. Colt, ed., pp. 70–75. London: British School of Archaeology in Jerusalem.

———. 1938. *Coins from Jerash, 1928–1934*. New York: American Numismatic Society.

Bendall, S. 2002. A neglected nineteenth century numismatist. *Numismatic Circular* 110: 261–264.

Betlyon, J. W. 1988. Coins from the 1985 Season of the Limes Arabicus Project. In *Preliminary Report on the 1985 Season of the Limes Arabicus Project*, S. T. Parker, ed., pp. 162–174. *Bulletin of the American Schools of Oriental Research. Supplemental Studies* 25.

Bijovsky, G. 1998. The Gush Halav hoard reconsidered. *'Atiqot* 35: 77–106.

———. 2002. The Coins. In S. Agady, M. Arazi, B. Arubas, S. Hadad, E. Khamis, and Y. Tsafrir, The Bet Shean Archaeological Project, 507–512. In *What Athens has to do with Jerusalem. Essays on classical, Jewish, and Early Christian art and archaeology in honor of Gideon Foerster*, Leonard V. Rutgers, ed., pp. 423–534. Leuven: Peeters.

Blake, R. P. 1942. The monetary reform of Anastasius and its economic implications. In *Studies in the history of culture*, pp. 84–97. Freeport NY: Books for Libraries Press.

Bonham's. 1980. *A catalogue of standard Byzantine and Dark Age gold coins, December 3*. London.

Boutin, S. *Collection N.K. Monnaies des Empires de Byzance*. Wetteren: Cultura, 1983.

Butcher, K. 2003. Archaeology of the Beirut Souks 1. Small change in ancient Beirut: the coin finds from BEY 006 and BEY 045: Iron Age, Hellenistic, Roman and Byzantine periods. *Berytus* 45–46, 2001–2002. Beirut: American University of Beirut.

Buttrey, T. V. 1981. Byzantine, medieval and modern coins and tokens. In *Greek, Roman, and Islamic coins from Sardis*, T. V. Buttrey, A. Johnson, K. M. Mac Kenzie, and M. L. Bates, pp. 204–224. Cambridge: Harvard University Press.

———. 1993. Calculating ancient coin production: facts and fantasies. *Numismatic Chronicle* 153: 335–351.

———. 1994. Calculating ancient coin production II: why it cannot be done. *Numismatic Chronicle* 154: 341–352.

———, and S. E Buttrey. 1997. Calculating ancient coin production, again. *American Journal of Numismatics* 9: 113–135.

de Callataÿ, F. 1995. Calculating ancient coin production: seeking a balance. *Numismatic Chronicle* 155: 289–311.

Callegher, B. *Catalogo delle monete bizantine, vandale, ostrogote e longobarde del Museo Bottacin*. Vol. I. Padova: Comune di Padova, Musei e biblioteche, 2000.

Callot, O. 2004. *Salamine de Chypre. XVI Les monnaies. Fouilles de la ville 1964–1974*. Paris: Boccard.

Callu, J.-P. 1982. Le tarif d'Abydos et la reforme monétaire d'Anastase. *Proceedings of the 9th International Congress of Numismatics, Berne, September 1979*, T. Hackens and R. Weiller, eds., pp. 731–740. Louvain-la-Neuve: Association internationale des numismates professionnels.

Carcasonne, C. 1987. *Methodes statistiques en numismatique*. Louvain-la-Neuve: Séminaire de Numismatique Marcel Hoc.

———, and J. Guey. 1978. Valeur statistique des petits échantillons. *Revue Belge de Numismatique* 124: 5–21.

———, and T. Hackens. 1981. *Statistique et numismatique: table ronde organisée par le Centre de mathématique sociale de l'Ecole des hautes études en sciences sociales de Paris et le Séminaire de Numismatique Marcel Hoc de l'Université Catholique de Louvain, Paris, 17–19 sept. 1979*. Strasbourg: Conseil de l'Europe, Assemblée parlementaire.

Casey, P. J. 1996. Justinian, the *limitanei*, and Arab-Byzantine relations in the 6th c. *Journal of Roman Archaeology* 9:214–222.

Christie's. 1986. *The Goodacre collection of Byzantine coins, April 22*. London.

Cox, D. 1959. Coins from the excavations at Curium, 1932–1953. *Numismatic Notes and Monographs* 145. New York: American Numismatic Society.

Curta, F. 1996. Invasion or inflation? Sixth to seventh century Byzantine coin hoards in Eastern and Southeastern Europe. *Annali di Istituto Italiano di Numismatica* 43: 65–224.

Delougaz, P. 1960. Coins. In *A Byzantine church at Khirbat Al-Karak*, P. Delougaz and R. C. Haines, pp. 50–52. Chicago: University of Chicago Press.

Demirel Gökalp, Z. 2007. *Yalvaç ve Isparta arkeoloji müzelerinde bulunan Bizans sikkeleri.* PhD dissertation. Anadolu Üniversitesi Sosyal Bilimler Enstitüsü.

Devreker, J. 1984. Les monnaies de Pessinonte. In *Les Fouilles de la Rijksuniversiteit te Gent a Pessinonte 1967–1973*, J. Devreker and M. Waelkens, eds., vol. I, pp. 173–215. Brugge: De Tempel.

Dimitrov, K. 1998. Poznorzymskie i wczesnobizantyjskie monety z odcinka iv w Novae z lat 294–612. *Novensia* 11: 99–112.

Duncan-Jones, R. 1994. *Money and government in the Roman Empire.* New York: Cambridge University Press.

Edwards, K. M. 1933. *Corinth VI: Coins, 1896–1929.* Cambridge, MA: Harvard University Press.

———. 1937. Report on the coins found in the excavations at Corinth during the years 1930–1935. *Hesperia* 6 (2): 241–256.

Erslev, K. ed. 1873. *Catalogue de la collection de monnaies de feu Christian Jürgensen Thomsen. Seconde partie: Les monnaies du moyen-age, tome I.* Copenhagen: Imprimerie de Thiele.

Esty, W. 1986. Estimating the size of a coinage. *Numismatic Chronicle* 146: 185–215.

Evans, DeRose J. 2006. *The joint expedition to Caesarea Maritima. Excavation reports. Volume VI. The coins and the Hellenistic, Roman, and Byzantine economy of Palestine.* Boston: American Schools of Oriental Research.

Fisher, J. E. 1984. Corinth excavations, 1977, forum southwest. *Hesperia* 53 (2): 217–250.

Fitzgerald, G. M. 1929. The coins. In *Excavations in the Tyropoeon Valley, Jerusalem 1927*, J. W. Crowfoot and G. M. Fitzgerald, pp. 103–132. London: Palestine Exploration Fund.

Foss, C. 1975. The Persians in Asia Minor and the end of Antiquity. *The English Historical Review* 90: 721–747.

———. Syria in transition. A.D. 550–750: an archaeological approach. *Dumbarton Oaks Papers* 51: 189–269.

Friedländer, J., and M. Pinder. *Die Münzen Justinians. Berlin, 1843.*

Fulco, W. J., and F. Zayadine. 1981. Coins from Samaria-Sebaste. *Annual of the Department of Antiquities Jordan* 25: 197–225.

Füeg, F. 1991. Die Solidusausgaben 717–803 in Konstantinopel. *Revue suisse de numismatique* 70: 35–54.

Gândilă, A. 2003–2005. Sixth-to-seventh century coin circulation in Dobrudja. *Cercetări Numismatice* 9–11: 109–166.

———. 2006–2007. Early Byzantine Capidava: the numismatic evidence. *Cercetări Numismatice* 12–13: 97–122.

———. 2008. Some aspects of the monetary circulation in the Byzantine province of Scythia during the 6th and 7th century. In *Numismatic, sphragistic and epigraphic contributions to the history of the Black Sea coast*, I. Lazarenko, ed., vol. 1, pp. 301–330. Varna, 2008.

Grierson, P. 1961. Coinage and money in the Byzantine Empire 498–c. 1090. In *Moneta e scambi nell'alto medioevo*, pp. 411–453. Spoleto: Presso La Sede del Centro.

———. 1965. The interpretation of coin finds. *Numismatic Chronicle* 5: i–xiii.

———. 1966. The interpretation of coin finds (2). *Numismatic Chronicle* 6: i–xxi.

———. 1967a. Byzantine coinage as source material. In *Proceedings of the XIII International Congress of Byzantine Studies, Oxford, 5–10 September 1966*, pp. 317–333. London: Oxford University Press.

———. 1967b. The monetary reforms of Anastasius and their economic consequences. In *International Numismatic Convention, Jerusalem 1963; The patterns of monetary development in Palestine and Phoenicia in Antiquity*, A. Kindler, ed., pp. 283–302. Tel-Aviv/Jerusalem: Schocken.

———. 1982. *Byzantine coins*. Los Angeles: University of California Press.

———. 1986. Circolazione monetaria e tesaurizzazione. In *La Cultura bizantina, oggetti e messaggio: moneta ed economia*, A. Guillou, ed., pp. 37–57. Rome: L'erma di Bretschneider.

———. 1998. *Memoir on the Coin Room*, Dumbarton Oaks Center for Byzantine Studies.

Hahn, W., and M. A. Metlich. 2000. *Money of the incipient Byzantine Empire*. Vienna: City Press.

Hamburger, H. 1956. Minute coins from Caesarea. *'Atiqot* 1: 115–138.

Hendy, M. F. 1985. *Studies in the Byzantine monetary economy c. 300–1450*. London: Cambridge University Press, 1985.

———. 1986. The coins. In *Excavations at Saraçhane in Istanbul*, R.M Harrison, M. V. Gill, M. Hendy, S. J. Hill and D. Brothwell, vol. I, pp. 278–313. Princeton: Princeton University Press.

———. 2007. *Roman, Byzantine and Latin Coins*, in *Kalenderhane in Istanbul. The excavations*, edited by Cecil L. Striker and Y. Doğan Kuban, pp. 175–276. Mainz: Verlag Philipp von Zabern.

Hennequin, G, and A. Abū-l-Faraj. 1978. *Les monnaies de Bālis*. Damascus: Institut Français de Damas.

Hohlfelder, R. L. 1978. *Kenchreai, eastern port of Corinth. III. The coins*. Leiden: Brill.

Iordanov, I., A. Koicev, and V. Mutafov. 1998. Srednovekovijat Ahtopol VI–XIII v. spored dannite numizmatikata i sfragistika. *Numizmatika i Sfragistika* 5, n. 2: 67–89.

Ireland, S. 2000. *Greek, Roman and Byzantine coins in the museum at Amasya*. London: Royal Numismatic Society.

———, and S. Atesogullari. 1996. The Ancient coins in Amasra Museum. In *Studies in ancient coinage from Turkey*, R. Ashton, ed., pp. 115–137. London: Royal Numismatic Society.

Isvoranu, T., and Gh. Poenaru Bordea. 2003. Monede bizantine de la Tomis şi împrejurimi în colecţia Institutului de Arheologie Vasile Pârvan. In *Simpozion de numismatică dedicat împlinirii a 125 de ani de la proclamarea independenţei României, Chişinău, 24–26 septembrie 2002, Comunicări, studii şi note*, pp. 137–161. Bucharest: Editura Enciclopedică.

Ivanišević, V. 1988. Vizantijski novac (491–1092) iz zairke Narodnog Myzeja y Pojarevci. *Numizmatičar* 11: 87–99.

Janković, Đ. 1981. *Podunavski deo oblasti Akvisa u VI i pocetkom VII veka*. Belgrade: Arheoloski institut.

Jantzen, U. 2004. *Die Wasserleitung des Eupalinos. Die Funde*. Bonn: Rudolf Habelt GmbH.

Katsari, C. 2003. The Statistical analysis of stray coins in museums: the Roman Provincial coinage. *Nomismatika Chronika* 22: 47–52.

Khazdan, A.P. 1954. Vizantijskie goroda v VII–XI vv. *Sovestkaja archeologija* 21: 164–183.

Kindler, A. 1989. The synagogue treasure of Meroth, Eastern Upper Galilee, Israel. In *Proceedings of the 10th International Congress of Numismatics, London, September 1986*, I. A. Carradice, ed., pp. 315–320. Wetteren: Cultura.

Kloetzli, G. 1970. Coins from Chorazin. *Liber Annuus* 20: 359–369.

Kruszynski, M. 1999. A group of Byzantine coins from Lebanon. *Notae Numismaticae* 3–4: 221–242.

Lampinen, P. 1992. The coins, preliminary report, 1990. In *Caesarea papers: Straton's Tower, Herod's Harbour, and Roman and Byzantine Caesarea*, R. L. Vann, ed., pp. 169–172. Ann Arbor, MI: University of Michigan.

Leuthold, E. 1952–1953. Monete bizantine rinvenute in Syria. *Rivista Italiana di Numismatica i Scienze Affini* 54–55: 31–49.

———. 1971. Monete bizantine rinvenute in Cirrestica. *Rivista Italiana di Numismatica i Scienze Affini* v. 73: 9–23.

Lightfoot, C. 2002. Byzantine Anatolia: reassessing the numismatic evidence. *Revue Numismatique* 158: 229–239.

Mac Isaac, J. D. 1987. Corinth: coins, 1925–1926. The Theater District and the Roman Villa. *Hesperia* 56 (2): 97–157.

———. 2005. Early Christian and later coin finds from Nemea. In *Excavations at Nemea III. The coins*, J. D. Mac Isaac and R. Knapp, pp. 183–237. Los Angeles: University of California Press.

Madgearu, A. 1996. The province of Scythia and the Avaro-Slavic invasions (576–626). *Balkan Studies* 37 (1): 35–61.

Mansfield, S. J. 1995a. Unknown (Near East), 1994 or before. *Numismatic Chronicle* 155: 348–354.

———. 1995b. Unknown (Near East), 1993 or before. *Numismatic Chronicle* 155: 354–358.

———. 2003. A hoard of twenty Byzantine copper coins. *Numismatic Chronicle* 163: 354–355.

Marot, T. 1998. *Las monedas del Macellum de Gerasa (Yaras, Jordania): aproximación a la circulación monetaria en la provincia de Arabia.* Madrid: Museo Casa de la Moneda.

Metcalf, D. M. 1958. Statistische Analyse bei der Auswertung von Münzfundmaterialen. *Jahrbuch fur Numismatik und Geldgeschichte* 9: 187–196.

———.1960. The currency of Byzantine Sirmia and Slavonia. *Hamburger Beiträge zur Numismatik* 14: 429–444.

———. 1964. Some Byzantine and Arab-Byzantine coins from Palaestina Prima. *Israel Numismatic Journal* 2 (3–4): 32–47.

———.1969. *The origins of the Anastasian currency reform.* Chicago: Argonaut.

———. 1991. Avar and Slav invasions into the Balkan peninsula (c. 575–625): the nature of the numismatic evidence. *Journal of Roman Archaeology* 4: 140–148.

———. 1976. *The copper coinage of Thessalonica under Justinian I.* Wien: Verlag der Osterreichischen Akademie der Wissenschaften.

———.2001. Monetary recession in the Middle Byzantine period: the numismatic evidence. *Numismatic Chronicle* 161: 111–155.

———, and S. Payne. 1965. Some Byzantine and Arab-Byzantine coins obtained in Jerusalem. *Numismatic Circular* 73: 130–2, 185–6, 208–10; 257–58.

Metcalf, W.E. 1975. A Heraclian hoard from Syria. *Museum Notes* 20: 109–137.

———. 1988. The joint reign gold of Justin I and Justinian I. In *Studies in Early Byzantine Gold Coinage*, Wolfgang Hahn and William E. Metcalf, eds., pp. 19–27. New York: American Numismatic Society.

———. 1995. Review of Duncan-Jones 1994. *Revue Suisse de Numismatique* 74: 145–159.

Mihailov, S. 2008. Vidovete nominali v monetnoto obrashtenie na vizantiiskite provintsii Ckitiia i Vtora Miziia (498–681 g.). In *Numismatic, sphragistic and epigraphic contributions to the history of the Black Sea coast*, I. Lazarenko, ed., vol. 1, pp. 278–300. Varna.

Milne, J. G. 1925. J. T. Wood's coins from Ephesus. *Numismatic Chronicle*: 385–391.

Mionnet, T. E. 1827. *De la rareté et du prix des médailles romaines*. Volume II, 2nd ed. Paris.

Mirnik, I. and A. Šemrov. 1997–1998. Byzantine Coins in the Zagreb Archaeological Museum numismatic collection. Anastasius I (A.D. 497–518)-Anastasius II (A.D. 713–715). *Vjesnik Arheološkog muzeja u Zagrebu* 30–31: 129–258.

Moorhead, T. S. N. 1997. The Late Roman, Byzantine and Umayyad periods at Tel Jezreel. *Tel Aviv* 24 (1): 129–166.

Morrisson, C. 1980. Les monnaies. In *Déhès (Syrie du nord) campagnes I–III (1976–1978), recherches sur l'habitat rural*, J.-P. Sodini, G. Tate, B. Bavant, S. Bavant, J.-L. Biscop, D. Orssaud, and C. Morrisson, pp. 267–287. Paris: Librairie Orientaliste Paul Geuthner.

———. 1981. Estimation du volume des emissions de *Solidi* de Tibère et Maurice à Carthage (578–602). In *Statistique et numismatique: table ronde organisée par le Centre de mathématique sociale de l'Ecole des hautes études en sciences sociales de Paris et le Séminaire de Numismatique Marcel Hoc de l'Université Catholique de Louvain, Paris, 17–19 sept. 1979*, C. Carcassone and T. Hackens, eds., pp. 267–284. Strasbourg: Conseil de l'Europe, Assemblée parlementaire.

———. 1988. The *Moneta Auri* under Justinian and Justin II, 537–578. In *Studies in Early Byzantine gold coinage*, Wolfgang Hahn and William E. Metcalf, eds., pp. 41–64. New York: American Numismatic Society.

———. 1989a. La monnaie en Syrie Byzantine. In *Archéologie et histoire de la Syrie II. La Syrie de l'époque achéménide à l'avènement de l'Islam*, J.-M. Dentzer and W. Orthmann, eds., pp. 187–204. Saarbrücken: Saarbrücker Druckerei und Verlag.

———. 1989b. Monnaie et prix a Byzance du V<sup>e</sup> au VII<sup>e</sup> siècle. In *Hommes et richesses dans l'Empire byzantin, tome I, IV<sup>e</sup>-VII<sup>e</sup> siècle*, 239–260. Paris: Lethielleux.

———. 1993. Die byzantinischen Münzen. In H. Voegtli, *Pergamenische Forschungen 8: Die Fundmünzen aus der Stadtgrabung von Pergamon*, 8–13. Berlin: Walter de Gruyter.

———. 1995. La diffusion de la monnaie de Constantinople: routes commerciales ou routes politiques? In *Constantinople and its hinterland*, C. Mango and G. Dagron, eds., pp. 77–89. Aldershot: Ashgate.

———. 1998. La circulation monétaire dans les Balkans à l'époque justinienne et post- justinienne. In *Acta XIII Congressus internationalis archaeologiae christianae*, N. Cambi, and E. Marin, eds., vol. II, pp. 919–930. Split, 1998.

———. 2001. La donation Schlumberger (1929). In *Trois donations byzantines au Cabinet des Médailles: Froehner (1925), Schlumberger (1929), Zacos (1998)*, D. Feissel, C. Morrisson, J.-C., Cheynet and B. Pitarkis, eds., pp. 21–50. Paris: Bibliothèque Nationale.

———. 2002. Byzantine money: its production and circulation. In *Economic history of Byzantium*, Angeliki Laiou, ed., pp. 909–966. Dumbarton Oaks.

———, and V. Ivanišević. 2006. Les emissions des VIᵉ-VIIᵉ siècles et leur circulation dans les Balkans. In *Les Trésors monétaires byzantins des Balkans et d'Asie Mineure (491–713)*, C. Morrisson, V. Popović, and V. Ivanišević, eds., pp. 41–73. Paris: Lethellieux.

———, V. Popović, and V. Ivanišević, eds. 2006. *Les Trésors monétaires byzantins des Balkans et d'Asie Mineure (491–713)*. Paris: Lethellieux.

Mosser, S. McA. 1935. *A bibliography of Byzantine coin hoards*. Numismatic Notes and Monographs 67. New York: American Numismatic Society.

Naismith, R. 2004. A hoard of Byzantine copper coins ending with the last year of Maurice. *Numismatic Chronicle* 164: 296–299.

Nicolaou, I. 1990. *Paphos II. The coins from the House of Dionysos*. Nicosia: Cosmos Press.

Noeske, H.-C. 2000. *Münzfunde aus Ägypten I. Die Münzfunde des ägyptischen Pilgerzentrums Abu Mina und die Vergleichsfunde aus den Diocesen Aegyptus und Oriens vom 4.-8. Jh. n.Chr.* 3 vols. Berlin: Mann.

Oberländer-Târnoveanu, E. 1996. Monnaies byzantines des VIIᵉ-Xᵉ siècles découvertes a Silistra dans la collection de l'Académicien Péricle Papahagi consevées au Cabinet des Medailles du Musée National d'Histoire de Roumanie. *Cercetǎri Numismatice* 7: 97–127.

———. 2003. La monnaie dans l'espace rural byzantin des Balkans Orientaux—un essai de synthèse au commencement du XXIᵉ siècle. *Peuce* 14: 341–412.

Ostrogorsky, G. 1959. Byzantine cities in the early middle ages. *Dumbarton Oaks Papers* 13: 45–66.

Phillips, M, and S. Tyler-Smith. 1998. A sixth-century hoard of nummi and five-nummi pieces. *Numismatic Chronicle* 158: 316–324.

Poenaru Bordea, Gh. 1981. Problèmes historiques de la Dobroudja (VIᵉ-VIIᵉ siècles) a la lumiére des monnaies byzantines traitées par des méthodes statistiques. In *Statistique et numismatique: table ronde organisée par le Centre de mathématique sociale de l'Ecole des hautes études en sciences sociales de Paris et le Séminaire de Numismatique Marcel Hoc de l'Université Catholique de Louvain, Paris, 17–19 sept. 1979*, C. Carcassone and T. Hackens, eds., pp. 365–377. Strasbourg: Conseil de l'Europe, Assemblée parlementaire.

———, R. Ocheşeanu, and Al. Popeea, 2004. *Monnaies Byzantines du Musée de Constanţa (Roumanie)*, Wetteren: Moneta.

Popescu, E. 2005. Le village en Scythie Mineure (Dobroudja) à l'époque proto-byzantine. In *Les villages dans l'Empire byzantin (IVᵉ-XVᵉ siecle)*, J. Lefort, C. Morrisson, and J.-P. Sodini, eds., pp. 363–380. Paris: Lethielleux.

Popović, V. 1975. Les témoins archéologiques des invasions avaro-slaves dans l'Illyricum byzantin. *Melanges de l'école française de Rome* 87 (1): 459–464.

————. 1978a. Catalogue des monnaies Byzantines du musée de Srem. In *Sirmium VIII*, Dj. Bošković, N. Duval, V. Popović, and G. Vallet, pp. 180–195. Rome/Belgrade: École Française de Rome/Institut Archéologique de Belgrade.

————. 1978b. La descente des Koutrigours, des Slaves et des Avars vers la Mer Egée: Le témoinage de l'archéologie. *Comptes Rendus de l'Academie des Inscriptions*: 596–648.

Pottier, H. 1983. *Analyse d'un trésor de monnaies en bronze enfoui au VIᵉ siècle en Syrie byzantine: contribution à la méthodologie numismatique*. Wetteren: Cultura.

————. 2004. Nouvelle approche de la livre byzantine du Vᵉ au VIIᵉ siècle. *Revue Belge de Numismatique et Sigillographie* 150: 51–133.

Prawdzic-Golemberski, E. J., and D. M. Metcalf. 1963. The circulation of Byzantine coins in the south-eastern frontiers of the Empire. *Numismatic Chronicle* 123: 83–92.

Radić, V., and V. Ivanisević. 2006. *Byzantine coins from the National Museum in Belgrade*. Belgrade.

Robertson, A. S. 1989. The accidents of survival. In *Proceedings of the 10th International Congress of Numismatics, London, September 1986*, I. A. Carradice, ed., pp. 315–320. Wetteren: Cultura.

Russell, K. W. 1985. The earthquake chronology of Palestine and northwest Arabia from the 2nd through the mid-8th century A.D. *Bulletin of the American Schools of Oriental Research* 260: 37–59.

Sabatier, J. 1862. *Description générale des monnaies Byzantines*. Paris, Chez Rollin et Feuardent.

de Saulcy, F. 1836. *Essai de classification des suites monétaires Byzantines*. Metz: Lamort.

Scheers, S. 1993. Catalogue of the coins found in 1992. In *Sagalassos II: Report on the third Excavation Campaign of 1992*, M. Waelkens and J. Poblome, eds., pp. 249–260. Leuven: Leuven University Press.

————. 1995. Catalogue of the coins found in 1993. In *Sagalassos III: Report on the fourth excavation campaign of 1993*, M. Waelkens and J. Poblome, eds., pp. 307–326. Leuven: Leuven University Press.

————, H. Vanhaverbeke, and J. Poblome. 1997. Coins found in 1994 and 1995. In *Sagalassos IV: report on the survey and excavation campaigns of 1994 and 1995*, M. Waelkens and J. Poblome, eds., pp. 315–350. Leuven: Leuven University Press.

Scheers, S. 2000. Coins found in 1996 and 1997. In *Sagalassos V: report on the survey and excavation campaigns of 1996–1997*, M. Waelkens and L. Loots, eds., pp. 509–549. Leuven: Leuven University Press.

Schindler, L. 1955. Die Reform des Kupfergeldes unter Konstantinos IV. *Numismatische Zeitschrift* 86: 33–35.

Sear, David. 1987. *Byzantine coins and their values*. London: Seaby.

Sheedy, K. 2001. Byzantine period coins. In *Pella in Jordan, 1979–1990: the coins*, K. Sheedy, A. R. Carson, and A. Walmsley, pp. 43–55 and pp. 129–145. Sydney: Adapa.

Spahiu, H. 1979–1980. Monedna bizantine të shekujve V-XIII të zbuluara në territorin e Shqipërisë/ Monnaies byzantines des Vᵉ-XIIIᵉ siècles découvertes sur le territoire de l'Albanie. *Iliria* 9–10: 353–422.

Spijkerman, A. 1975. *Cafarnao III. Catalogo delle monede de la città*. Jerusalem: Pubblicazioni dello Studium Biblicum Franciscanum 19.

Soleirol, M. *Catalogue des monnaies byzantines qui composent la collection de M. Soleirol*. Metz: Lamort, 1853.

Sommer, A. S. *Katalog der Byzantinischen Münzen. Göttingen: Universitätsverlag Göttingen, 2003*.

Sotheby's. 1990. *The William Herbert Hunt collection. Highly important Byzantine coins, I, December 5–6*. New York.

Sotheby's. 1991. *The William Herbert Hunt collection. Highly important Byzantine coins, II, June 21*. New York.

Spink. 2000. *The Dr. Anton C. R. Dreesmann collection of ancient coins, Part II: Byzantine and early European gold coins*, July 13, London.

Taylor, T. 1818. Iamblichus. *Life of* Pythagoras. Translated by Thomas Taylor. London: J. M. Watkins.

Taylor, G. 1977. A hoard of small module coins of Anastasius. *Coin Hoards* 3: 87.

Thomsen, R. 1986. The Graeco-Roman coins. In *Hama, fouilles et recherches, 1931–1938. III*, A. Papanicolaou Christensen, R. Thomsen, and G. Ploug, pp. 59–69. Copenhague: Nationalmuseet.

Thompson, M. 1954. *The Athenian agora, v. 2, coins from the Roman through the Venetian period*. Princeton: The American School of Classical Studies at Athens.

Todd, R. 1987. A late sixth-century hoard from northern Syria. *Numismatic Chronicle* 147: 176–182.

Tolstoi, J. 1912–1914. *Monnaies byzantines*. Saint-Petersburg.

Torbatov, S. 2002. *Monetnata circulaciia v gradishteto kraj Odartsi*. Tărnovo: Faber.

Tushingham, A. D. 1972. *The excavations at Dibon (Dhībân) in Moab. The third campaign 1952–53*. Cambridge: The American Schools of Oriental Research.

Vorderstrasse, T. 2005. Coin circulation in some Syrian villages (5th–11th Centuries). In *Les villages dans l'Empire byzantin (IVᵉ-XVᵉ siecle)*, J. Lefort, C. Morrisson, and J.-P. Sodini, eds., pp. 494–510. Paris: Lethielleux.

Waage, D. 1952. *Antioch-on-the-Orontes, vol. IV, part 2: Greek, Roman, Byzantine and Crusaders' coins*. Princeton: Department of Art and Archaeology of Princeton.

Walmsley, A. 1999. Coin frequencies in sixth and seventh century Palestine and

Arabia: Social and economic implications. *Journal of the Economic and Social History of the Orient* 42 (3): 326–350.

Waner, M, and Z. Safrai. 2001. A catalogue of coin hoards and the *shelf life* of coins in Palestine hoards during the Roman and Byzantine periods. *Liber Annuus* 51: 305–336.

Whitby, M. 1988. *The Emperor Maurice and his historian: Theophylact Simocatta on Persian and Balkan warfare.* Oxford: Clarendon Press.

de Wilde, G. 1997. Monnaies au Musée de Pessinonte. *Epigraphica Anatolica* 28: 101–114.

Zhekova, Zh. 2006. *Moneti i monetno obrashtenie v srednovekovniia Shumen.* Sofia: Iupi-Tp.

Yannopoulos, P. 1987. Inflation, dévaluation et réévaluation à la transition des mondes romain et byzantin. In *Histoire économique de l'antiquité: bilans et contributions de savants belges présentés dans une réunion interuniversitaire,* T. Hackens and P. Marchetti, eds., pp. 123–133. Louvain-la-Neuve: Séminaire de numismatique Marcel Hoc, Collége Erasme.

Fig. A. Justinian I—Constantinople Mint
(% *nummia*/year of reign)

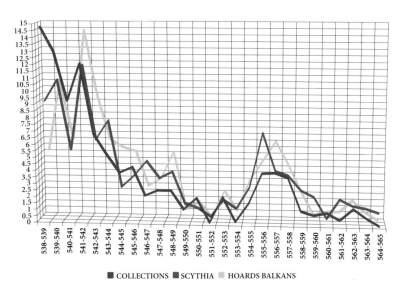

■ COLLECTIONS   ■ SCYTHIA   ▨ HOARDS BALKANS

Fig. B. Justin II
(% *nummia*/year of reign)

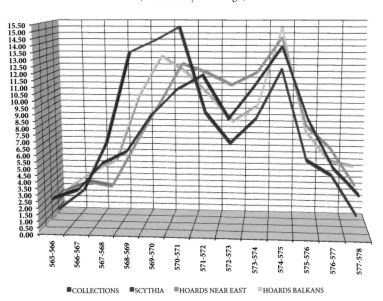

■COLLECTIONS   ■SCYTHIA   ■HOARDS NEAR EAST   ▨HOARDS BALKANS

Fig. C. Maurice Tiberius—Antioch Mint
(% *nummia*/year of reign)

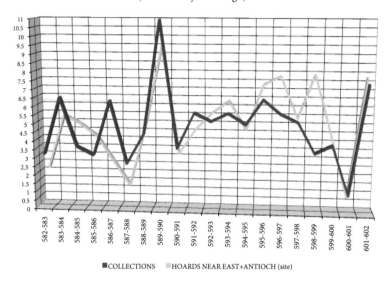

■ COLLECTIONS     ▬ HOARDS NEAR EAST+ANTIOCH (site)

Fig. D. Heraclius
(% *nummia*/year of reign 610–617)

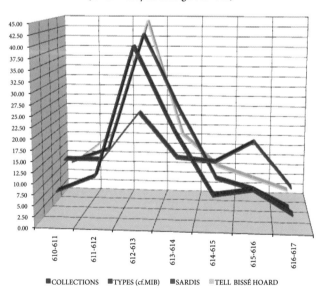

■ COLLECTIONS    ■ TYPES (cf.MIB)    ■ SARDIS    ▬ TELL BISSÉ HOARD

Fig. 1. *Nummia*/year of reform (%)

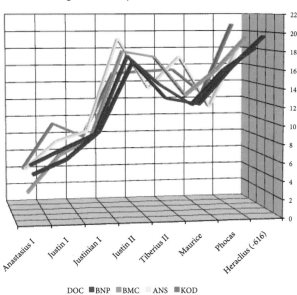

DOC ■BNP ■BMC ░ANS ■KOD

Fig. 2a. *Nummia*/year of reform (%)

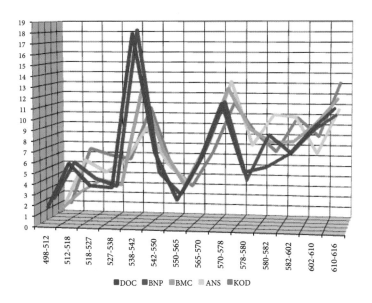

■DOC ■BNP ■BMC ░ANS ■KOD

Fig. 2b. *Solidi*/year of reform (%)

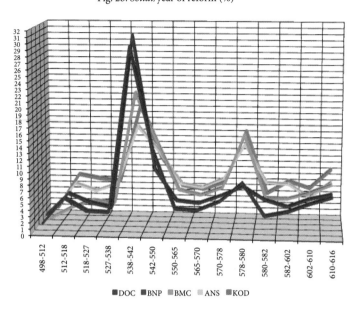

Fig. 3. *Nummia*/year 538–616 (%)

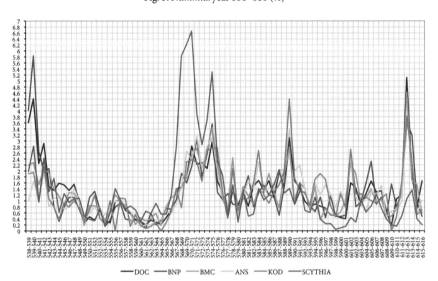

Fig. 4. Thessalonica Mint (565–602)
(% coins/year)

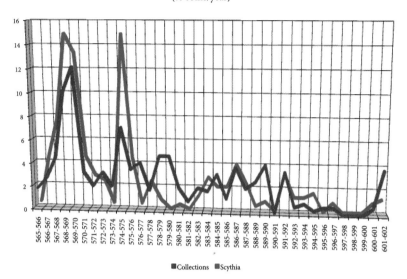

■Collections ■Scythia

Fig. 5a. Selected locations in the Balkans
(% *nummia*/year of reform)

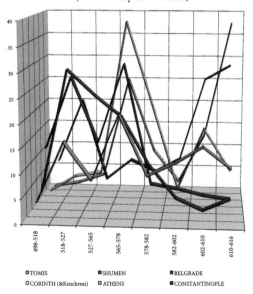

▣TOMIS                    ■SHUMEN                 ■BELGRADE
▢CORINTH (&Kenchreai)    ▢ATHENS                 ■CONSTANTINOPLE

Fig. 5b. Selected locations in Anatolia
(% *nummia*/year of reform)

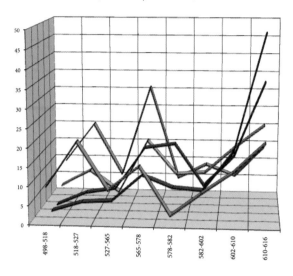

□ AMASYA    ■ SARDIS    ■ SIDE    □ PISIDIAN ANTIOCH    ■ MELITENE

Fig. 5c. Selected locations in the Near East
(% *nummia*/year of reform)

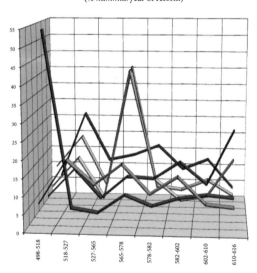

□ ANTIOCH    ■ BERYTUS    ■ CAESAREA MARITIMA    □ PELLA    □ GERASA    ■ NESSANA

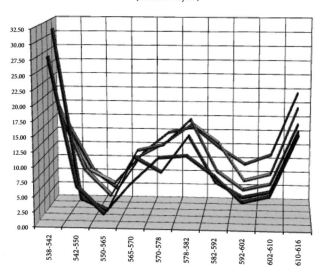

Fig. 6. Constantinople mint
(% *nummia*/year)

Fig. 6a. Mints 498–616 (%)

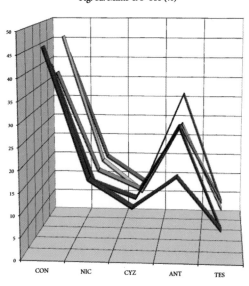

Fig. 6b. Mints 498–616 (%)

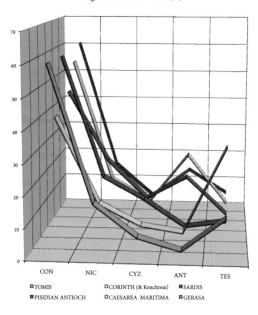

- TOMIS
- PISIDIAN ANTIOCH
- CORINTH (& Kenchreai)
- CAESAREA MARITIMA
- SARDIS
- GERASA

Fig. 7a. Mints 498–512 (%)

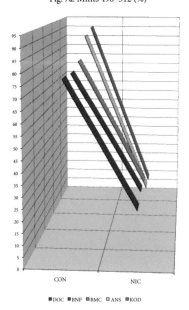

- DOC ■BNP ■BMC □ANS ■KOD

Fig. 7b. Mints 498–512 (%)

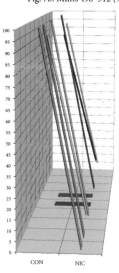

- TOMIS
- AMASYA
- ANTIOCH
- CORINTH (& Kenchreai)
- SARDIS
- CASEAREA MARITIMA
- CONSTANTINOPLE
- PISIDIAN ANTIOCH
- GERASA

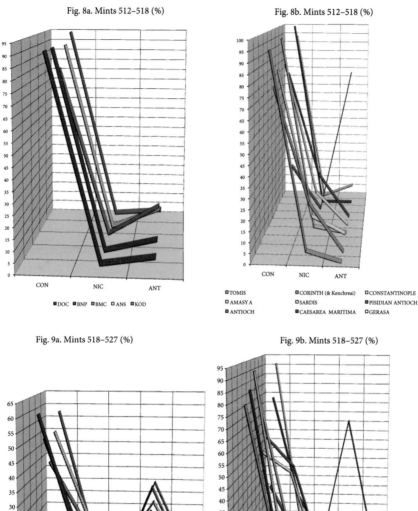

Fig. 8a. Mints 512–518 (%)

Fig. 8b. Mints 512–518 (%)

Fig. 9a. Mints 518–527 (%)

Fig. 9b. Mints 518–527 (%)

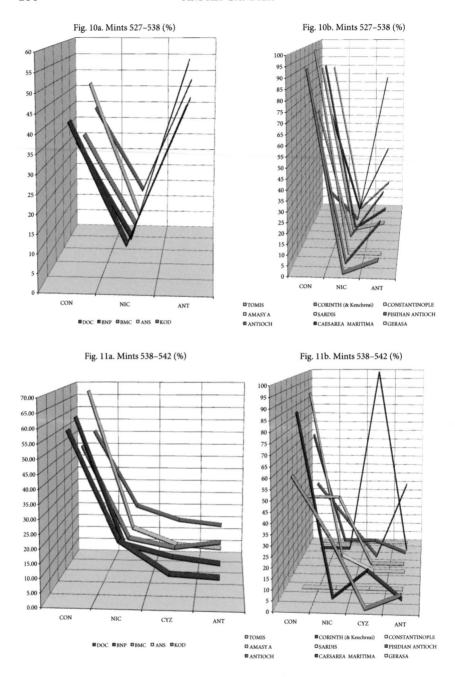

Fig. 10a. Mints 527–538 (%)

Fig. 10b. Mints 527–538 (%)

Fig. 11a. Mints 538–542 (%)

Fig. 11b. Mints 538–542 (%)

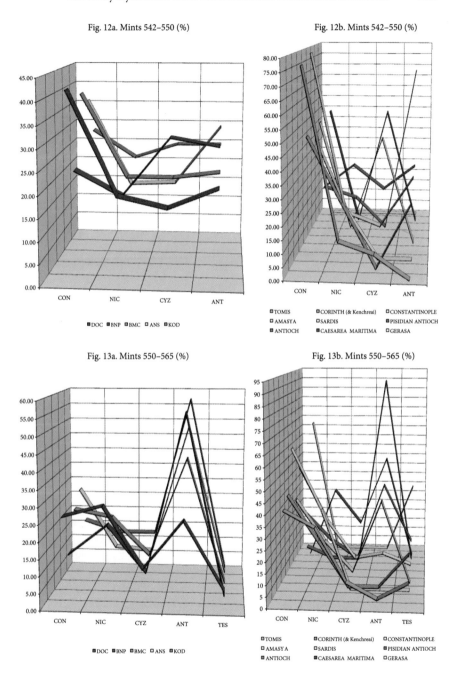

Fig. 12a. Mints 542–550 (%)

Fig. 12b. Mints 542–550 (%)

Fig. 13a. Mints 550–565 (%)

Fig. 13b. Mints 550–565 (%)

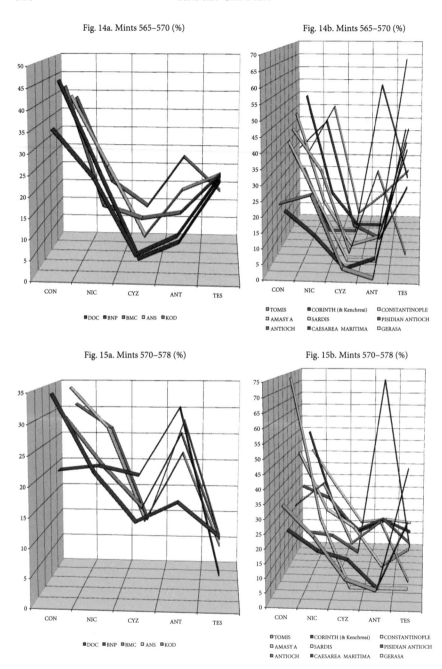

Fig. 14a. Mints 565–570 (%)

Fig. 14b. Mints 565–570 (%)

■DOC ■BNP ■BMC □ANS ■KOD

□TOMIS          ■CORINTH (& Kenchreai)    □CONSTANTINOPLE
□AMASYA         □SARDIS                   ■PISIDIAN ANTIOCH
■ANTIOCH        ■CAESAREA MARITIMA        □GERASA

Fig. 15a. Mints 570–578 (%)

Fig. 15b. Mints 570–578 (%)

■DOC ■BNP ■BMC □ANS ■KOD

□TOMIS          ■CORINTH (& Kenchreai)    □CONSTANTINOPLE
□AMASYA         □SARDIS                   ■PISIDIAN ANTIOCH
■ANTIOCH        ■CAESAREA MARITIMA        □GERASA

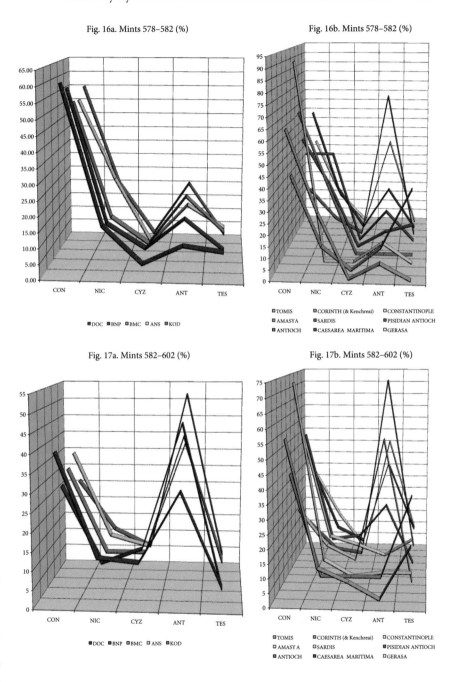

Fig. 16a. Mints 578–582 (%)

Fig. 16b. Mints 578–582 (%)

■DOC ■BNP ◨BMC ◻ANS ◨KOD

◨TOMIS          ◨CORINTH (& Kenchreai)    ◻CONSTANTINOPLE
◨AMASYA         ◨SARDIS                   ■PISIDIAN ANTIOCH
◨ANTIOCH        ■CAESAREA MARITIMA        ◻GERASA

Fig. 17a. Mints 582–602 (%)

Fig. 17b. Mints 582–602 (%)

■DOC ■BNP ◨BMC ◻ANS ◨KOD

◨TOMIS          ◨CORINTH (& Kenchreai)    ◻CONSTANTINOPLE
◻AMASYA         ◨SARDIS                   ■PISIDIAN ANTIOCH
◨ANTIOCH        ■CAESAREA MARITIMA        ◻GERASA

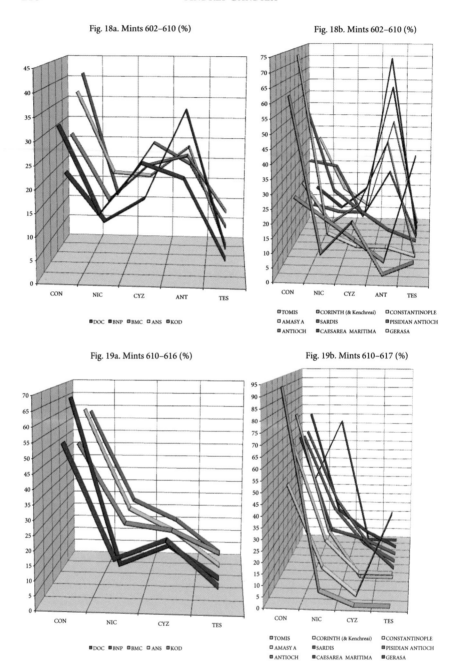

Fig. 18a. Mints 602–610 (%)

Fig. 18b. Mints 602–610 (%)

Fig. 19a. Mints 610–616 (%)

Fig. 19b. Mints 610–617 (%)

Fig. 20a. Denominations 498–616 (%)

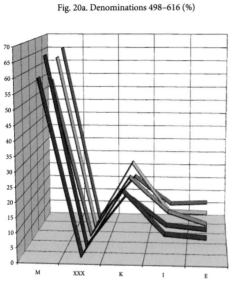

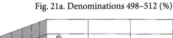

■DOC ■BNP ■BMC □ANS ■KOD

Fig. 20b. Denominations 498–616 (%)

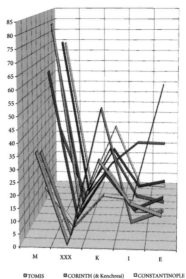

| □TOMIS | □CORINTH (& Kenchreai) | □CONSTANTINOPLE |
| ■SARDIS | □AMASYA | ■PISIDIAN ANTIOCH |
| ■ANTIOCH | ■CAESAREA MARITIMA | □GERASA |

Fig. 21a. Denominations 498–512 (%)

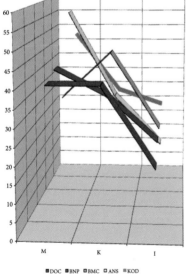

■DOC ■BNP ■BMC □ANS ■KOD

Fig. 21b. Denominations 498–512 (%)

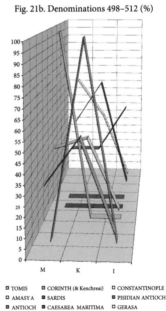

| □ TOMIS | □ CORINTH (& Kenchreai) | □ CONSTANTINOPLE |
| □ AMASYA | ■ SARDIS | ■ PISIDIAN ANTIOCH |
| ■ ANTIOCH | ■ CAESAREA MARITIMA | □ GERASA |

Fig. 22a. Denominations 512–518 (%)

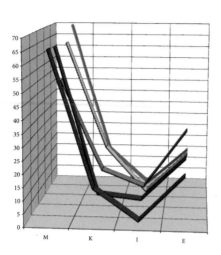

■DOC ■BNP ■BMC □ANS ■KOD

Fig. 22b. Denominations 512–518 (%)

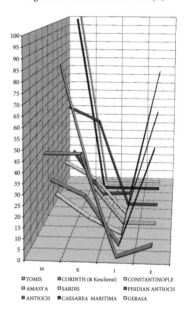

□TOMIS □CORINTH (& Kenchreai) □CONSTANTINOPLE
□AMASYA □SARDIS ■PISIDIAN ANTIOCH
■ANTIOCH ■CAESAREA MARITIMA □GERASA

Fig. 23a. Denominations 518–527 (%)

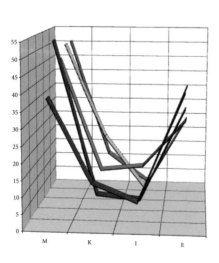

■DOC ■BNP ■BMC □ANS ■KOD

Fig. 23b. Denominations 518–527 (%)

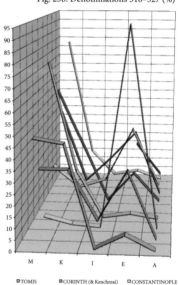

□TOMIS □CORINTH (& Kenchreai) □CONSTANTINOPLE
□AMASYA □SARDIS ■PISIDIAN ANTIOCH
■ANTIOCH ■CAESAREA MARITIMA □GERASA

Fig. 24a. Denominations 527–538 (%)

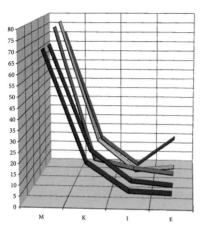

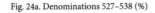

■ DOC  ■ BNP  ■ BMC  ▢ ANS  ■ KOD

Fig. 24b. Denominations 527–538 (%)

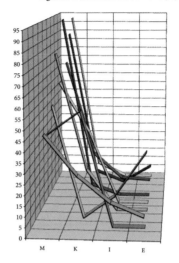

▢ TOMIS           ▢ CORINTH (& Kenchreai)      ▢ CONSTANTINOPLE
▢ AMASYA          ▢ SARDIS                      ■ PISIDIAN ANTIOCH
■ ANTIOCH         ■ CAESAREA MARITIMA           ▢ GERASA

Fig. 25a. Denominations 538–542 (%)

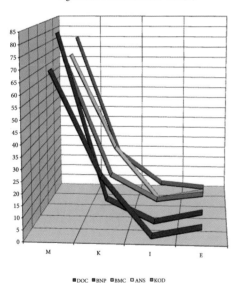

■ DOC  ■ BNP  ■ BMC  ▢ ANS  ■ KOD

Fig. 25b. Denominations 538–542 (%)

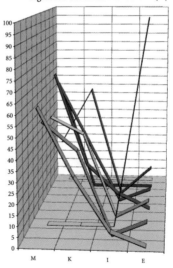

▢ TOMIS           ▢ CORINTH (& Kenchreai)      ▢ CONSTANTINOPLE
▢ AMASYA          ■ SARDIS                      ■ PISIDIAN ANTIOCH
■ ANTIOCH         ■ CAESAREA MARITIMA           ▢ GERASA

Fig. 26a. Denominations 542–550 (%)

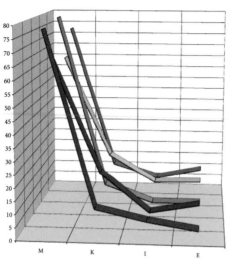

■DOC  ■BNP  ■BMC  □ANS  ■KOD

Fig. 26b. Denominations 542–550 (%)

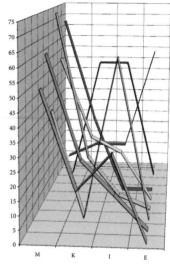

□TOMIS              □CORINTH (& Kenchreai)   □CONSTANTINOPLE
□AMASYA            □SARDIS                        ■PISIDIAN ANTIOCH
■ANTIOCH           ■CAESAREA MARITIMA       □GERASA

Fig. 27a. Denominations 550–565 (%)

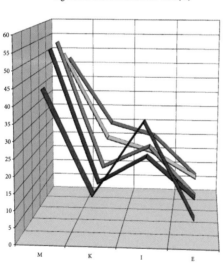

■DOC  ■BNP  ■BMC  □ANS   KOD

Fig. 27b. Denominations 550–565 (%)

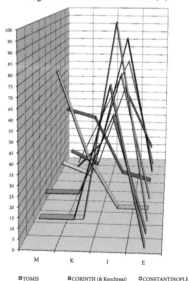

□TOMIS              □CORINTH (& Kenchreai)   □CONSTANTINOPLE
□AMASYA            □SARDIS                        ■PISIDIAN ANTIOCH
■ANTIOCH           ■CAESAREA MARITIMA       □GERASA

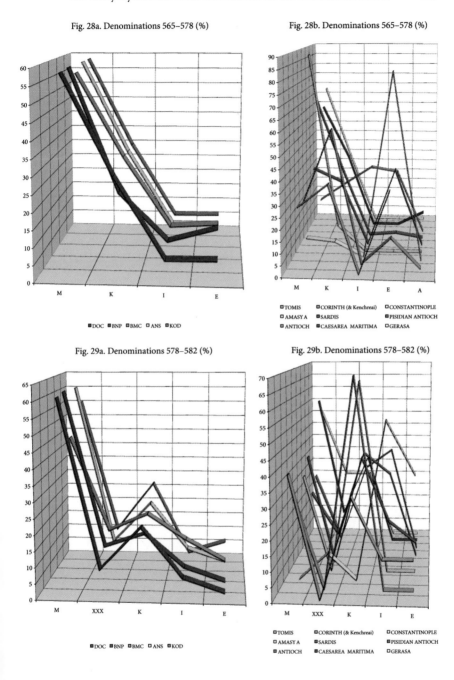

Fig. 28a. Denominations 565–578 (%)

Fig. 28b. Denominations 565–578 (%)

■DOC ■BNP ■BMC □ANS ■KOD

□TOMIS □CORINTH (& Kenchreai) □CONSTANTINOPLE
□AMASYA ■SARDIS ■PISIDIAN ANTIOCH
■ANTIOCH ■CAESAREA MARITIMA □GERASA

Fig. 29a. Denominations 578–582 (%)

Fig. 29b. Denominations 578–582 (%)

■DOC ■BNP ■BMC □ANS ■KOD

□TOMIS □CORINTH (& Kenchreai) □CONSTANTINOPLE
□AMASYA ■SARDIS ■PISIDIAN ANTIOCH
■ANTIOCH ■CAESAREA MARITIMA □GERASA

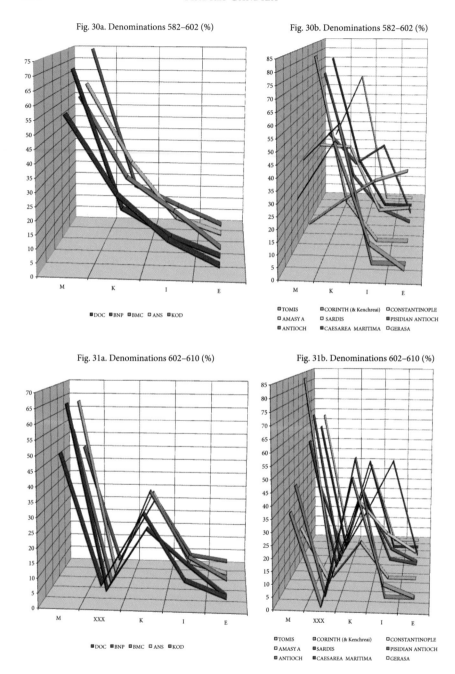

Fig. 30a. Denominations 582–602 (%)

■ DOC  ■ BNP  ■ BMC  □ ANS  ■ KOD

Fig. 30b. Denominations 582–602 (%)

■ TOMIS          □ CORINTH (& Kenchreai)   □ CONSTANTINOPLE
□ AMASYA         □ SARDIS                  ■ PISIDIAN ANTIOCH
■ ANTIOCH        ■ CAESAREA MARITIMA       □ GERASA

Fig. 31a. Denominations 602–610 (%)

■ DOC  ■ BNP  ■ BMC  □ ANS  ■ KOD

Fig. 31b. Denominations 602–610 (%)

■ TOMIS          □ CORINTH (& Kenchreai)   □ CONSTANTINOPLE
□ AMASYA         ■ SARDIS                  ■ PISIDIAN ANTIOCH
■ ANTIOCH        ■ CAESAREA MARITIMA       □ GERASA

Fig. 32a. Denominations 610–616 (%)

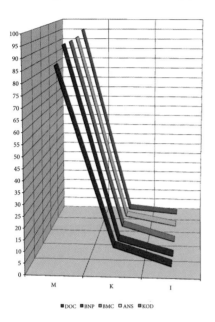

■DOC ■BNP ■BMC □ANS ■KOD

Fig. 32b. Denominations 610–616 (%)

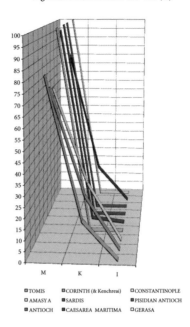

□TOMIS       □CORINTH (& Kenchreai)    □CONSTANTINOPLE
□AMASYA      ■SARDIS                    ■PISIDIAN ANTIOCH
■ANTIOCH     ■CAESAREA MARITIMA        □GERASA

Plates

Plate 1

1

2

3

4

5

6

7

8

9

10

The Northern Syria 2007 Hoard of Athenian Owls

Plate 2

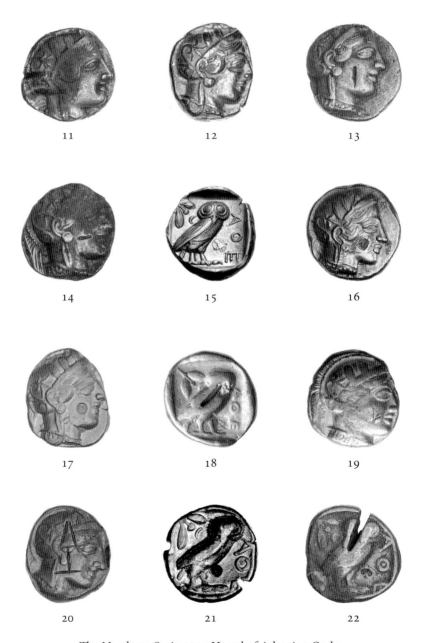

The Northern Syria 2007 Hoard of Athenian Owls

Plate 3

23

24

25

26

27

28

29

30

31

32

33

34

The Northern Syria 2007 Hoard of Athenian Owls

Plate 4

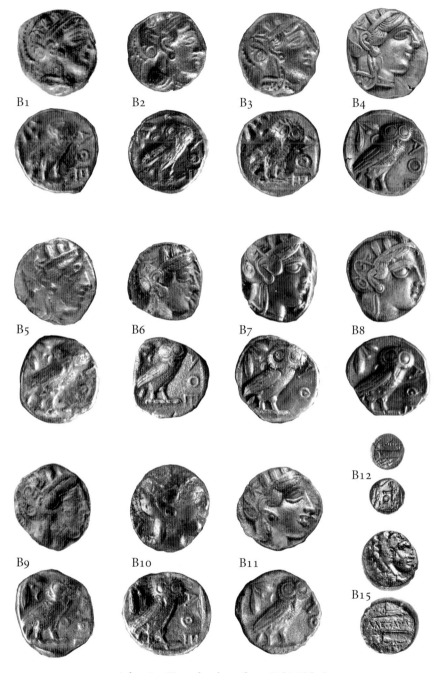

B1  B2  B3  B4

B5  B6  B7  B8

B9  B10  B11

B12

B15

Athenian Tetradrachms from Tel Mikhal

Plate 5

1  2  3

4  5  6

7
The Eras of Pamphylia

Plate 6

8

9

10

11

12

13

14

The Eras of Pamphylia

Plate 7

15       16       17

18       19

The Eras of Pamphylia

Plate 8

Antiochus III Hoard

Plate 9

Antiochus III Hoard

Plate 10

27 28 30 31

34 38 39 40

42 43 44 45

Antiochus III Hoard

Plate 11

Antiochus III Hoard

Plate 12

59    60    62    63

64    65    66    67

68    69    70    71

Antiochus III Hoard

Plate 13

72    73

74    75    76    77

Antiochus III Hoard

Plate 14

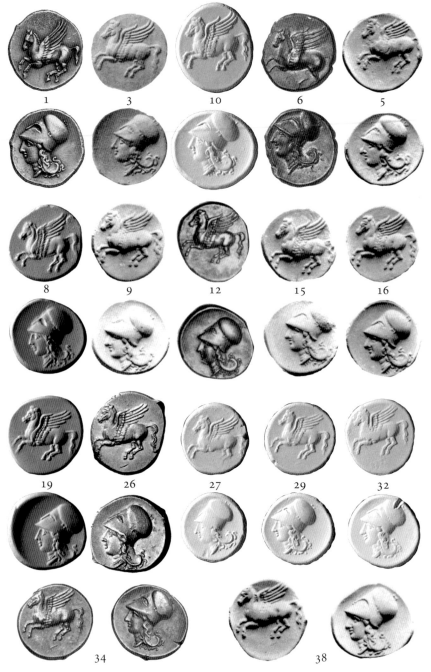

1     3     10     6     5

8     9     12     15     16

19     26     27     29     32

34     38

G. Gorini, The Die Sequence of Medma Silver Staters, *AJN* 20 (2008), pp. 143–154

Plate 15

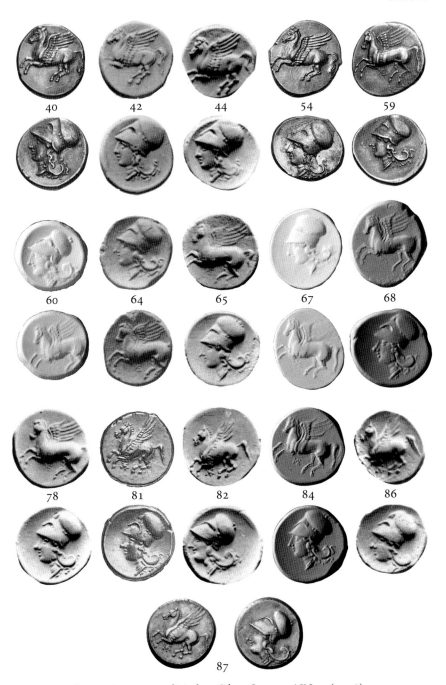

G. Gorini, The Die Sequence of Medma Silver Staters, *AJN* 20 (2008), pp. 143–154